CW00853676

Content

Acknowledgements

My first thank you goes my amazing husband. He met me shortly after I escaped from a completely different life he didn't know or understand, and he stayed by my side through it all. He listened to my horror stories as my sounding board. He was there for me to unload all my traumas. Even when things were hard, he kept a smile and a sense of humor. I couldn't say thank you enough times and I still believe he was my light when I was in my darkest place. I love him so much and I'm so excited to share the next chapter of our life together.

My second thank you goes to my brother, Daniel. We shared so many traumatic experiences together and he understands me in a way most people never will. I love our phone conversations where we talk about the traumas and laugh because of the progress we've made since then. I'm thankful he has forgiven me for so many things and has chosen to keep me in his life. He's become one of my best friends.

I also want to thank my husband's family. I came from a huge community and leaving that community was extremely difficult, despite its level of toxicity. I wanted more than anything for my children to have a loving support system. My in-laws have become my family in a way I never thought I could have again. I'm so thankful for their love and support, especially when it comes to the love they have given my kids. I love and appreciate them so much.

I also want to thank everyone who supported me when I left my community and offered their advice, home, or kind word when I needed it most. My journey has been difficult at times, but the people I have met along the way have done so much to make it better and easier.

Lastly, I want to thank everyone who encouraged me to write this book and listened to my story. It went a long way in validating my story and helping my healing process.

Chapter 1
Home Birth

Natalie let out a long breath and took a moment to relax her tired muscles, as another painful contraction finally let go of her overworked body. She had been laboring for hours, though her concept of time was lost to the timing of what was happening within her own body. When she had finally begun her first labor, she had no idea what to expect, and she couldn't wait to meet her beautiful baby. She hadn't anticipated just how exhausting and painful the process would be. After many hours, she finally felt like she was understanding the process and was more prepared to work with her body than against it.

"Get ready for the next one," her husband, Paul told her gently, as her body began to tighten again.

Lightening pain shot through her back, making it impossible to completely relax as she had been instructed. She grabbed a nearby pillow and let out a scream, as the pain completely engulfed her for half a minute. It finally released her again to give her a few moments to catch her breath. Each break from the pain seemed to be shorter than the last, and she hoped this was a sign she was getting close.

When does this end? she thought, feeling restless.

As painful as this experience was, she was happy to have her husband by her side. The fact that outside these walls, even with her own family, he would never acknowledge her as his wife didn't even cross her mind. Despite being in love with another man at the time, she married him nearly five years ago. She became wife number five in a small spiritual ceremony with only her parents, his parents, his other wives, and a few other witnesses privileged enough to go to the most private weddings within the community. She hadn't even had a reception and most of her friends had not been invited or even told the wedding was happening.

Sometimes it still felt like yesterday she gave her life to one man. He had already given his life to four other women before her. She had been a young teenager, only sixteen at the time, but she knew she was ready to start her family and become a mother. Her father had also made it very clear that this was the man who would ensure her entrance to heaven. Living the law of Celestial marriage would qualify her to make it to the highest degree of glory where angels can create worlds and everyone lived in harmony.

An intense pain, unlike any she had ever felt began to grow deep inside her. Before she could comprehend what was happening, the pain began to change and continued to intensify. There were no rest periods this time. Panic began to set in, as a whole new level of pain engulfed her entire body. She felt as though she was about to be split open from the inside.

"I see the head," she heard her husband's voice from far away.

I'm going to die, she thought nearly oblivious to what he was doing down below. *I can't do this anymore. The pain is just too much.*

"One more push," she heard her husband gently command.

His voice was like a lighthouse in the most painful darkness, and it was oddly comforting. With everything she had, she followed her body's instinct and gave one more push.

"Again," she heard his voice say more firmly.

Fighting back tears, she felt her body tighten again. Her control was lost. It seemed her body was naturally trying to expel her child, and her level of pain had reached a level she could no longer put into words.

"The head is out," he told her hoping to motivate her to push again.

The pressure had eased but was replaced by a sharp stabbing pain.

"The shoulder is stuck, don't push."

Exhausted and frustrated, Natalie didn't know if she could push even if she had wanted to. Luckily, she didn't have to. She had already done enough work.

"It's a girl," Paul's eyes were gleaming as he pulled his daughter the rest of the way out.

In an instant, it was as though the pain had gone away completely. She could nearly feel the rush of hormones flooding her body. She had never had an ultrasound or any other form of medical intervention during her whole pregnancy. Her husband had acted as her midwife. Her check-ups included simple measuring of her stomach and checking for a heartbeat with a doppler. For the first time in the last nine months, she could finally envision her life with her daughter.

"Is she okay?" Natalie asked after a moment, feeling as though they had been down there too long. She wanted to meet her new daughter.

"The cord is wrapped around her neck," her husband explained calmly.

A small surge of panic crept up and Natalie forced it back down. Her husband was as close to God as any man could be. If anyone could protect her daughter, it would be him. Exhaustion was beginning to set in, when finally, Paul placed her daughter gently in her arms.

"She's beautiful," she expressed as tears welled in her eyes. She had been praying to God to bless her with a baby for years, and it had finally happened. The night her daughter was conceived went through her mind as she remembered the falling snow and the struggle to drive up the road. Because of the storm, they nearly didn't make it to the home where she lived with her grandmother, Ethel. She had been worried she would never be able to have a baby, but miraculously, her daughter was conceived that night in the same room she was now entering the world.

Despite only being in his late twenties, Paul had married many other women in the five years since Natalie had been married. The first one had been difficult, but she came into Paul's family with the expectation of him acquiring more wives. However, she had never thought it would be so many or so quickly. When the wives after her quickly became pregnant before she did, her heart hurt to have a child of her own. Maybe her daughter's birth would finally put an end to the rumors. Maybe now, she would be considered one of the "favorite wives" after having a child of her own. The rumor of God punishing her for not being one with her husband could finally be put to rest as well. That one definitely hurt.

"Her color doesn't look right," Natalie was suddenly snapped back to the reality of where she was and what was happening.

Paul came over and glanced at their daughter, and realized she was turning a dark purple. She was not receiving enough oxygen from her tiny lungs. He quickly took his daughter from her mother and pulled out his phone. He left the room to make a call. Natalie knew better than to question his authority or even make a suggestion. The idea of going to the hospital didn't even enter her own exhausted mind as she struggled to quiet the nagging voice in her head.

Your daughter is being punished for your sins, her mind repeated the same mantra all the women were told when there were problems in childbirth or with the health of their children.

Please God, she prayed silently, looking up to the ceiling. *Please protect my baby.*

"Daniel is on his way," Paul stated as he walked back into the room holding his silent daughter. "He's bringing the oxygen machine."

Natalie tried not to panic. She needed to trust her husband. He was the leader of the Order and the man on the watchtower, and nothing could go wrong in his hands. Despite the fact they had never gone on a honeymoon, had never lived together, or had ever spent more than a couple of consecutive days together, Natalie loved her husband in the only way she knew how.

A knock at the door sent a sigh of relief running through Natalie. Her daughter could now get the oxygen she needed to keep her alive.

"Looks like we had a baby," Daniel laughed as he walked into the quiet room.

Daniel noticed two of Paul's other wives sitting in the living room waiting. He followed their gaze towards the bedroom as he began setting up the oxygen machine without instruction. Though he was the older brother, he was used to taking orders from his younger brother. Sometimes Daniel felt like he should have been the leader of the Order, but Paul was more popular among his peers.

"You made it," Paul exclaimed as he entered the room, startling Daniel as he made the final preparations to work the large machine.

Paul brought his daughter to the machine, and both men began hooking the tubes to the small, seven-pound baby girl. When the vitals began to register on the equipment, Paul realized she had been in worse shape than he had originally thought.

8

"She's lucky to be alive right now," Daniel exclaimed, realizing the seriousness of the situation. "God must have a very special plan for this girl."

"She's definitely a special little girl," Paul said with a soft smile in his daughter's direction.

"We're in for a long night," Daniel continued, as the baby finally began to return to a normal color. "You get some sleep, and I'll take the first shift."

Paul didn't argue. He plumped down on the couch next to his brother and fell fast asleep. His spiritual wife was already snoring in a restless sleep in the bedroom.

Natalie awoke from her exhaustion and looked around her. She was still lying in her bed where she had just given birth only hours before. It was still dark out, so she knew she hadn't been sleeping more than a couple of hours. The rest of the house was silent except for some faint snoring coming from the living room. Paul must be sleeping in the next room. Her daughter must still be with him. Unable to get out of bed from the pain of her tugging stitches, she laid back down.

It wasn't long before the snoring stopped, and she heard conversation in the next room. Paul poked his head in.

"You're awake," he smiled and entered the room, holding her beautiful daughter in the dark red blanket Grandma Ethel had made for her.

"How's she doing?" Natalie asked already knowing the answer. The smile on her husband's face told her all was right with the world.

"She's a tough little girl," Paul said softly as he handed his daughter back to her mother. "God must have a very special plan for her."

Natalie took her daughter and held her close. She

remembered the promise she had made to God when she was praying to conceive. If God would give her a baby, she promised to raise that baby in God's work. Her child would grow to be a powerful force for good. She fully intended to keep her promise.

Natalie was not from generations of polygamy, as many from this lifestyle are. Her grandfather had been a part of the mainstream LDS church, which banned the practice of polygamy in 1890. It was a requirement of signing the Manifesto to make Utah a state. The Manifesto didn't dissolve current polygamous marriages, but it did prevent new ones. Utah was officially able to be admitted as a state in 1896. Some leaders continued to practice the law secretly, even entering new plural marriages until 1904. Joseph F. Smith officially disavowed polygamy before Congress in 1904. The church ordered new plural marriages were not to be performed, and those who disobeyed were excommunicated from the LDS church.

Natalie's grandfather, Elden Kingston, found this information through his own research, and came to his own conclusion. The practice was stopped because of the laws of the land, and not because God commanded it to be stopped. He believed God's laws were higher than man's laws, and the LDS church must have fallen away from God. They no longer practiced plural marriage.

Elden officially established the "Order" on January 1st, 1935. His original home is still in the Order and became nicknamed, "the home place". Natalie was lucky enough to be living and giving birth to her children in the first house of the Order. It is near the "holy spot", where the first leader, her grandfather, went to pray during his times of leadership.

"How's she doing?" Ethel asked as she popped her head in, breaking Natalie's train of thought.

"Did Paul leave?" Natalie asked, surprised when she didn't hear anyone in the living room.

She had hoped he would stick around for a bit, but being her first baby, she hadn't known what to expect.

"Yeah, he did." Grandma whispered as she took the sleeping baby from Natalie's arms.

A pang of disappointment shot through her heart as she wiped away a tear.

It's probably just baby hormones.

Everyone had warned her about those. She was thankful she would have her grandma's help. Her grandmother was a great cook and she kept the house cleaned so Natalie didn't have to. Despite being twenty-one, she was not exactly the most domesticated woman in her community.

Chapter 2
Early Childhood

Though my mother had her hands full with three young children, she did her best to love her children and give them nice things. During the summer, she would take us to Jone's Dairy in Taylorsville, Utah to get us an ice cream cone, and pet the goats in their goat pen behind the store. On the way home from work, she would stop at the farm where her mother lived and let us visit for some time.

During the Christmas season, she would take us to the mall and let us visit Santa. We loved to see all the great decorations in the store. She would drive around to see Christmas lights almost every night after work, because she usually worked late. We lived thirty minutes from most of my dad's stores, banks, and anywhere else my mom worked, which made our journey almost convenient.

Though many kids in the order didn't have enough to eat, my mother was on the WIC program and we always had cereals like Kix and King Vitamin. Despite how hard my mother worked, she always appeared to be happy and smiling.

After giving birth to her fourth child, my mother was soon unable to pay for child care, even with the extremely low rates in our community. There were also rumors of abuse and neglect circulating within the daycares in our community as well, and my mother did try to protect us during these early years. My mother was working two jobs at this time. She would wake up at 6am to go work at my father's accounting office and after her shift ended there, she would work for his brother, Daniel, at his answering service company. I remember multiple times we would be picked up from my grandmother's house to go back to my mom's work, where she would put us to bed in a double bed in the back. The bed was reserved for employees to sleep, but my mother was always working so it was usually available for us. Some mornings, I would wake up to find my mother asleep in the bed next to us. I never understood how she could work so much.

After a few months of this, the answering service soon stopped allowing children to sleep in the back. They were left unattended and things had been damaged. My mom wasn't the only young mother bringing her kids to work with her. My grandmother finally agreed to allow us to stay with her while my mother worked.

My grandmother lived about five minutes away from our home at the "home place" in Bountiful, Utah, which made it a convenient place for my mother to drop us off in the mornings. It took her about thirty minutes to drive to the central location of the majority of my dad's businesses. She would drop us off in the morning with no shoes, full diapers, and pajamas for those who couldn't dress themselves.

My mom was always rushing in the mornings. Our house was way too loud for 6am. My siblings and I would all pile into my mother's old gray van and go back to sleep. We were never buckled in a car seat or even a seat belt for that matter. I don't ever remember wearing a seatbelt when my mom drove us anywhere. It wasn't until I became much older and began riding with other people in our community that I even learned the actual purpose of a seatbelt.

As we pulled into my grandmother's driveway every morning, I remember hearing the rooster crow and smelling the stink of the Great Salt Lake and animal manure in the distance. On the way to the farm, my mother would ask me to recite the Perfecting Meditations, which was written by my great grandfather as words of wisdom to live by. I could only remember the first paragraph, but there were a lot of big words for a five-year-old. When we went into the house, so early in the morning, most everyone was still in bed. We were plopped on the couch before my mother ran back out the door, and we usually fell back to sleep.

When we woke up, my uncles were usually watching cartoons like Aladdin, Teenage Mutant Ninja Turtles, and Anamaniacs, before Anamaniacs was banned by my grandmother's husband, Adam*.

On the days Adam* had spent the night, he would wake everyone up at seven in the morning for mediations. It was known around the group that all members were supposed to meditate every day for five minutes. The special times were at seven am, noon, and seven pm. This showed unity and higher living in the community. On normal days, when Adam* was not there, everyone slept in.

When everyone was out of bed, we would be fed raw oats, raisons, and raw milk, which was usually way too sour and way too creamy. Our dishes would usually be an old carton that once held cottage cheese or sour cream and a spoon that was either plastic or way too big for our tiny mouths. While we enjoyed WIC foods at my mom's home, my grandmother's home was a different story. Most of our food came from the garbage my grandfather picked up for the animals on the farm. Rarely did we have any food that had not expired or that we were not cutting the moldy parts off melons and cantaloupes. Cheese was rare at my mother's house because it was so expensive, but at my grandmother's house, they found huge bricks of it in the garbage. Once the mold was cut off, it tasted great.

Myrna had been the first wife in her previous marriage to my biological grandpa, Lloyd, when she gave birth to my mother. Her husband had died in a mining accident just weeks before she discovered she was pregnant with her second child. Her sister Janice* was married to Adam.* After my grandmother's husband died, things worked out for her to marry Janice's* husband. It was not abnormal for a woman to marry her sister's husband in our community. In fact, it happened all the time. In some instances, it seemed, men would marry one sister to get another. The men would justify this by using the story of Jacob from the bible. He wanted to marry a girl named Rachel, but her older sister Leah was unmarried. Rachel and Leah's father told Jacob he could only marry Rachel if he married Leah first.

Where my great grandmother had been an impeccable housekeeper, my grandmother was not. There were always dishes with week old food piled high on the tables, counters, and in the sinks. She had plenty of dishes, but it was usually easier to wash some old carton that contained last night's cottage cheese than to try to wash week old food off the actual dishes. None of us had even seen a commercial dishwasher.

My grandmother's house had a finished top floor, but the basement with all the bedrooms was still concrete flooring and exposed wiring. It had a finished bathroom and the laundry room was off to the right. The house only had one bedroom upstairs and three bedrooms downstairs. My grandmother had eight children and lacked space, so her husband attached a trailer to an outside door instead of building a porch. This added another bedroom and a large playroom. The trailer was always very cold. Whoever was in the bedroom, was given three or four large quilts my grandmother had quilted to try to keep warm.

In the wintertime it was too cold to sleep in the

trailer. The playroom was eventually converted to a storage unit where her husband stored old computers, guns, and things he thought might make money at his pawn shop. Realistically, it was all a scene from hoarders gone wild with a few valuable items thrown in.

My grandmother had been a public-school teacher before she committed to the duties of faithful housewife. She was always more interested in projects that stimulated her mind as opposed to the manual labor of housework and parenting. She spoke fluent Spanish from her years of teaching. Education was important to her and she loved to read. She also enjoyed gardening and sewing, but these were the only things she did regularly to put her in the category of housewife. Most of her kids ran around without shoes and socks. In fact, my feet are still calloused and have very little feeling to this day. The driveway was made of rocks and we were able to take it bare feet at a run.

Most of my memories at the farm are good ones. Our main activity at the farm was scavenging through the garbage pile behind the large hay barn and most of the main houses. It was a slab of concrete where the farm workers would collect old, expired food from local grocery stores to feed the animals. There would be large piles of boxes full of hostess cookies, twinkies, cupcakes, yogurt, cottage cheese, and other things we weren't able to buy because of our low incomes and strange health beliefs. The old food would be fed to the farm animals if we didn't get to it first.

Everyone from the farm came from poor families. My grandmother's husband owned pawnshops and had done well for himself, but because she was not the first wife, you couldn't see that in my grandmother's home or any of her belongings. She drove run down vehicles that were known for their embarrassing aesthetics, but they lasted forever. It was the same for all the other women on the farm. Most of them were second, third, or fourth wives, which meant they didn't get any income or support from their husbands. Most of them ate food from the garbage. My grandmother got a deal from the nearby bakery to collect all their outdated bread. She would take that bread to church on Sunday and sell it to earn an income.

My two best friends came from the poorest family on the farm. They were two sisters who looked nothing alike. Brenda*, was older, and had blue eyes and blonde hair. Many guys would have actually found her attractive if she had been from a different family. Catherine*, was a year or so older than me, and had the thickest, fiery red hair I had ever seen. Her green eyes and large chest set her apart from other girls, but she had more of a homely look to her and her short stature didn't help the situation.

Their personalities were as different as their appearance. While Brenda* was loud and outgoing, Catherine* was quiet and reserved. They had been teased in public school for being polygamous and even the families in the Order treated them as outcasts. I didn't care though. They were nice to me and we had great memories on the farm together, playing dolls, sneaking into my aunt's makeup, and gathering as much sugary food from "the back" as we could carry.

As a child, I had never seen a middle-class home. Everyone I knew lived in poverty or close to it. I didn't see my grandmother's house as anything but normal. When I went to Brenda* and Catherine's* house, I felt like I was in a lower-class home. I never saw their mom home and their front door didn't shut completely. Any time I walked into the house, there were kids from the farm who didn't live there. There was no supervision, so naturally, this is where most of the kids socialized. It didn't matter that the house was in worse condition than my grandmother's. None of us kids cared that there were ants and spiders crawling all over the floor from the rotten food and the cracks in the home. I don't remember seeing animals inside the house, but I remember cat fur all over their couches.

I would spend hours playing with Brenda* and Catherine* until the sun started to go down and you could hear my grandmother calling,

"Ryan*!" "Dylan*!".

This was everyone's cue to go home and start dinner. Brenda* was responsible for making dinner in her home before her mother came home and Catherine* was responsible for sweeping the kitchen. They were supposed to be finished with their chores before their mom came home, but they never started until everyone else was called home. Their mother came home shortly after that. Their brother Richard* was my age, and he was often hit with a belt when his mother came home. Brenda* and Catherine* were hit on occasion, but Richard* seemed to get the worst of it. I once asked them why they didn't just do their chores before their mother came home. Their response was, "It would take us a year to complete our chores." With the condition their house was in, they were probably right.

After my grandmother's stew-of-some-kind dinner, we would continue playing indoors the rest of the night. Sometimes we would sneak out to the front yard and play "No Bears are out Tonight" or if my grandmother was in a good mood, she would allow us to play for a couple of hours before bed. About ten o'clock, my aunts and uncles were sent to their rooms to sleep. My siblings and I would spread out our blankets on the floor and couches and go to sleep. Sometimes my grandmother would allow television on, but most of the time, we were left alone in the dark to go to sleep until my mother came home. She usually didn't arrive until well past midnight.

On the days that Brenda's* and Catherine's* mom stayed home, they were not allowed to go outside. Their mother would force them to stay inside and do chores all day. The chores were rarely completed, and often times they would sneak out of the house when their mom wasn't looking. Their mom would force them to stand in the corner or sit on a chair for time out and they would quietly sneak out. One time their older brother Ron* came outside holding a chair to his butt. When we asked why he was doing this, he explained that his mother told him he would get a hard spanking if his butt left that chair. We laughed and turned it into a game of tag.

The older boys would often climb to the top of the cilos and throw rotten produce off them. I was afraid of heights and never dared climb more than a few feet up the cilo, but I often saw Ron* and Dylan* hanging off them as though they had no fear of the thirty feet drop to the cement below.

One of the farm workers would be so angry with them for throwing produce all over the ground and would chase them around with his shotgun in his old brown pickup truck. It may not have started out brown, but with all the mud caked on, it appeared a dirty brown color. I thought it was a game the couple of times I happened to be with them, because we never actually got caught, until we did.

The farm worker ran Ron* down and tackled him to the ground. Ron* was usually much faster, but this time, he tripped and went down. The farmer was much bigger and was able to wrestle Ron* to the ground. I stood with my uncles and some other kids from the farm as we hid behind the haystacks and watched as the farmer tied Ron's* arms

19

behind his back. I looked on in horror as he tossed him into the back of his pickup truck. I seemed to be the only one upset by what was happening.

We waited an hour or so before we went to the farmer's trailer and peaked inside. His dirty, brown truck was gone. We peaked into the window to find Ron* tied in a bedroom in the trailer. Because I was the smallest, I was hoisted up to the window and went to unlock the door for the rest of the rescue team. The trailer was the filthiest I had seen around. I couldn't believe someone lived here. Everything was covered in dirt as though it had been exposed to the elements and had never been wiped down. I brushed past a chair on my way to the door and found a layer of dirt on my jeans.

After releasing Ron's* bonds, the rescue team rushed out of the trailer. Ron* seemed unfazed that he had just been held captive by a kid with a shotgun and everyone else appeared to be having a good time.

"David's coming!" Someone shouted, certain they had spotted the farmer.

I was too scared to wait around to see if it was true. I ran away with Brenda* and Catherine* to play games that didn't involve people holding guns.

The summer at the farm was ending, and school would be starting in two weeks. Though I was born into a chaotic environment, I never knew it up to this point. I had my friends from the farm and was learning to read with my grandmother. My mother was gone most of the time for work, but my grandmother had become more of a mother to me. I didn't miss my biological mother when she was gone. I felt safe and stable. It only took one day for this to change.

I was playing in my uncle's room with some other

boys from the farm. Brenda,* Catherine,* and Ron* had all gone home. I didn't even think about the fact that I was the only girl in the room. Why would I? I was with my uncle and the other boys he was always with. Even when the conversation turned from the game on the floor to the most recent R rated movie Dylan* had just watched, I wasn't worried. He watched the movie without permission, of course. Adam* didn't want us to have a television in the house, let alone R rated movies.

Dylan*, asked me to shut the door. Because I looked up to my uncle, I didn't think anything of it. I was excited to be included in their game for once. Usually, I was kicked out when they were doing things they weren't supposed to. When Dylan* looked at me though, I saw something different in his eyes. I saw something I had never seen before. As I looked at the other boys, some of them looked nervous. I suddenly felt like meat in a circle of rabid dogs.

I grew very uncomfortable. When Dylan* told me to take my pants off, I didn't know how to respond.

"But boys can't see girls without their clothes on," I protested, trying to buy some time to figure out what was going on.

"You have to do what I say because I'm older," Dylan* said pulling his authority card on me, and I did as I was told.

Tears welled in my eyes as some of the boys took this opportunity to leave. I wished just one of them would have asked me to do the same or suggested another activity. Anything to protect me.

When the tears cleared enough for me to see again, there were fewer people there, but I didn't notice who they were anymore. I wanted to scream or cry for help. I willed someone to please just walk in and stop this, but no one came.

Before I knew it, my pants were in the corner and Dylan* had commanded me to lay on the floor in front of him and a couple of the boys who remained. We were in a basement and most of the floor was unfinished cement. I was so cold. I closed my eyes as tight as I could as each of them took turns touching me. First, over my Hanes flower panties and then underneath. I couldn't stop the tears anymore, and they flowed freely.

My concept of time was warped from the combination of my young age and the horror of what was happening to me, until finally, it was over. The boys had each left and I was lying on an area rug over a cement floor. I rushed to find my pants and put them on before anyone could come back. After I awkwardly struggled to get them back on, I ran to the unfinished closet under the stairs and made myself as small as I possibly could. I wrapped my arms around my legs and started to cry.

Why did this happen? Why do I feel this way? Why do I feel so icky inside?

I had been beaten by my uncles and it had been painful. This was different. This was a pain on the inside that I couldn't pinpoint and I didn't understand. I just couldn't shake the feeling of shame and embarrassment. Boys weren't supposed to see girls without their clothes on. It was one of the first lessons I had been taught, and the way I felt only confirmed what had happened was wrong. Dylan* was someone I knew and trusted. He was not supposed to ever hurt me. I couldn't help but feel I had done something wrong and that I was a bad girl now. Somehow, this was all my fault.

After the incident, I hid under the stairs until my mother came back. When I heard her voice upstairs, I ran to her seeking protection and comfort.

"I want to go home," I whimpered as she began a conversation with my grandmother.

It was an odd request, because I never wanted to leave my grandmother's house. Unfortunately, she was either too naive or too uninvolved in her children to think much of it. She granted my request to leave immediately, but she brought me back the next day even though I didn't want to go.

For the next two weeks, I tried to stay close to my grandmother. We probably read the "Lion and the Mouse" a hundred times, but she was in her room often and we weren't allowed to be in there.

Whenever Dylan* could get me alone, he would try to offer me soda and candy. At first, I thought he was trying to make up for hurting me, but I soon learned it was just the opposite. He thought that he could bribe me to continue doing sexual things with him. After a couple of weeks of being touched by him, I had gotten over the initial shock of it. Any communication with him from then forward was painful and confusing.

"If you tell anyone, they are going to think you are a bad girl," Dylan* would often tell me referring to the abuse he had not only caused, but had encouraged his friends to take part in.

"If you tell anyone, I'll beat you up."

I remembered the last time he had gotten mad at me, Dylan* had thrown a large sized rock at my head. I only remember a quick dull pain where the rock had hit, and then the world went black.

"It was an accident!" he shouted when I woke up.

I was laying on the ground where I had been standing, and Dylan* and some of his friends were standing over me with their eyes wide. I had a terrible

23

headache for the rest of the day and just wanted to sleep.

"If you tell anyone, I'll do it again."

I kept my mouth shut.

Another time, he was throwing a letter opener around and when I looked over at my infant sister Rachel*, it was sticking out of her head. He started screaming and Rachel didn't even seem to notice. My grandmother came outside and saw a the letter opener sticking out of her small head. She called my mom to come take her to a hospital.

"Paul doesn't want us to go to the hospital," my mom declared.

My grandmother pulled it out herself and I remember blood spurting everywhere as my grandmother ran to grab a towel. The white towel was soon dark red as the blood soaked through and my mother's hand over the wound was unsuccessful at stopping the bleeding as well. My mom rushed my sister to see Paul, and I didn't see them again for the rest of the night. It seemed for the first time, Dylan* was punished for something he had done, as I remember my grandmother yelling at him for hours.

"She could have died!" we could all hear my grandmother's voice throughout the house.

What Dylan* didn't know is that I had no intention of ever reliving this experience by telling anyone. Besides the fact, that telling would only get me into trouble and I didn't want everyone to think I was a bad girl.

Finally, two weeks later, the abuse finally ended. I started Kindergarten in the public school across the street from my house and would no longer be at my grandmother's house for long hours. My mom would be unable to leave work to pick me up after school, and my only option was to walk home afterwards. My younger siblings would be taken to a babysitter during the day, and I would be home alone for hours until my mom came home after her work day.

I had always been a quick learner, and I was never one to get into trouble, but I found myself unable to connect and socialize with most of the other kids in my class. I became drawn to a tall, black boy named Josh, who was known for getting in trouble. If the teacher asked him to do something he didn't want to do, he would throw a tantrum and walk out of the classroom.

After a couple of times of this, the teacher no longer chased him. He would generally go sit in the hall and sulk, so I guess she figured he would be fine. Josh and I connected in a way I was unable to with any of the other kids. I suspected his dad was abusing him, and he didn't deny it when I asked. Eventually, I started sneaking out of class shortly after he would walk out. He was my only friend.

Stealing had never been something I had thought about before Josh, but after seeing him do it, it made sense. He showed me his backpack with all the quarters he was stealing from his mom. My mother would never buy me things from the store. She used our lack of money as the reason to not buy anything. Josh had all this nice stuff with money he stole from his mom. My mom never bought me candy, and that was what I wanted.

I started stealing from Mrs. Henderson's candy jar on her desk. I didn't take much at first, but I became greedy. It was working so well. I could steal handfuls of candy and take them home to my siblings. I wanted them to have nice things too. Josh was soon transferred out of our class, but his habit stayed with me.

After months of stealing my teacher's candy, she

finally discovered what was happening.

"Does anyone know who took the candy on my desk?" Mrs. Henderson asked moments after I had just taken a handful and shoved it into my pocket.

"Nicole did it," claimed a young blonde girl named Tiffany, as she looked up from her notebook she had been writing in.

I didn't know if she really knew it was me or if she simply hated me. We weren't exactly in the same circle of friends.

I wasn't a great liar when I was confronted. In fact, I couldn't even get words out when she asked me if the accusation was true. Mrs. Henderson took me to the principal's office to call my mom when she saw my pockets full of the stolen candy.

My mom was shocked at what I had done.

"Why would you steal her candy?" she asked.

I knew stealing was wrong. We learned about it in Sunday school.

"Is that where all that candy was coming from?" she asked as though the answer wasn't obvious.

I had been bringing home candy for weeks. I claimed my teacher gave to me as a prize. My mom was so proud of me for sharing with my siblings, but she never suspected it might be stolen.

"You're going to have to tell Uncle Paul," she told me at the end of the conversation.

I hadn't said much because my teacher was standing next to me, and my mom realized the conversation was going nowhere.

I knew Paul was the leader of the Order, but I did not know he was my dad at this time. I thought the leader would have better things to do with his time, but I knew my mother was upset and I didn't want to make it worse. My mom was never consistent in her punishments and more than likely, we would never speak about this incident again. Quite frankly, I wasn't too worried about getting in trouble with my mom. She never punished us. I was more embarrassed about being caught and having everyone in my class look at me the way they did.

When I came home that night, my mother didn't bring up the situation again. I had suspected I would be getting off without a punishment, and it looked as though I was right. It wasn't until Sunday evening rolled around and I found myself in my mom's van driving to some unknown destination. We found ourselves in a poverty-stricken neighborhood I recognized from a babysitter I had maybe one or two times in the past.

Why are we at Jenny's house?*

I was surprised when we parked next door to Jenny'*s at the old rundown church. I was even more surprised when we went inside the church.

Paul was surrounded by a group of the numbered men in our church. When a man becomes so high in the church class system, he is given a number to signify his standing in the church. The man who started the order is number one and each number was given out consecutively to those who joined in the early days of the church. After the Order became much larger, numbers were no longer given in order. Paul and the man who would receive the number, would pray and get divine inspiration from God. Paul is number nine. Paul's dad, Ortell, is number eight.

As my mom and I waited for Paul to finish meeting after meeting, hours passed. My mind wandered, and I thought about why we could be here. I soon realized I hadn't gotten out of the stealing incident as I had thought. I prepared myself for a long speech from the leader of the Order and was determined to never steal again. The whole situation was humiliating, and it was getting late. I just wanted to go home and go to sleep.

Finally, the last man left the church. It was eerie with only the three of us sitting in such a large empty building. You could hear the echo of the smallest sounds in the large meeting room. I had never been to a church meeting in here, but I couldn't imagine being able to hear it with the echo from the children.

"Nicole has been stealing candy," my mother began before anyone else could get a word out.

"Is that true?" he asked after gathering his thoughts.

"She's been taking it for weeks and giving it to the kids," my mom continued without allowing me a word.

Without another word to me, Paul turned to my mom.

"Will you go ask Jenny* if she has a wooden spoon or something you can borrow?" he asked her.

Almost too eagerly, my mother rushed out to follow his command.

My stomach dropped.

Was he seriously going to hit me? Did he even have the right to hit me?

I didn't know him personally, but he had seemed like a nice guy.

"Stealing is wrong," he began his long lecture. It went on for about fifteen minutes or so, but I couldn't focus on what he was saying as the fear continued to grow the longer my mom was gone.

"I'm going to spank you," he continued, bringing my thoughts back to the present. "I'm going to spank you, because I love you. I'm going to spank you because I want you to know this is wrong. I'm going to spank you, and it's going to hurt me more than it will hurt you."

Fear only grew as my mother came back. I could hardly believe what she had brought back with her. Instead of a wooden or metal spoon, my mother had managed to come back with a metal L-shaped object that looked as though it had been removed from an old bed frame or utility shelf. There was no way he was going to hit me with that. I could see the rust clearly glinting in the low lighting of the church. I was wrong.

"You can wait in here," he instructed my mother as he took me by the hand roughly. He led me to a smaller, darker room off to the side of the large room.

I was afraid of the dark at this point, and I was uncomfortable being alone with a man after what Dylan* had done to me. To make matters worse, Paul instructed me to pull down my pants.

Dylan's* abuse came flooding back and my eyes welled with tears. I was helpless, drowning, and he hadn't even hit me yet. With no choice, I complied with his request, and he bent me over his knee. The whole thing was demeaning.

"I'm going to spank you, because I love you," he began. "This is going to hurt me more than it will hurt you."

I wanted to argue that just forcing me to remove my pants was hurting me more than him, but I kept silent as I felt violated again. Then the pain came. He hit me with the bar again and again. I screamed after the fourth or fifth time and I wanted so badly to take the bar from him and hit him over the head with it. The pain was unbearable, and I lost count after the sixth time. At one point, the pain was less intense, and I thought maybe I had blacked out. The next hit proved I was still conscious.

Finally, it was over. I was sobbing.

"I want you to stand in the corner and think about what you've done," he said coldly.

With that, he left the room and closed the door behind him.

The room was consumed with darkness, and I felt like I couldn't breathe. Despite my anger for my father, I couldn't be alone. I was afraid of the dark because of my abuse. I stood in that corner feeling violated all over again, and in that moment, I hated Paul with a hate I had never had before. I hated Dylan*.

I couldn't even remember what I was standing there for anymore. I just hated. I hated my mother for bringing back that bar.

Why couldn't she get a normal wooden spoon like he had asked? Why did she let him hit me?

I don't know how long I stood in that corner. After it was over, Paul hugged me. I was in too much pain to fight it or hug him back even if I had wanted to. My mom tried to talk to me on the way home, but I wouldn't speak to her. This was the second time she was supposed to protect me and didn't. I didn't know it at the time, but her neglect would only get much worse.

Chapter 3
Abuse

My mother kept me home for weeks after Paul's abuse. I was horrified to find bruises all up and down my back, buttocks, and my upper legs. I hadn't even remembered being hit in all those places. My body ached for weeks as the bruises healed, and my mother left me alone for those two weeks. She didn't bring up the incident again, and neither did I. I had nothing to say to her.

She finally went back to work and I went back to Kindergarten. I was no longer the quiet, reserved child I had been. I became angry. There was a young boy named Lincoln who had picked on my friend, Jamie, before my abuse happened. He became my target. If he was mean to her, I would chase him down and knock him into the ground. Jamie was a sweet, blonde girl with Nala earrings from the Disney Show, The Lion King. I was so jealous of her new clothes and pierced ears. I knew I would never have those things, but sometimes she would give me some of her lunch or her new toys. She shared her things with me and I protected her from bullies.

After school, I would walk home and be alone for hours before my mom came home from work with her other kids. I was lonely at home, but any time I mentioned playdates with kids from school, my mother would dismiss the suggestion. I never understood why, and after months of asking my mom, it never happened. Finally, school was over. My mom went back to work. My siblings and I went back to the farm part of the time, and other times went from babysitter to babysitter.

One day, my mother sat my siblings and I down for one of her attempted "family meetings" she had whenever she was feeling extra obedient to my father.

"Uncle Paul is planning a camping trip with a bunch of girls and he wants to know if you would like to go."

It was ironic how suggestions were often worded to make it sound as though you had a choice in the matter. I had never been allowed to go camping. I had asked to visit my aunt who lived about two hours away, but I was never able to make even that happen. Yes, I wanted to go camping.

"Well some of the girls claimed that you've been very mean to them," my mom continued, taking the conversation in a completely new direction than I had expected.

"Who?"

She named a bunch of girls I had gone to Sunday school with. I had never really had a personal interaction with any of them. I was at a loss for words.

Maybe I didn't want to go camping with them?

This was the first "Girl's Outing" my father's wives orchestrated to allow Paul to spend time with his hundreds of children. Every year, the wives planned a "girl's outing" and a "boy's outing". Paul would put it in his schedule and make sure he was on the trip. He would assign the food and preparation to the wives, and Dena*, the second wife, would delegate assignments to all the other wives who had children old enough to go on the outing.

I was six years old when we went on the first outing, and we went to the Bountiful Mountains. Paul kept his camper at my mom's house because it was the "home place" and had extra space. I remember helping him clean out the camper to get ready for this trip. There were many other times we cleaned the camper together because he would take one of his wives camping for a birthday or anniversary as well. Except during the times of abuse, Paul was a generally happy and pleasant person to be around. I

32

don't ever remember seeing him sad in my youth. He made jokes and sang out of tune, even though he was a talented singer. Unfortunately, I saw more of his abuse as I got older.

Late one night, Paul came home and just as he normally did, he went into the kitchen to dish himself some food my mom had previously prepared for him. The nights Paul came home were the only nights my mother seemed to try to be a wife and mother. She would take the day off work and clean her house spotless and make chicken and mashed potatoes. I don't know if that was his favorite meal or if it was just a meal my mother did well, but it was delicious all the times she allowed us kids to have some, which was rarely. Most of the time we would eat cereal while she finished the meal for my dad. When we did eat her dinner, it was the one time in our life when dinner included a salad, though she never put tomatoes in it because Paul didn't like tomatoes. To this day, I still don't like tomatoes. All the kids knew if they came home from school and the house was clean, Paul was coming over.

As Paul settled in to eat his food, one of the kids had gotten my eighteen-month old baby sister a bowl of cereal. It was not one of our special nights. Many times, we would watch Paul enjoy his food when we had either had cereal, or nothing for dinner. He never shared with us.

On this occasion, we were given cereal. Rachel* had brought her dish into the living room to eat with Paul, who was sitting on the couch enjoying his meal. After telling her twice to go into the kitchen with her dish, and getting nowhere, he lashed out and spanked her. Her cereal flew everywhere from the ceiling to the carpet to the walls. Paul was livid. Setting his food on the couch, he grabbed Rachel* and hit her on her little diaper.

When Rachel* started screaming, Paul told her to be quiet and when she didn't, he grabbed her and took her into the bathroom. My brother and I rushed to clean up the carpet where the cereal had spilled, in hopes of helping the situation. We could all hear Paul hitting her again and again, telling her to be quiet. When she continued to cry, he would hit her again for being disobedient.

My mom quickly instructed the kids to go to their rooms for bed. Not knowing what else to do, we ran up the stairs as my baby sister's screams echoed through the house. My mom closed our bedroom doors, something she had never done in the past. She must have thought it would hide my sister's screams and the sound of Paul hitting her over and over again, and yelling at her to be quiet and stop crying. It didn't. We heard everything.

This is wrong! I should be protecting my baby sister, a part of me shouted.

My eyes welled up with tears as I wondered if I would ever have any control in my world that seemed so out of control. After what seemed like hours passed, my guilt continued to build.

What if he killed her? What if he beat her until she died?

I should stop this.

She's my sister. She's a baby!

Once again, I found myself hating Paul and my mother. Parents are supposed to protect their children.

Finally, I heard my mom coming up the stairs and my poor baby sister was breathing heavily and sniffling, struggling to calm down.

She was still alive!

I pretended to be asleep as my mom opened my bedroom door and put Rachel* on the bed and left. She didn't give her a kiss or try to comfort her. Rachel* was plopped on the bed and left alone in the dark.

My heart hurt as I heard her trying to stop the most tired, pathetic whine I had ever heard out of an infant. She must have cried until she was too exhausted or hurt to cry anymore.

I was left in the pitch black with my two little sisters. I crawled closer to Rachel* on the bed we shared and put my hand on her, hoping to comfort her. She startled when I touched her and acted as though she might start screaming again, and I prayed she would stay quiet. When I called out to her, she realized it was me and settled down again.

"I'm so sorry," I mumbled as tears began to flow freely. "I'm here. I will never let this happen again."

I was determined to keep my promise.

As the summer ended, I was excited to start school again. My younger brother, Dustin* would be going to public school with me, and I would have someone to walk home with after school. I was starting first grade and Dustin* would be going to all day Kindergarten. I'm not sure if my mom worked it out with the school or if they offered all-day Kindergarten, but my brother was in school until I got out to walk home with him. My teacher was Mrs. Hill and I really liked her. I was determined to avoid getting in trouble at school because school was my favorite place. I became a model student.

About half way through the year, Dustin* began coming home from school with bruises.

"What happened?" I demanded to know.

"Nothing," he mumbled.

When my mom came home, I made sure she knew as well.

"What happened?" my mom asked.

"Nothing!" my brother yelled.

To my dismay, my mother let it go.

"That's your kid!" I yelled at my mom. "Do something."

When she continued to do nothing, I wouldn't let it go.

He finally admitted that two brothers named Hollace and Walker were bullying him.

They were much bigger boys and had a reputation for bullying. I was tall for my age and quite strong. I marched right up to those boys the next day.

"Leave my brother alone!"

Though amused that I had the courage to stand up to them, they didn't take me seriously.

"You're a little girl," Hollace began. "You can't do nothing."

I punched Hollace in the face. When Walker went to attack me, I punched him in the stomach. As both boys sat crying on the ground, I explained my position again.

If you ever touch my brother again, it will be worse."

They never touched Dustin* again, and they later became good friends with my brother after that. I never got in trouble because the boys would never admit they were beat up by a girl. I promised I would never stand by and do nothing again. I couldn't do anything for Rachel*, but I could protect Dustin*. My mom laughed when she heard the story of Hollace and Walker and even though Dustin* was embarrassed that his sister had to step in, I think he appreciated it in the end.

Being home all the time was boring for me. Dustin* didn't mind it. He went home and was fine watching cartoons till my mom came home. I was bored out of my mind. When I was playing outside one day, against my

36

mother's wishes, the girl who lived across the street from me came over to talk to me.

"What are you doing?" she asked innocently. I fell in love with her short blonde hair and her high pitched feminine voice.

We got into a conversation about something or other and became best friends after that. I never told my mom about my new friend, because I knew she would try to end it. Tasha had everything I wanted. She was the youngest of three girls in a family with a mother and a father who came home every night. When she asked me about my dad, I told her I didn't have one. As far as I knew, I had never met him. My mother had concocted a story that his name was Steven Allen and he traveled all the time for work. When I asked if I could meet my father, she assured me I would meet him someday. I kept waiting for someday. Maybe we could all be a family like Tasha's family. I didn't realize it at the time, but my life was about to change in some big ways, but they would only get me farther away from the traditional family I wanted.

.

Chapter 4
Polygamy

My mom usually celebrated the holidays with her mom and siblings, but when Thanksgiving came around this year, we went to Paul's family party. It turned out to be all his brothers and their families as well. The food was not good and there were too many people to organize any kind of games or activities. I didn't really know anyone there and I was not close to anyone. The following week I found myself at our next-door neighbor's house to be babysat. I didn't think anything of it until I was swinging on the swing-set with my friend, Mia.*

"Do you know why you're here?" she asked as though she was just about to explain a simple fact of life, and not completely shatter mine.

"My grandma is sick," I answered.

That was the story my mom had told, and I had no reason to not believe her. I didn't even think about the fact that my grandmother was never sick.

"Your grandma is dead," she calmly explained as though I was stupid for not knowing this fact.

I was upset she knew before me, and I questioned her further. She told me she didn't know much. I hoped she was lying. We hadn't been to my grandmother's house in about a month, which was unusual for us. The farm was close by and my mother depended on her for everything from caring for her kids to feeding her. My mother would never survive without her.

I was unable to play with Mia* for the rest of the day. This news was unbelievable for me. It was unusual for us to be at Mia's* house. Her mother was our next-door neighbor. Though she was a member of the Order, she was not one of my father's wives, nor directly related to my mother in any way. She lived next door, but we almost never talked except when I would play with Mia* during the summers. Our mothers were not close though and she would have been one of the last people on my mother's lists of babysitters.

Finally, my mother returned from wherever she had been. The sun had almost gone down and I had some time to process the news of my grandmother's death. I had so many questions.

Who would take care of us now? Where would we go when my mom worked? Who would read with me? Would we still go to the farm? What happens when people die?

I remember hugging my mother tightly when she finally returned home. I could feel the cold of her skin and clothing and smell her older woman's perfume. I felt safe for a moment before the world came crashing down. My mother's little sister Leah* had married my father years after my mother married him and was currently pregnant with her second child. My mom was also pregnant with her fifth child. Leah* was still living with her mom. Her mom had just died. Who would take care of everyone?

I never saw my mom cry over the death of her mother. It was strange for me and made it difficult to believe the death had happened at all until the next day at the funeral. This was where I faced my grandmother's dead body in an open casket. Maybe God could bring her back to life. I remember staring at her for a few minutes willing her to open her eyes. I didn't understand death or the permanence of it. When I kept trying to talk to my mother about it, she explained that she was in fact dead, but she dismissed any conversation about it. My mother's sisters all dealt with their mother's death differently. Jennifer* was cold. Leah* became teary eyed whenever she talked about it, and Ashley* sobbed unprovoked. Her sons Ryan* and Dylan* were young teenagers and went through the motions.

After my grandmother's funeral, my family had a potluck dinner for family and friends. I wasn't hungry. I grabbed a single red rose from the flowers and the program from her funeral and went to my room. I stared at her picture for hours as everything sunk in. When I finally realized she was never coming back, I began sobbing. I missed her so much. She was more of a mother to me than my own mother had ever been. She was the one who taught me to read. She was the one who bathed me on the rare occasions we were bathed. She was the one who tucked me in before she went to bed. She couldn't really be gone. I sobbed for hours until I finally fell asleep.

"Nicole," I heard a whisper from somewhere far away.

When I opened my eyes, I thought I had imagined it. I felt trapped in that moment right between dreaming and awake and I was unable to lift my head to follow the voice. The moonlight was shining directly on a point in front of me, directly in the center of my room.

I thought I saw a figure standing there and I tried to get up. My body felt unresponsive and my mind seemed peacefully blank. My heart was strangely at peace.

"You can do this," came the whisper again, though this time seemed closer.

I thought the figure was my grandmother, but logically, that didn't make sense. Still, she was so clear in her red dress from the funeral. She was so beautiful and seemed so happy and she also seemed younger than she had the last time I saw her alive.

"Don't leave me," I begged. Even if it wasn't real, it

was better than the reality of her being gone.

"You can do this," she said again softly.

My eyes filled with tears and I was no longer stuck between awake and dreaming. As soon as I realized I was completely awake, she was gone.

I would have given anything to go back and be with her for just one more minute. When I realized I couldn't go back, I began sobbing again. The moon was still shining, but now the only thing in front of me was the ugly blue carpet covering my bedroom floor. My grandmother was really gone, but at that moment, I knew she was watching over me.

After my grandmother's death, my life began to change in so many big ways. My mom's younger sister and sister wife, Leah* moved into my mother's basement with her baby. Her and my mother were both pregnant and due at the same time. A month before their due date, their younger sister, Ashley*, who was fifteen at the time, became the fifth wife to my father's oldest son.

I didn't understand polygamy until Leah* moved into my mother's house. We had never spent a lot of time with any of my father's other wives and all the kids went to school with each other and only half of us knew who our fathers were at the time.

When my mother went into labor with her fifth baby, she paged Paul on his pager. She understood her labors by now and knew when she was close to delivering. Paul didn't show up until his wives were in active labor and about ready to push the baby out. He felt like it was a waste of time to be there until that point. He wasn't there to support his wives, he was there to deliver a baby. My mother wanted only Paul at her deliveries, so she labored on her own for many hours alone. She would finally call

Paul to come catch the baby.

A week after Paul delivered my mother's fifth baby, Leah* went into labor with her second baby just downstairs from my mother's bedroom. Paul had gone out of town shortly after my mother's delivery with another wife. Leah* continued to page Paul over and over throughout the hours of her labor. Usually he would at least call back, but after having no answer, Leah* called Patricia*, Paul's first wife to ask her to get ahold of him.

The first wife generally has the most power in a family and can generally get ahold of her husband. Patricia* refused to tell Leah where Paul was or give him the message that she was in labor. Leah* finally felt like she was getting too close to wait. To avoid having a baby by herself, she called her father and a midwife to come deliver her baby. Paul didn't ever make it to her second birth.

Leah* was not one of the favorite wives and made it very clear that she knew this to everyone who would listen. She was overweight, so she wasn't pretty. She was emotionally immature, so she didn't understand the manipulation required to play the game in polygamy. She was the puppy dog.

If my dad said "Jump,"

She asked, "How high?"

My father knew he could treat her like the dirt beneath his shoe, and she would not complain. If she ever did complain, he would scold and belittle her for questioning her husband. He would dangle the possibility of love or a trip in front of her to get her to repent. Because she was so emotionally immature, she didn't realize she was being played not only by her sister wives, but also her husband.

In the polygamy I knew, your sister wives are not

42

your friends. They are your competition. Your siblings from other mothers are not your friends. They are also your competition. The first wife is automatically one of the favorite wives. She was married first and will always have the title of legal wife, except in very rare circumstances. This gives her more power. She has more access to his schedule and more time with him, because she has the most power over the family. The husband is the head of the family, and the first wife is like his right hand.

After my mother delivered her fifth child, she decided to try her hand at being a stay at home mom. Paul insisted she needed an income, and a lot of the women in the community began starting home daycares after they had more than three or four kids. They could no longer afford to pay daycare while they went to work, and the husband didn't pay child support. My mother lived about thirty minutes from the women in Paul's family, but one of Daniel's wives, Heidi, lived two minutes away. They decided my mom would get licensed with the state because Heidi had her kids taken away by DCFS on more than one occasion. They knew the state would not grant a license for her to open a daycare. They considered just watching each other's kids, but the state offered a food

The other favorite wives are generally the prettiest. Sex is used as currency. If your husband wants to have sex with you, it grants you more privileges. Favorite wives do things for their husband sexually to please him. Favorite wives go on more trips with their husband, have nicer houses, have more nights with their husband, and those nights are less interrupted by other issues. Favorite wives are a higher priority than non-favorite wives. Leah's* advice for me was to make sure I did what I could to be a first wife. It was the only way to be sure to be one of the favorite wives.

check if the provider was licensed. They both knew neither of them could afford to pay the other enough to make it worth it, and the food check would be the reason the plan would work.

My mother began her daycare. It went well for a week or so before problems began. Heidi's kids were incredibly disrespectful and destructive. They ran away when they didn't like someone telling them what to do and they were violent towards the animals on the property. My mom wasn't someone with a lot of patience, and these kids required the patience of a saint. My mom began making excuses for needing to leave the daycare, and asked Ashley*, her little sister to care for all the kids while she was gone. Ashley*, who was only a young teenager herself, was supposed to be downstairs helping Leah* while she was on bedrest for a difficult pregnancy. My mother continued to ask Ashley* to watch her daycare for her and Leah" ended up miscarrying her baby.

Megan* was the oldest of Heidi's children, and we became friends. She was a compulsive liar and had some emotional problems from years of physical and sexual abuse. We would run away whenever Ashley* was in charge. She would tie us up in the bathroom for hours when we did something wrong or beat us with a wooden spoon. She belittled us and called us names. Megan* and I would sneak out and go back to her house and play in her apple orchard or play with the few toys she had in her bedroom.

During one of our escapes, we were playing in her bedroom, when a couple of boys climbed in her window. I hadn't known anyone else was coming to play and I didn't know these boys. I had seen some of them at church, but I wasn't sure of their names. They started talking to us, and I saw a change in Megan*. She became flirtatious with the boys. The mood became uncomfortable, and before I knew it, one boy pinned Megan* down and began taking her pants off.

Everything seemed to happen so quickly. I tried to leave, but the other boys blocked my exit. I looked over at my friend and could only see strange movements before I felt my own pants come off. I didn't realize what was happening. I thought the boys were playing a game, but I was scared. When one boy pushed me down onto the floor, I tried to get up to leave. I couldn't move. The other boy had pinned me down. I closed my eyes and heard the first boy comment that something wouldn't fit. I opened my eyes to see him pick up a yellow toy bat off the floor. I couldn't have been more confused.

Before I could try to figure out what was happening, I felt like my body was being ripped apart from the inside and I screamed in pain.

"Hold still, I have to loosen it up!" the boy shouted to me.

I couldn't see through the tears streaming down my face as I looked at the white ceiling above me. I couldn't see between my legs because I was still restrained, but I felt like I was on fire. I thought I was going to die.

Just then, we all heard the front door open down the hall. The boys jumped up and threw us our clothes.

"Get dressed," one of them hissed at us.

In a daze, I did as I was told just before Lana*, one of Daniel's wives walked in. Apparently, Ashely* had called her when Megan* and I had gone missing and she had come to help find us. When she questioned us, I couldn't stop crying.

"What's wrong?" she asked me, without really worrying about it.

I couldn't speak. The yellow toy bat on the floor

caught my eye from the corner where it had quickly been tossed. It was covered in blood. I nearly vomited as I realized the blood was mine.

"Go home," Lana* told me.

She took Megan* back to her mom.

I ran out the door as quickly as I could, afraid that the boys might chase me and hurt me again. I could hardly stand because I was still in so much pain, but I made it to the orchard behind my house. The boys were not behind me and I couldn't go anymore. I sat behind a tree and began to sob. I looked down at my jeans and they were blood stained.

What happened to me?

After sitting in the woods for what felt like hours, I regained my composure and walked home. I went straight to my bedroom and took off my blood-stained jeans and underwear before putting on clean ones. I took the old ones to the big black garbage outside. I didn't want anyone to find them and I didn't want to ever see them again anyways.

I never snuck out with Megan* again. I would watch the other kids for Ashley* while she tried to chase down Heidi's kids. Luckily, Ashley* refused to watch Heidi's kids shortly after that, and my mother had decided to get a job instead of being home. She claimed the state's rules for daycare were too strict. She didn't think the kids needed fruits and vegetables with lunch and dinner as the state requested. She felt like her whole food check was going to feeding the kids instead of paying her. I guess she missed the point of the food check.

While, I once had very little to do with Paul's family, it seemed they were now suddenly everywhere. Leah* had moved into my mom's basement, and my father's third wife, Rhonda* was living out of town on the Washaki Ranch up north. When she came to Salt Lake for church and family gatherings, she needed somewhere to stay. She began staying with a different wife every weekend.

Rhonda* had more than ten children who also needed a place to stay when they came to visit. During the weekends they stayed with us, things were overcrowded and there was no chance for a shower. I hated those weekends. We had three of my dad's wives and twenty plus children staying in a five-bedroom house. The fact that Rhonda's* children were rude and violent only made matters worse.

One night, when they were over, I was walking through the living room to get a diaper for my mom. The boys had set up their bed on the floor and I could barely see them. One of the boys reached up and grabbed my crotch painfully hard.

At first, I thought it was only an accident, but later that night, he, snuck into my room and began to fondle me. I pretended to be asleep, but that seemed to only encourage him. I pretended to begin to stir awake, but that did nothing. Once again, I laid there as another of my family members violated me. The abuse continued every weekend they stayed with us for months. Suddenly they were no longer allowed to stay with anyone except Diana*, who was the sixth wife. I found out much later that he had done the same thing to many of his half and full sisters and he wasn't allowed to stay at the other wives houses anymore. One of the girls told her older brother and Paul found out what he was doing.

Despite the drama going on at home, my neighbor Mia* and I became closer as friends. We would play together every day and she became someone I could feel myself growing close to. There was always a wall between us because I could never tell her about the abuse in my life. I didn't think she would understand. I was right. She teased me about sleeping with my mom at seven years old. I could never tell her about the multiple times my half-brother had come into my room at night.

Our friendship hit a wall as I was unable to be open with her about my life. That wall grew thicker as she began saying things about my mother and her poor parenting and neglect. She made comments about my sibling's lack of manners, personal hygiene, and cleanliness. Our yard and our house were in the same condition as everyone else I had grown up with, and yes, it was filthy. I knew her house was clean, and her parents were both present in their children's lives. Her father had three wives at one time, but one had left him many years before. Having a smaller family seemed to work out better for them. Though I knew what she was saying was true, I didn't enjoy being attacked in this way.

During one of our fights, she shoved me hard enough to break my collar bone. I stood up and began to cry. I walked home, unable to move my arm. She looked like she felt so ashamed, but I didn't care. I was in pain and she had shoved me on purpose. When my mom tried to look at it, I couldn't move it. My mom tried to call Paul but as he usually was, Paul was in a meeting. She wasn't sure what to do, so she called Adam*.

Though Adam* was not her biological father, he was the closest thing she would ever have to one. Adam* told her to bring me to Salt Lake and he would make sure I got a meeting with Paul to look at it. When Adam* saw me in tears, he tried to get Paul to talk to us, but he was too busy. Adam's pawn shops were doing very well financially, and it put him in a position to help some guys out in business deals from time to time. If we ever needed anything, it seemed that Adam* always knew a guy. Fortunately for me, one of the guys he knew, just happened to be a doctor.

Adam* gave his buddy a call, and thirty minutes later, we were driving to Dr. Taylor's house on the hill in Bountiful, Utah. Though he was resentful of my mother's biological father, Lloyd, and he never tried to hide it, Adam* took care of my mom. He openly called Lloyd a "womanizer" and "boozer" and other things that were just not true. I believe Adam* harbored a jealousy towards Lloyd because my grandmother married him first. But, for all Adam's* shortcomings, he was the only person who ever took care of my mother when her own mother passed away. None of Lloyd's own family ever reached out for her, except for one of Lloyd's sisters who had left the community many years before. This put her in a situation where my mother could not have accepted her help even if she had wanted to. It would have shown her disloyalty to my father because she was not allowed to associate with people outside the community.

Adam* was my mother's only support. He would bring over produce and food for us. Despite the fact it was from the garbage, and we were forced to cut moldy sections out of the food, it was far greater than anything anyone else had ever done for us. It was also more than most women in the community had. If our doors broke, Adam* sent one of his boys to fix it. When our heater went out, Adam's* sons fixed it.

My mother was not an easy woman to deal with, and she did not appreciate him for what he did for her. In fact, she had the nerve to complain to my father that they were not getting things done in a timely manner. My father's response to her complaint infuriated me. Instead of pointing out all the things they had done for her, he

49

berated her and told her if they weren't getting things done in time, she should be responsible enough to find someone else to do it. This was always my father's attitude. Find someone else to do it.

Paul had still been in meetings all day and hadn't even called to check on me. I was in excruciating pain during the winding, bumpy, thirty-minute ride. When we finally arrived, Doctor Taylor asked me to have a seat on his couch and gave me an orange drink. He told me to drink the whole thing. It clearly tasted like a medicine and not a beverage, but I was in too much pain to be worried about what might be in it. Doctor Taylor went off with my mother, Adam* and Janice*, who was his first and only wife after my grandmother died, to show them his new million-dollar home. I suspected Doctor Taylor and Adam* were in the middle of a pissing contest, but I knew this was more medical care than anyone I knew ever received and I was grateful. I was in a real doctor's house! Also, the orange drink was making me feel much better, so I rested on the couch while they went for the grand tour.

After the tour, we all piled back into the car and followed Doctor Taylor down the hill to his office. He opened his medical facility for us and completed my x-rays himself. My left collar bone had been completely broken and it wasn't a bone they could cast. He told me I would be in a back brace for six weeks or longer until the bone healed.

After finishing at the Doctor, my mom brought me back to Jenny's* house to wait for Paul to finish his meetings. I just wanted to go home, but my mother insisted that Paul wanted to see me. I believe my mother just wanted some sympathy and attention from him, whether it was for my sake or hers, I didn't know.

We waited for hours while people who were leaving

the church after meetings with my father, stopped by one by one to see how I was doing. It wasn't my dad's attention, but it was something for my mom. She repeated the story of what happened over and over to everyone who came over. I had been given something for pain and was happy to lie on the bed and relax. The one benefit to my mom's need for attention was that I did not have to speak to single person who came to see me. They wished me to get well and I said thank you as they left.

Finally, Paul showed up. I guess he figured he would appear uncaring if he didn't at least make an appearance for his little girl. He appeared to be annoyed when he came into the room to see me.

"You know there are easier ways to get my attention," he commented, though I wasn't sure if it was directed towards my mother or me.

I didn't care. I wasn't the one who wanted to stay and wait for him. I didn't need his attention. I had needed medical care, and once again, Adam* was doing what my father should have. Paul didn't ask about my follow up care or anything about my condition.

"I'm glad you're okay," he said after only being there for five minutes or so. He went back to the church for his next meeting.

As soon as he walked out the door, my mother seemed irritated, "It's time to go."

My back brace made it difficult for me to get up.

"Help," I begged through my grogginess.

Jenny,* who was another of my dad's wives I was never close to, took my good hand and helped me to my feet. My mother was already out the door.

I remember hating that back brace. Every week I went to see Doctor Taylor to tighten it and to do more x-rays to be sure the bone was healing properly. Despite being a seven-year-old who could no longer run or play, I received very little sympathy from my mother. I dressed myself despite the pain and continued my own care.

A week after the incident, Mia* came to my house to ask me if I was still mad at her. No one had told her the severity of my injury. I told her.

"I'm so sorry," she said sincerely. "Will you forgive me?"

I had nearly forgotten all about her role in the incident. It was a struggle to figure out how to bathe myself. I wasn't worried about what she had done and I was no longer angry with her. I had however, lost interest in being her friend. Her mother seemed to agree, because I was later told that her mother had forbidden us to play together anymore.

After my back brace came off, I was relieved to be able to have full mobility again. I didn't use my mobility for good however, and my abuse from Kindergarten had obviously done nothing to solve the problem. I began stealing again. Abuse doesn't teach kids to be good people. It instills fear. Once I got over that fear, there was nothing to stop me from making the same mistake.

I began stealing from the Order's grocery store. At first, it was a little candy bar here and there, but soon, it escalated. I began taking large bags of candy. I soon told my brother Dustin* about it, and he stood watch while I took the items.

We continued this system for months before Jenny*, happened to be shopping the same time as my mother. She saw me take a bag of candy and put it in my backpack. Dustin* ran out to the car to avoid getting caught, but I knew there was no way out of it. I had been down this road before. Jenny* told my mom what she had seen, and my mother rolled her eyes. She was clearly not happy to be back down this road again. She grabbed my backpack, and in front of the whole store, made a huge scene taking everything out and putting it back on the shelf. Her tactic had been far more effective than my father's. It was humiliating. She grabbed my hand and we immediately left the store.

My mother seemed determined to put an end to this behavior. When I stole candy in Kindergarten, she seemed to step back and allow Paul to handle it. This time, she seemed to take control of the situation. When we got in the car, she began.

"Why would you take something that doesn't belong to you?"

"I wanted some candy," I explained.

"Do you realize that Karen works so hard to make that store successful?"

"No."

"If everyone stole from the store, what would happen?"

"I don't know."

"The Order would lose a lot of money and we wouldn't have a grocery store."

The next day she took me back to the store and forced me to apologize to Karen and give back all the candy I had taken. She didn't hit me once, but her lesson is one that stuck with me.

Chapter 5
Trouble

Growing up as the oldest child, I was given more responsibility than your typical seven-year-old. My mom began leaving me home alone with my siblings for short periods of time while she went up the street to her friend's house to get her hair done or just to socialize. It would be hours at a time before we would hear from her again and she asked me to watch my four younger siblings. Caleb was the youngest at the time at about 9 months old. He had just started crawling.

My mother hadn't taught me to change diapers yet, and when Caleb had a disgusting diaper, Dustin* and I were unsure what to do. We grabbed the baby powder, as many wipes as we could find, and a diaper. Dustin* held him down while I opened the diaper. The smell was overwhelming. I dumped as much baby powder into the diaper as I could. Eventually, the only smell was the strong baby powder and I was able to remove the diaper and wipe as much as I could. I put the other diaper back on and realized it was backwards, but it was on. Baby powder was officially renamed as the "messy extinguisher" in our house.

Another day, I decided I would make suckers while my mom was gone. I started the honey cooking on the stove and went upstairs to check on the kids. I must have forgotten about it and left it on the stove for too long, because we all began to smell smoke. I remembered the honey on the stove and rushed downstairs to a house full of smoke. I turned off the stove and began opening windows before my mother came home, but I didn't get the house cleaned out in time and the honey had burned to the pan, making it completely useless. This gave Dustin* the idea that the stove could make less edible things edible, and when my mother came home on a different occasion, my brother Dustin* was standing in front of an oven fire roasting an apple. It was a miracle our house hadn't burned down yet.

I was a good student up to this point, and I absolutely loved school. I was getting ready to start second grade at the public school across the street, and the year could not start soon enough. Some of my friends from first grade were in the same class and I was excited to see them again. I had missed them. I was not allowed to see them during the summer because I was not allowed to socialize with people outside my community, though I didn't know this at the time. I only knew our old saying, "School friends stay at school."

My brother would be going into first grade at the public school with me, and my little sister would be starting preschool in an Order household.

On my first day of school, I recognized Chonsey, a pretty little Mexican girl with a white mother and Mexican father. She had been in my class in first grade and had asked me if we could do a play date sometime during the summer. I never gave her an answer because my parents would never allow it, and I didn't have a logical explanation for it. I couldn't very well explain to her that her skin color meant she carried the curse of Cain from the bible, or the fact that because she wasn't in the Order, she would not be going to heaven.

I hoped she wouldn't remember the fact that I had ignored her request all summer, and when I sat down next to her, she didn't seem to. She gave me a small smile as the teacher entered shortly afterwards and asked for everyone's attention. After welcoming us back for the year, we started right in on academics.

At lunchtime, I followed Chonsey to the cafeteria and we sat together. Hilary*, who had also been my friend the previous year, was someone I had seen throughout the summer. She was also in the Order and we were in the same Sunday school class together, but she was a year older than me in elementary school because my birthday had missed the deadline. Her father owned a carpet company and wasn't high up in the Order class system because he wasn't from the Kingston bloodline, so our families didn't mingle much. The fact that we lived two minutes away from each other was the only reason we were in the same elementary school.

I didn't understand the bloodline theory at the time, even though it was so ingrained in my culture, and there was no way to ignore it. The theory was introduced by Ortell, my grandfather on my father's side. He had been the leader of the Order before Paul, my father. He died two years before I was born.

When Ortell had worked on the farm, he began breeding cattle. He took great interest in trying to breed the best cattle to get best calves. He then applied this theory to the Order mating system and believed his family had the best bloodline. He thought if he kept everyone in his family marrying each other, the bloodline would become more and more pure over the years. Unfortunately, he hadn't taken a basic genetics class to learn the difference between dominant and recessive genes and that many genetic diseases and birth defects occur when mixing the same recessive genes. For two diverse people who are not related, the chances of having the same recessive genes are incredibly small, and the likelihood of genetic disorders and birth defects is greatly reduced. When relatives marry, they will almost certainly have the same recessive genes and it's only a matter of time before those birth defects and genetic disorders start showing up in the population.

As the year went on, I began growing closer to Hilary*. We went to the same church and the same school, which gave us more to talk about than Chonsey and I, despite being in different grades. My mother was still letting me walk home from school with my brother Dustin*, and we would be home for hours before my mother returned. I asked Dustin* to keep it quiet, and I started going to Hilary's* house after school. Her cousin Tina*, who was also our age, and in the Order would come over sometimes and we would play together. Hilary* would make up wild stories about a killer who left a dead body in her backyard.

One day, I walked home hours after school had ended, but before my mother was supposed to be home from work. When I turned into the driveway and saw her van parked, my heart sank. I knew she would be angry, but more because of her lack of control in the situation. I didn't feel like she really cared about my well-being at all. When I walked in the door, I watched her slam the phone down. Her eyes were wild, and she was visibly shaking.

"Where have you been?" she demanded.

"I went to Hillary's*."

"Why?"

"Because you weren't home!"

"You left Dustin* home alone?"

"No!" I yelled. "You did!"

She had no response to that. I should have known the issue was not over though. When she sent me to my room, I was too young to understand the Order games at this time. Just because she was through with the confrontation, didn't mean she wouldn't go behind my back and try to manipulate the situation to make me do what she wanted. That's exactly what she did.

My life had always been unstable and chaotic. It seemed that once I got my footing and adjusted to the last new thing, something else was always coming on the horizon. The next Sunday brought the next obstacle.

Multiple grades were going on a field trip to the home place to learn about the early history of the Order. I found it funny that my Sunday school class was going to my house for a field trip, but everyone else thought it was great. We each piled into our assigned cars to make the trip.

Gina* was a girl I had seen around, but we weren't close. She was in the Sunday school class just younger than me, but we happened to be in the same car together for the field trip, and we started talking.

"My dad is Paul," she said loudly for everyone in the car to hear. "But my mom said I can't tell anyone because it's a secret."

I didn't respond to this. I remembered Paul beating me and my sister and I wasn't too impressed with him, but I was not going to tell Gina* this. He was still the leader of the Order.

"Paul's your dad too!" she told me.

"No, he's not," I objected. "My dad's name is Steven and he's always out of town for work."

"That's just what they tell you when you're little," Gina* explained, happy to have information that none of the other kids in the car had.

We argued for a few minutes until one of the teachers broke off the argument.

"Why don't you guys ask your moms about this."

Gina* continued the conversation quietly. Only special kids get to be Uncle Paul's kids and I was special.

After my conversation, just as I had every Sunday before, I went to tell Paul goodbye after church. My mother

58

insisted we always make sure to do this, as did countless other parents. There were hundreds of kids lined up to give Paul a hug and a kiss after church. I had assumed we were showing respect and love to the leader of the Order. It wasn't until this Sunday that I realized these kids may all be his kids. As I looked at all these kids, I shook my head. There was no way one man had that many kids.

"Is Paul my dad?" I asked my mom on the drive home from church that day.

She didn't appear surprised by the question. She was more interested in how I got the information.

"Gina told me."

She still didn't seem upset or even interested in my question. She instructed me to talk to "Uncle Paul" about it. This was always the answer she gave when I asked a question she either didn't know the answer, or didn't want to talk about it.

My mother had never talked to me directly about my relationship with Paul. She explained his position in the church as the leader, but never his relationship to me as his daughter. I had always envisioned my dad doing a very special job for God, and as soon as he was done with his job, he would come home and want to build a relationship with me. I had played the scene in my mind a hundred times of him coming home and telling me how much he loved and missed me. I wanted, more than anything to hear how he wished he didn't have to be gone. If Paul was my dad, it meant my father had known where I was the whole time and had every chance of having a relationship with me.

I thought about the time I had walked in and saw my mom and Paul naked in my mom's bed. At the time, I thought it was okay only because Paul was the leader. My mom had always taught only your husband can see you naked. As these thoughts went through my head, my heart sank with disappointment and I knew Gina* was right. Paul is my dad. No one is ever coming to save me.

About a week after I learned the devastating news about my father, Paul came to stay at our house. My mom dragged me out of bed at about midnight because Paul wanted to talk to me. I was wearing a revealing slip undergarment instead of pajamas because we never had air conditioning, and I asked my mom if I could change into something more appropriate. She didn't want to keep my new daddy waiting.

Embarrassed about my revealing outfit, I sat on Paul's lap. It wasn't clear at the time, but this was the first conversation I had ever had with my father about polygamy. He began by explaining how special his marriage with my mother is, and how it's so important for them to have that kind of marriage in God's Kingdom. He continued talking about a great responsibility to build the Kingdom of God and part of that was in a special marriage.

He never once used the word polygamy or plural marriage. My father had a way of talking for hours and hours without ever making a clear point. Now, I understand that he felt plural marriage was the key to building God's Kingdom, but at the time, his vague line of bullshit was just confusing for a seven-year-old.

When I went to school the morning after my father's confession, I could hardly keep my eyes open. He had kept me up well past three in the morning and didn't seem to care about it being a school night. Even though my world was chaotic on a daily basis, it seemed Paul's visits made the situation even worse. He didn't seem to be concerned with anything already going on in the household such as school, work, or other responsibilities. Luckily, his visits were not frequent.

When Hilary* came to the lunch table she noticed I was not myself. When she asked me about it, I didn't feel the need to lie to her. She was in the Order, and Paul had explained the Order was God's work. She was in God's work and she should probably know about the special marriages too.

Hilary* could barely keep her composure when I told her my father's identity.

"Why didn't you tell me?" she asked with a mixture of hurt and surprise.

"I just found out," I assured her. I didn't want to tell her, but my father's identity wasn't a fact I was happy or proud of. Her positive reaction made me even less inclined to share my true feelings.

"If I was your best friend, you would have told me!" She accused. "There's no way you didn't know."

That was a good point. Why didn't I know?

"You're so lucky to have your dad be the leader," she went on. "Does that mean you automatically go to heaven?"

I didn't share her enthusiasm.

"Please promise not to tell anyone," I said. "It's a secret and no one is supposed to know."

"Why?" she asked.

"I don't know," I answered her honestly.

"I promise I won't tell anyone," she assured me.

Unfortunately, the second we were alone with Chonsey in the bathroom, she couldn't hide her reaction. My secret was out in the open.

"Hilary*!" I couldn't believe it. My secret was out. My mom and new daddy were going to be so mad at me. I had been trusted with this very important information and I wasn't strong enough to keep it to myself.

"She's not even in our same church," Hilary* went

on. "It's not like your mom or dad are even going to know you told anyone."

That still didn't make me feel better. I didn't know how, but somehow, they would know. God would probably tell them.

Chonsey didn't seem to care that my father was the leader of our church, but I was so angry. I stormed out of the bathroom and refused to speak to Hilary*. It was two weeks before Christmas break and I ignored her for all of it. Unfortunately, I never got the chance to make up with her because the next major change in both of our lives was just around the bend.

Chapter 6
Submerged in Insanity

"Sometimes I wish I wasn't born in the Order. But I would have nothing without the Order. I just want to be normal."

About a week into Christmas break, my mom informed me I would no longer be going to school across the street. My first reaction thought she was no longer allowing me to go to school at all. I loved school. School was a safe place in my chaotic life. I had been student of the month in my first-grade class. The teacher asked me to read to the class during story time because I was already a fluent reader. My teachers adored me and expressed how smart I was. My file in first grade claimed I read like a sixth grader, and I was on the same path in second grade. They were announcing student of the month after Christmas break and my teacher had suggested it would be me. Why did my mom insist on ruining everything good in my life?

After my emotional outburst, my mom, cold as ice, calmly explained the situation.

"Your dad has put a new school in place, and you will be going there."

Uncle Paul wanted me to go to his school to be with his kids. Even after learning my father's identity, I was not allowed to call him dad. I thought it was this way for all of Paul's kids, but I soon learned only the first wives' kids could call their father "dad" or "daddy." Many of the first wives children used this opportunity to bully the kids of the subsequent wives. They were better than us because they were his "real" kids.

Maybe a new school wouldn't be so bad. I had still not made up with Hilary*, and Chonsey didn't understand why I was so upset, so she took her side. They would sit at a different lunch table and just look at me. I knew they were talking about me. Maybe this was a time for a new start with new friends.

Hilary's* dad also chose this time to take his entire family, which included her mom and her siblings, and leave the Order abruptly. It was shortly after I left public school, and I hadn't heard anything about the situation until I asked my mom why she wasn't at church or Sunday school anymore.

"Her dad made the wrong choice and has decided to leave the Kingdom of God," my mother told me in the saddest tone I had ever heard her use. I didn't even hear her use that tone when her mom died.

I was not allowed to see Hilary* or her family again, because they were now going to hell for leaving God's work. I never spoke to my best friend again.

At the end of Christmas break, my mom drove me to my new "school". It wasn't a school at all, though. It was the house belonging to the community midwife who delivered most of the women's babies at their home births. She had been married to Ortell, the previous leader, before he passed away. She was getting older, now, and she had done fairly well for herself as the midwife. Her house had been one of the only ones with a room big enough to fit twenty or so desks and children at the same time. She was asked to provide her home to use as the second-grade classroom. None of the other grades were in her home, though. Mothers found themselves driving all over the Salt Lake City valley to take all their children to school at a different house in that first year.

The lack of one building wasn't the only strange aspect to the first year of the "Order school". Kathleen's house had two stories and only the basement was used for school. We were not allowed to go upstairs under any circumstance, except to be picked up and dropped off. There were a few children allowed to go upstairs when the lady from the food program showed up. One of the adults was using this opportunity to collect a food check for running a daycare for "relative care". This allowed them to collect a check without needing a daycare license for compliance. Whenever the food lady would show up, a select group of kids would eat their lunch upstairs to be claimed for the food check. The rest of us were told to eat our food very quietly downstairs, because we didn't want her to hear us. I was jealous because it was always the same kids who ate upstairs. Everyone knew they were the favorite. I was not one of them. Rather than running a school, my father had put an illegal day care in place of a quality education.

After a couple of weeks at my new school, I hated it. I begged my mom to send me back to public school. The kids at my new school were mean and they made mean comments about people of color. They were racist and bigoted. We were taught in school, that black people carried the mark of Cain from the bible story of Cain and Abel.

The story goes: Cain was jealous of his righteous brother Abel, and one day he killed him. God sent Cain away and cursed him with a "black mark." My family interpreted this to mean black skin. We were not allowed to talk or associate with outsiders, but especially people with dark skin. The darker their skin, the worse they were because they carried more of the mark. We used the term "nigger" and "faggot" often, though I didn't know what the word "faggot" was referring to until I was much older. It wasn't unusual to hear a five-year old at church notice a black person walking by, and yell, "Mom, there's a nigger!"

The mother would then quickly usher her child into the building to avoid the person of color becoming offended. Many of them did become offended. My mom reprimanded us from yelling this because she said they would beat us up if they heard us call them that.

"Why?" I remember asking. "Why would they be mad if that's what they are called?"

"Because they don't like being niggers either, and when you call them that, it makes them feel bad."

On one girl's outing, we were camping at a lake, and my father had gone away to gas up the jet skis late at night to use the next day. There was a Polynesian family camping in the spot next to ours. I walked past them, following some of my sisters to the bathroom. One of my other sisters shortly walked in after us and said very loudly,

"Did you see those big niggers sitting out there?" I rolled my eyes and didn't say anything. I was used to those kinds of comments by now. When I walked out of the bathroom, one of the Polynesian women called me over to her. My other sisters were frightened, but because I had gone to school with people of color, I knew they weren't so bad.

"Did your sister call us niggers?" she asked me point blank. I didn't know how to answer. This woman was not happy, and I was so embarrassed.

"Because we aren't black," she continued. "We're Tongan."

"I'm sorry," I told the lady sincerely. I didn't know what else to say. This woman seemed genuinely nice. "I'll let her know that her comment was mean."

The lady seemed satisfied with my answer and I went back to my group. Paul returned shortly and ordered everyone to stay in their tents and not come out. We left early the next morning.

66

Racism wasn't the only new downside to my education. The boys talked about sex in a very crass and demeaning way. They objectified women's bodies in a very disrespectful way that a child of second grade should not be able to do. I didn't understand how disrespect towards women could be so ingrained in my culture, and I wouldn't understand for many years. The sexual comments were not age appropriate, and because of my past abuse, they were extremely difficult, especially when directed at me.

My mom refused to listen to my complaints and my academia started to fall behind. My mom blamed my struggles on the fact that public school was not as advanced as the Order school, but it was impossible to focus on academics with the lack of resources, structure, and teacher experience. Sister Dora* had been a babysitter who worked mostly with toddlers. She was now expected to design and run a second-grade classroom with nothing more than a Christian curriculum and a desire to help children. She didn't have a college degree, let alone a teaching degree. She walked into a situation set up for failure.

Sister Dora* did her best. She ran her classroom the way she had run her daycare. I know because I had been in her daycare years before. She locked the kids in a closet and turned out the lights when they misbehaved. She tried calling parents a few times, but most parents felt like their child was her problem during school hours. The classroom was chaotic, the kids were disobedient and out of control, and the parents were exhausted from running to five different schools twice a day before and after a full workday.

We were forced to memorize different seminary material directly pertaining to the Order, such as the ABC Order standards, Articles of Faith, and Perfecting

Meditations. This was a much greater focus than the core subjects like math and reading. History lessons were changed to match the Order perception. When we were supposed to be learning about the Civil War, our teacher explained that the war had taken place, but focused more on the assassination of Abraham Lincoln. The Order version was that Lincoln was assassinated by a man of God because after he got rid of slavery, he would try to get rid of polygamy. There is no evidence of this in the history books.

When we learned about the Titanic, which is a strange subject for a history class, we learned that God sunk the Titanic because the men on the ship were wicked and thought they had tricked God. God forced the ship to sink because they were not humble and doing as God wanted them to.

In our science classes, we were told black people had an extra bone in their leg and they could jump higher than a white person because of it. We were taught black people came from monkeys, but white people came from God. Our lessons denied evolution completely and this time was used to teach the creationist perspective from the bible.

I did my best to survive the chaotic environment I had once only been in my home. It was now everywhere. When I tried to make friends, I would talk about my old school and my old friends. When I showed pictures, the kids would make fun of me because a lot of my friends were brown or black. We didn't see color in public school, but in this school, that was all they saw.

I started making up stories to fit in and excite my classmates. When I came to school late because of a dentist appointment, I told everyone I had gone on a date with "my boyfriend." I convinced one of my new friends to make up a story with me about a man that lived behind my house and saved us from a kidnapper. I knew the man's name and we had gone to pet his horses a couple of times, so when some of the kids had come to my house for holidays, my story checked out.

I was very athletic and could beat anyone in a jump rope competition. My half-brother, Ken*, challenged me to a jump rope contest every single day and could never beat me. He practiced all during recess and finally, at the very end of the school year, he finally beat me. I challenged him to a rematch and he declined. He had won, and he would never compete with me again. It didn't matter. I was finally learning to play this game.

Sister Dora* became concerned about my outlandish stories and addressed her concern with my mother. When my mother asked if any of the stories were true, I admitted they were not. When she asked why I was telling them, I told her the truth. The kids like me more when I tell them stories and they don't make fun of me for having black friends. When I brought up the boyfriend story, the boys stopped objectifying me and started asking me questions about what it was like to have a real date.

After our conversation, Sister Dora* made everyone put their head on their desk while she yelled at them for their inappropriate comments. She said if she heard another whiff of those kinds of comments, she would call Brother Paul and let us tell him the comment. I don't think most of them had even realized there was anything wrong with their comments. They were only voicing what was clearly so ingrained in our culture even though the adults didn't want to admit it, when confronted with it. Everyone had the most respect for the leader of the Order and even though the comments didn't stop, they happened less and the kids were more careful about getting caught. The kids respected the leader, but they couldn't change the environment that was happening in their home.

My academic education continued to decline, but I was learning more and more about my odd situation. I had gone to school with normal kids who had talked about normal lives in public school, but this was a world I had never experienced or understood. Most of my classmates had never gone to a public school and had not had anything contradict Order teachings for them. My couple of years of public school had been enough to cause questions.

Desperate for some answers, I thought my mother's room would be the best place to start. I had noticed some files in one of her drawers, and one day when she was not home, I began looking through them. I found a file with my name on it and pulled it out. Inside was my birth certificate and my social security card. When I looked at the father's name, it was not Paul Kingston.

According to my birth certificate, my father was a man named Steven Allen. Digging further, I stumbled upon my mother's old driver's license. Her last name was Dye. My dad's last name was Kingston. Maybe I could just pick my own last name when I got older?

When I asked my aunts about this, they explained to me. In the Order, only the first wife could take her husband's last name. All the spiritual wives would pick their last name and then legally change their name on their driver's license. It was one perk about being a spiritual wife. You could pick any last name you wanted. I later learned, my mom had opened the phone book and stuck her finger on the page. That was the last name she went with and it is currently my maiden name. As I dug even further, I discovered a small red journal with my mother's handwriting in it.

After carefully putting everything else back, I took the red journal to my bedroom. As I read her journal, my heart sank. She had been in love with a young man from the Order who was about her age. They had been on group dates together, and he had talked to my mother about being together. My mother had wanted to marry him, but she was told only Paul would get her into heaven. If she had married this man, she would have been his first wife. Leah* had made it clear to me that the first wife is the favorite wife. Why would she pick Paul when she could have been the favorite wife?

I asked my mom about what I had found, and she was calm with her responses. Sometimes when we are young, and we don't know any better, we have certain feelings because the Devil is trying to tempt us. She thought she might like to marry someone else when she was young, but she said she would never have what she has now if she had married the other man. What did she have now?

Later, I talked to Leah* and learned the other man had left shortly after my mother was married and is now doing well for himself. He's running multiple businesses in California and is wealthy. If she had married him, she would have a husband, a house, and her kids would have a dad. I didn't hide my feeling that she had definitely made the wrong choice in marriage. Even when she pointed out the fact that I wouldn't be here if she hadn't married Paul didn't change my mind. If God had a spirit that was going to come to Earth, he wouldn't punish them because someone made a different choice in marriage.

My second-grade school year was finally coming to a close and I couldn't be happier. I wanted to get as far away from these people as I could. Ashley*, my mother's younger sister, had been married at the young age of fifteen and given birth to her first child only months after her sixteenth birthday. She knew nothing about raising a baby and her husband had about five other wives who felt like they needed his attention.

Even if her husband didn't have multiple wives, it was uncommon for the men to help with the children in any way. The father's showed up to the birth most of the time, and then left shortly afterwards. They came back to check on the woman after a couple of days if she had stitches needing to be removed, but they didn't even seem to notice the children until they were about eleven years old, which was when they were approaching marriage and working age.

One night, Ashley* came into our house with her screaming newborn. She had no clue how to handle the situation. Apparently, her little boy was coughing or had colic. My mother helped her throughout the night and Ashley* was at our house more than her own tiny little apartment for the next six months. Her husband had set up her apartment shortly after she was married, and even though it was extremely small, I was jealous. She was a young kid with her own place and her own baby.

Sometimes my mom would let me stay with Ashley* to help her, but the neighborhood was dangerous, and we often were awoken by gunshots in the distance, or loud knocks on the door by homeless drunks looking for food or a place to crash for the night. I knew my mother was uncomfortable with the idea of me staying there, but I didn't understand the danger at the time.

Little did I know the outside was not the only danger around me. Though I didn't hear anything at the time, things were not only changing dramatically in my life, but for the community I was growing up in as well. At the end of my second-grade year, on May 22nd, the end of an era occurred. Miles away, my cousin, whom I had never met, Maryanne, was taken to the Order's ranch, Washaki, by her father Daniel, and beaten with a belt, nearly to death. Though this was not the first time Daniel had done something like this, it was the first time he was ever caught. Maryanne had the courage to do something no one in our group had ever been able to do. She ran to a gas station a couple of miles up the road and called the police. She had been forced to marry Daniel's brother, David, who was also her uncle, at the young age of sixteen. He was thirty-three. She had tried to leave on numerous occasions and had been sneaking out for months before her marriage and in the few months after they were married. Her breaking point was not when David raped her three months after their "spiritual" marriage, but after her father had nearly beat her to death.

Though abuse happened frequently in the Order, it was generally kept very quiet and only the people within the families knew the details or the extent of it. Maryanne's situation was no exception. I had never met Maryanne and didn't know anything about her runaway. I was busy preparing for my own spiritual death. I was eight years old and it was time to be baptized.

I remember very little about my baptism, except the long Sunday school lesson about what it means to be baptized. My teacher had brought a board to class with a nail in it. She explained to the class that the nail is like a sin. Every time you sin you hit the nail and it goes deeper in the board. When you're baptized, it's like taking the nail out of the board. You still have a mark where your sins are, but the nail is gone, and you are forgiven. This was the beginning of the extensive studying required to be baptized.

Our religion is identical to the original LDS doctrine.

We believed in the "three degrees of glory", which is basically three levels of heaven. The Celestial Kingdom was reserved for only God's highest people. This only included people from the Order because even the LDS church was not living God's higher principles of plural marriage and united order. The next level, the Terrestial is reserved for all the good people of the world who tried to live right but didn't know the higher laws of God. The next level is the Telestial, which is reserved for those who knew the higher laws of God but chose to do something else. This included anyone who is born in the Order but chose to leave. The last level is hell. This is reserved for the murderers and anyone who tried to hurt the Order. After weeks of memorizing this doctrine, I was finally baptized.

"Sister Nicole Marie Allen Kingston, having been commissioned by Jesus Christ, I baptize you in the name of the father, the son, and the holy ghost. Amen."

With those words I was completely dunked under the water from head to toe to wash away my sins of the past eight years. "Every time you do something wrong, it's like pounding the nail further into the board. When you are baptized, it is like removing the nail. There is still a mark there, but the nail is gone." Those words came to my mind during my baptism.

After my baptism I didn't feel different. I remember the water was nice and cold on a scorching hot day. I was given a blessing where ten or twelve men put their hands on my head. I don't remember anything the blessing said because my blessing was long after everyone else's and it was dark by the time it was finally my turn. I was exhausted and even fell asleep during the last half of my blessing. There was nothing special about it for me. My mother's sister, Leah* would often remind me every time I wasn't in line with my father that I had been baptized and that I would not go to heaven if I got too many bad marks. She seemed to enjoy antagonizing me and my siblings, and I soon learned this was normal when two sisters were married to the same man.

One morning, all the bathrooms upstairs were full. I figured it was early, and Leah* was probably still asleep. She would never notice if I quickly used her bathroom. When I went downstairs, I was half asleep and didn't register the blood trail from the kitchen sink leading into the bathroom. It wasn't until I was sitting on the toilet after closing the door that I noticed a bedpan completely full of what looked like blood and small body parts. I nearly vomited as I finished and rushed upstairs. I told my mom what I had seen, and she rushed downstairs to the scene.

I learned later that Leah* had miscarried and lost her baby. I had heard stories of so many women who had miscarriages and they had never sounded serious before. Some women would miscarry alone in the church bathroom during the service and stay for the rest of the service. It wasn't abnormal to see a woman pregnant and then suddenly, you would see her, and she would be thin again. Everyone acted as though it was normal. I couldn't help but think that much blood could not be normal. If you judged from Leah* and her calm disposition and lack of emotion when she talked about it, it really wasn't a big deal.

I had always loved animals and especially after leaving the farm, I grew attached to my cat, Tiger. He was a small orange tabby cat we found when he was only a kitten. His mother had been a stray cat and all her other kittens had run off to find other homes. Tiger stayed behind and finally, he let me pick him up and he became mine.

When one day, he wouldn't get up or eat, I ran to my mom to ask her what to do. She looked at him, and in her eyes, I knew she didn't think he would make it, but she allowed me to try. I gave him tuna fish, which my mom would generally not allow. I gave him milk, which my mom told me was not good for cats because it gave them dhiarrea. He wouldn't eat anything. He just laid there with his tongue hanging out. If anyone touched him, he would hiss, but he wasn't strong enough to lash out. Wanting to try anything, I asked my mom to make him some greendrink. She told me it couldn't hurt, and she made the disgusting green smoothie that everyone in our group swore by. They believed it could cure cancer. It contained large amounts of comfrey, garlic, and every family added their own touch to it in hopes of making it as healthy as possible. I just wanted it to cure my cat.

Unfortunately, my cat seemed to only hate me for trying to feed him green drink, and he did not improve. I went to bed with a heavy heart and prayed to God to heal him. I promised over and over that I would do anything if God would heal my cat. I had heard so many stories from the Sunday school about the power of prayers. Many people claimed they would find things they were so sure were gone, and that people who had been sick were suddenly cured by the power of prayer.

As I prayed, my sister came rushing into my room to tell me that my mom had called my uncles and they were going to kill my cat. She went into gory details about their conversation about how they were going to do it. Would they shoot him? Would they put him in a bag and run him over with the car? Would they snap his neck? I couldn't speak as each horrible detail came pouring out of her mouth like word vomit. I prayed harder that God would heal him before my uncles were able to get to my house. I finally cried myself to sleep.

The next morning, the sun was shining in my

window and it seemed later than my mother generally let me sleep. The house was quiet, which was abnormal for a house of so many kids. Finally, the previous night came back to me. Was Tiger dead? I climbed out of bed and went downstairs to the table. I ate my oats in silence. I couldn't ask my mom about my cat without breaking down, and I didn't want my mom to think I was a cry baby. I finished my oats and went outside. I couldn't see anything out of the ordinary, but I just knew my cat was gone. I could only hope they left the body for me to bury.

A brown box next to the mulberry tree caught my eye. It had not been there last night. I knew he was in it. As I looked inside, I was right. I couldn't see his face, but I saw the orange fur and a little paw poking out. I went to my favorite hiding spot next to my clubhouse and buried him there. I rolled a large rock to make a gravestone and put flowers on the grave when I was done. I told him how much I loved him and how much I would miss him. He had been my best friend. We had many cats, but Tiger was mine. He loved me, and I loved him.

After my little funeral, I stood on the porch watching his grave. I couldn't quite go in, and my mom walked past me. She didn't say a word, and she didn't have to. She put her hand on my shoulder and for the first time since I could remember, she hugged me. She was never affectionate with her kids and we never felt loved, but today was different. When she let go and went back inside, I felt empty. I hadn't realized how much I needed my mom and her love, and how little I was getting of it. I wished she would have hugged me longer, especially since it would be many years before she would hug me again.

Shortly after Tiger died, summer ended, and it was time to start school again. I was going into the third grade. This year I would be going to school at another woman's house named Lana*. She had also been my babysitter at one time, and she was nice. She wouldn't be my teacher though. My class was taught by Sister Laney*, who also happened to be one of my dad's wives. I had no idea what number she was, and frankly, it really didn't matter. I really liked Sister Laney* and was starting to get along better with my classmates. I went to school with a boy named Jake*, who was Maryanne's full brother. This was the first I heard about Maryanne's runaway and only because it was difficult to hide because it was going to court.

When I initially heard the story of what the police were claiming, I knew deep down that it was true. Megan* had told me stories of Daniel beating her and her siblings, and even her mom got her share of it as well. Jake* tried to convince everyone that the story wasn't possible because Daniel was out of town at the time, but that was only what his mother had told him. It was true. Daniel was out of town that night. Daniel had picked up Maryanne and had taken her out of town to Washaki, where he beat her. This was the first time I had ever heard about anyone leaving the Order. I couldn't believe it. The idea had never crossed my mind before that and I didn't know it was possible.

As Maryanne's case went forward, my mother and everyone else talked about it as though the police and everyone were only trying to persecute the Order. They believed that Maryanne was possessed by the Devil and this was why she was saying these things to try to hurt her father. Very few people talked about the abuse. A couple of people were quick to deny the abuse, but most of the rumors in the Order didn't even touch the subject. It seemed everyone was extremely blind to the idea that there was abuse involved. I didn't see it at the time, but if they were to acknowledge Maryanne's abuse, they may start to see their own.

Maryanne's case did something remarkable for the group. Daniel was sentenced and served 28 weeks in jail for felony child abuse and David served four years for incest and unlawful sexual misconduct with a minor. This was the first time any of the men had ever been held responsible and even punished for abusing their victims. My father completely stopped hitting his kids as far as I'm aware after his brothers went to prison for abuse. Daniel became more careful about which of his wives and children he abused. If he knew he could get away with it, he would abuse them. If he thought they might be like Maryanne, he didn't.

Not only did this discourage some of the men from beating their wives and children with no consequences, it opened the group up to public scrutiny. The leaders of the Order had been free to do whatever they wanted without any consequences. Maryanne's case was a wakeup call for them. They were no longer invincible and free to hurt anyone they chose. The public didn't like the story they were seeing about polygamy, something they thought didn't exist anymore.

Maryanne ended up suing the Order and everyone whose names she could remember shortly after Daniel and David served their sentence. The Order easily filed a counter lawsuit against Maryanne. My father went to law school and was a practicing lawyer. Maryanne later dropped the lawsuit after everyone realized how much time and money would be wasted on the project. Maryanne didn't realize it at the time, but despite losing that lawsuit, she did something for so many of the victims of the Order that had never been done before. She showed us all that we had options. It was as though we were all sheep in a cage. As we watched her get out of the cage, even if we weren't ready or even if we didn't want to get out, that option was forever in our minds now. I had never met her, but I secretly admired her.

Chapter 7
Fears of the Outside

"What would you say if someone asked you, 'Do you know Paul Kingston?"
"I don't know."
"Well, who is your dad?"
"I don't know."

Fear of police and authority was just as ingrained in our culture as the abuse and disrespect towards women. Our church lessons consistently told stories of the raids that happened during our grandparent's time. Because we were God's people, Satan consistently tried to persecute us and hurt us. As Maryanne's case progressed, the leaders of the community used her case to plant even more fear in the minds of their followers. Instead of some distant story that happened long ago, we were now talking about real persecutions happening now.

Whenever Daniel or David had a court date, we were told to fast and pray for God to protect them from the persecutions. When my mother helped me say prayers at night, we were asked to watch over Daniel and David to free them from persecution and harm. When they finally went to prison, we were told to pray for their safe return. While Daniel and David were known as child abusers and molesters on the outside, they were martyrs for everyone in their community.

Maryanne's case caused a lot of changes within the community that none of the followers understood at the time. It planted a fear in the leader's mind that worked both for and against their followers. On the one hand, men were now more conscious and afraid of beating their wives and children. On the other hand, the leader's forced a tight control upon the community. The children were pulled out of public school and forced to attend the Order schools, despite the poor education and lack of facility. Women were forced to get off any public assistance such as food stamps, WIC, and medical assistance. Now that the group was under public scrutiny, Paul knew he could be charged with welfare fraud the way his father had been.

John Ortell had encouraged his "spiritual" wives to get on government assistance and claim they were single mothers. Eventually the government caught on, and sued Ortell for the fraud. Instead of admitting wrongdoing or proceeding with the case, Ortell settled for an approximate sum of $200,000 dollars and the case went away. They became more careful about their fraudulent activities, but they never ended the practice famously known as "bleeding the beast."

We went from living off the government to living off nothing. These programs were never replaced in the community. The women were told to work harder to support their families if they ever complained about the lack of resources to provide for their families. The men provided nothing except the assurance of a roof over their head. Most the wives had their living conditions go from bad to worse. They were being paid less than minimum wage and supporting more than ten children. They were expected to pay rent to their husbands for the roof over their head. When they spent more than their income every month, their husbands would berate and belittle them for it.

None of the women were ever kicked out of their homes for not paying, because they were more valuable for their children's potential to work than for their own. However, the fear of not meeting their payment obligations was very stressful for them. Many chose to pay their husband rent instead of buying food for their multiple children. My mother was fortunate enough to have Adam*, and he continued to give us food from the garbage. We were fortunate compared to many women in the community.

Before Maryanne's case, though our Christmas was small, my mother tried to do something for us. She would buy each child a couple of toys and then spend some money on much needed socks, clothes, and shoes. The toys were never expensive, but they were something. She would find something at the secondhand store for us. She didn't know her children very well, and she never got us anything we really wanted, but there was something exciting about waking up on Christmas morning and seeing all the presents under the tree.

All the kids knew the good gifts would be from my aunts and uncles. My aunt Jennifer* would always give me something with horses on it, because she knew I loved horses. We both shared horses as our favorite animal. She had married my father's brother and hadn't had any children, so she spoiled her nieces and nephews. Jennifer* was eleven years older than me and always my favorite aunt. I loved when she came to our house. Sometimes she would take us to church when my mom was on bed rest from a pregnancy and she always had some candy in her car. She wore a Victoria's Secret perfume called "Love Spell" and it became my favorite as well. While my other aunts and uncles didn't really try to connect with us, Jennifer* was different.

After Maryanne's case and my mother having no additional assistance, our Christmas became even smaller. My mom loved Christmas and did what she could to make the season nice. She would make Christmas candy and fill our stockings with a small toy, some homemade candy, and an orange from the box of oranges Paul gave all his wives for Christmas. On a good year, we might get a piece of chocolate and a candy cane. Stockings were always my favorite part of Christmas morning and this is how I found out who Santa Claus was. Most parents try to hide presents from the kids, and though my mom pretended to try, I don't think she really did. If I was out shopping with her and we found something on sale, she would buy it. I would see it on Christmas morning. Eventually, she would get even more lazy about it and ask the older kids to wrap all the presents. I would wrap Dustin's* presents and he would wrap mine. Together we would wrap all the other kids' presents. We were all very young when we learned Santa's identity.

Paul wasn't ever physically or emotionally present during Christmas. His seventh wife's birthday was on Christmas Eve, so he spent every Christmas with her family. A couple of days before or a couple of days after Christmas he would drop off a box of oranges and a bag of oats. If it was a good year, we might get a box of hamburger from the Washaki Ranch as well. Some years he was too busy to even drop it off himself. He would send his older sons to deliver the packages.

After Daniel and David went to prison, the control got even tighter. Paul began having meetings with his kids to teach them what to say if an authority figure ever questioned them. I remember rehearsing in my mind over and over about what I would say if ever a cop asked me about my father. He would walk up and down the aisle and ask each kid in the room what to say.

"What would you say if someone asked you, 'Do you know Paul Kingston?'"

"I don't know," the poor kid would respond if he knew the correct answer.

"Well, who is your dad?"

84

"I don't know."

Some of us got creative, and played completely dumb about what a father was, and with my dad's sense of humor, he loved it. He couldn't contain his pride that his children would never betray him. The irony in the story is that we really didn't know what a father was, but I guess Paul didn't get that.

Just as every polygamous family does, my family was growing. My mom had just given birth to her sixth child, a boy, though I was in my own world at this time. I was finishing up third grade with Sister Laney*, and I got along with her very well. While most of the other teachers showed up to get a paycheck, Sister Laney* seemed to enjoy her job. She encouraged us to sing and put on plays and be creative. She helped me catch up academically after falling so far behind in the joke that was my second-grade year. I loved Sister Laney* so much. I even organized a surprise birthday party for her birthday. I assigned everyone to bring a treat, and we asked Lana* if some of us could show up early in the morning to decorate before she came to teach. The look on her face was priceless.

After my third-grade year ended, Paul announced our school would be getting a building. No one was more excited than the mothers who had to drive all their kids across the valley to get them to a different house for school every morning. Though the school would not be an actual school, it was better than anything anyone had hoped for. My dad had bought a business complex meant for multiple businesses and put a couple of classrooms in each of the complexes. The classrooms were not connected from the inside. We had to go outside to get to the lunchroom, which was converted into a P.E. gym outside lunch time. They had found a metal slide that was very hot in the summer and had some sharp edges on the side. It was only used for a year before none of the kids would try it anymore. They put in some bars to act as monkey bars and there was a rock garden on the edge from the business building next to it. They fenced in the space in between the business complex and the neighboring building and this was their outside play area. The area was gravel and concrete, so they put rubber padding underneath the monkey bars. The building was not finished, and you could still see the exposed wiring in the ceiling where workers were still putting the building together. Some of the halls were still concrete and hadn't had tile laid yet. The building was a work in progress, but it was more than we had ever had.

The new building wasn't the biggest problem the teacher's ran into. The students learned from the very beginning that they outnumbered the teachers. I went into fourth grade and I was thrust even deeper into my strange culture. I was spending all day being immersed in the culture of my cult. This had never happened for anyone in our community in the past, and no one could anticipate the level of behavioral problems that would come out. Paul was shocked. So many of these kids had been abused or neglected in some form or another and at varying levels and had not been taught any life skills. When they were all put in the same place, everyone's behavior became worse.

Sister Mona's* fifth grade class was the worst. The students would throw chairs and books at her, they would never listen to anything she had to say, and when they were asked to turn in homework or do any work, they refused. Mona* called in substitutes for half the year and refused to return after her first year. In fact, less than fifty percent of the teachers who taught the first year would come back for a second year. I was in fourth grade, and though we weren't a violent class, we didn't listen. I didn't get along well with Paul's daughters because of their stuck-up attitude and need to be anorexically skinny so I made friends with Daniel's girls who were naturally anorexically skinny. This was from being starved by their parents instead of purposefully doing it to be skinny. My best friends were Anna*, who was Megan's* full sister and had skipped a grade to be in my class, Sara*, who had been in public school until her mom was forced to pull her kids out and put them in Order school to be in line with her husband, and Randy*, whose mom was one of Daniel's favorite wives and received far less abuse than most of the other wives.

My fourth-grade teacher was Sister Sandra*. She had been my preschool teacher and Sunday school teacher at one point and was getting too old to be putting up with a bunch of preteens. We didn't listen, and she didn't really seem to care if we did. She put up with much less than the other teachers. When we disobeyed her, she would send us to the office to call our mom. There was always someone from her class in the office on the phone throughout the day and after a few months it was no longer a punishment. It gave us a chance to get out of the classroom and go for a walk. Some days we would ditch class and sit on the empty school bus Daniel had acquired. We had one yellow bus with peeling paint that looked as though it had needed a new paint job for years, and an ugly dark blue bus in the same condition. Why the bus was blue, I'll never know, but Daniel had a knack for finding and buying junk for a great deal.

I had been friends with Megan* for a brief period in our childhood, but after our traumatic rape together, I held onto some resentments toward her for either getting me in the situation or not warning me beforehand. I wasn't sure which. I became best friends with her little sister though, and never told her about the trauma I experienced with her older sister in her home. After hearing Anna's* stories though, I found it more difficult to be angry with her sister. I had known Daniel was abusive, but I had never seen it for myself or heard any specific details. Those details are kept quiet from everyone else and abuse isn't talked about. As young girls ditching class, we had little to do besides talk. I was horrified about what I heard.

Anna's* mother, Heidi, had her children taken from her by DCFS multiple times because of calls by neighbors and schools. When Daniel would get upset, he would become violently angry. The situation of Maryanne being beaten nearly to death was not abnormal. The only difference was Maryanne came to a breaking point. It wasn't the first time Daniel had beaten her and if she would have stayed, it would not have been the last. Anna* told me of the time Daniel was angry with her mother and pushed her down the stairs when she was seven months pregnant. She never went to a doctor, even when she miscarried the baby, and it was never reported. There were times Daniel would beat the kids with boards, sticks, belts, whatever he could find. Anna* explained that Megan*, being the oldest, would step in to defend her brothers and sisters, and she would be beaten because of it. Anna* had been beaten by her father, but she explained it to be nothing compared to what Megan* had gone through. At one point, Megan* became the person who called DCFS. She would hold the phone and a broom at her father as she dialed the number. DCFS kept sending the kids back despite the numerous reports and Megan's* testimony of what her father was doing to her mother and siblings. She never gave up though. She kept calling and calling. She put her parents through hell. Maybe Maryanne gave her hope that one day she might get out too. Or maybe she was just desperate.

One Sunday as a practical joke, Anna* and Randy* hid the fliers for the grocery store that were supposed to be distributed to all the members after church. When they found out there would be a meeting with Daniel after church, both girls were terrified.

"What's wrong?" I asked as I watched them waiting for the meeting.

We stole some flyers and Daniel wants to have a meeting."

"We get in trouble all the time," I reminded them. "It's not a big deal."

Maybe not for you," Randy* sobbed. "Your dad doesn't beat you!"

I remember holding Anna* as she sobbed on my shoulder. Randy* thought the beating would be worse if she kept him waiting, so she went on ahead of Anna*. I don't know if Anna* was so familiar with the abuse or if she knew it didn't matter. Instead of fear when she went into that meeting, her eyes showed defeat.

Chapter 8
Preparing for Tragedy

As fourth grade went on, my life seemed to calm down, while Anna's* seemed to get more complicated. Her and her sister, Megan* were very close. At the young age of fourteen, Megan's* uncle from her mother's side of the family began pursuing her for marriage. At the time, I didn't have a lot of first-hand experience or knowledge of the courting process within my community. I knew people would pray to God and then God would tell their parents and them who they should marry. As far as I knew, there was no courting happening outside that process. I knew Megan's* uncle was in his forties and already had two other wives, one of which, we were all sure had a mental disorder. She was nice enough, but she told us strange stories and laughed at socially awkward times.

Anna* seemed confused by what was happening at home and my only sexual experience had been abuse. At the time, I was told marriage was such an amazing and sacred thing. I couldn't believe my abuse would be anything like what I would experience with my potential husband, so I was of no help to Anna*. I soon learned Megan* was sneaking out with this much older uncle. He was telling her they could start doing sexual things because they were already married in heaven and the earthly marriage didn't matter. When her mother walked in on her doing sexual things with this older uncle, she said and did nothing. She turned a blind eye. In Megan's*, Anna's*, and my mind, this confirmed that what this man was doing was not wrong. They continued courting for months, which is abnormal. Engagements were usually very short, but everyone was afraid Megan* might turn around and follow in Maryanne's footsteps with another court case. They were not wrong.

After finishing my first year at the new Ensign Learning Center, I became closer to my aunts, Jennifer* and Ashley*. They were both much older than I was, and they were married. Ashley* had multiple kids, and Jennifer* didn't have any. She had been pregnant, but she had a miscarriage. I never heard of her becoming pregnant again. Whenever I would ask when she would have a baby, she wouldn't give a clear answer. I didn't know there were problems in her marriage at this point. In fact, aside from Leah's* comments when I was much younger, I didn't know there could be problems after marriage. Marriage is taught to be the highlight of your life. It's your calling from God to find the right person and marry them. From the time you can talk, you always ask God to help you marry the right one when saying personal prayers. I was now talking to person number two about an unhappy marriage.

As I began my fifth-grade year, the community wasn't the only place my father was trying to control. With the new building being very close to being finished and the teachers having more of a handle on the behavioral problems, the teachers started implementing more and more rules. They implemented a dress code which prohibited tank tops, shorts, belly shirts, open-toed shoes, and any artwork a teacher found offensive. Boys and girls were separated and not allowed to have any classes together and were not allowed to sit at the same table during lunch period.

My new teacher was Sister Michelle* and everyone hated her. She was incredibly strict, and her class was always known to be the best behaved. Every morning she would do a uniform check. Most teachers would only discipline a student for dress code if they happened to catch it. Sister Michelle* would ask every student to stand

91

and stretch their arms as far up as they could. If any skin was showing, their clothing was against the dress code and they were forced to call their parent to bring them a new shirt to class. I spent a lot of time in the office waiting for someone to bring me a shirt that year. Other times I was sent home for my pants being too tight.

As much as I hated Sister Michelle*, though, my grades began to come up. She taught her students and made learning fun. We played games to learn history and science and she incorporated a lot of free reading time into her curriculum. I loved reading and would spend all my free time with a novel of some kind.

My mom loved reading as well and would sit in the cookbook aisle, at the library for hours while I was able to freely explore. It was my favorite place in the whole world. After Paul showed up to my house and caught me reading some novels, he demanded my mom stop taking me to the library anymore or at least monitor the books I was reading. She tried to monitor, and she would ask me what my book was about. I would make up a story about kids always doing what their parents want them to, a girl who loved her dad and always wanted to be like him, or some other plot that would teach me to be blindly obedient. Eventually she realized I was lying, and she stopped taking me to the library. I refused to have my only mental stimulation taken from me. I began walking to the library. My mom relented and realized it was safer for her to drive me there instead of me walking by myself in the outside world and I think she secretly missed her cookbooks. I noticed she started making me return all my library books or put them in my room whenever Paul spent the night. I'm guessing it wasn't a subject she wanted to talk to him about.

My mom began pushing me to socialize with Paul's

family. Sara's* mom had rebelled against her husband and had taken her kids out of the Order school because she wasn't able to pick them up and her husband refused to offer any suggestions. He felt like they were her kids and she needed to figure it out. It wasn't something he had time for. Her solution was to put her kids back in public school and the bus would take them home. They would stay home alone until she could come home. She had tried to start a daycare to be home with her kids, but because she was a rebellious wife, none of the women in the Order would bring their children to her for care, so she began taking clients outside the Order without permission. One of her clients called DCFS on her, and because of the state of her house and her lack of cooperation with them, her kids were taken from her. After finally getting them back, there was no way the state would license her to run a home daycare again.

As I was getting older and approaching eleven years old, my mom felt like I was drifting away from the Order beliefs. She would often tell me stories of her friends and how most of them ended up leaving the Order. She was so grateful the Lord had allowed her to be married at a young age to keep her on the right path. She seemed to have the same idea in mind for me. Suddenly, we were attending every family event in Paul's growing family. Surprisingly, I felt like I enjoyed attending. The anorexic, self-righteous, princesses stopped bothering me so much and we found to actually have some things in common. We were a bunch of little girls with low self-esteem and hopes of being more than we were someday.

I was becoming closer with Gina*, the same girl who informed me of my father's identity many years before. We went to school together and then she went to work at the payroll office with her mom after school. She had gotten her job when she was eight years old and had been working there since. I was almost eleven and I had never been employed. I begged my mom to let me get a job. She told me that wasn't her decision. If I wanted to be employed, I would need to convince my father I was ready for that responsibility. It was a privilege to have a job and serve God's Kingdom. If you weren't worthy, you couldn't have one. Later, I realized Gina* got a job because her mom was the boss of the payroll office and she didn't want to pay for daycare. There was nothing for the kids to do at the office. The adults made them work to keep them out of trouble.

Finally, shortly after my eleventh birthday, Paul allowed me to work at the payroll office with Gina*. My job involved putting old checks in numerical order and filing invoices or check stubs for the payroll, accounts payable, and the accounts receivable department. I was being paid a little over three dollars an hour, but for an eleven-year-old who didn't have any expenses and didn't understand money, I didn't mind.

I wasn't allowed to spend any of what I earned. It went onto my "statement" which applies to the Order's banking system. When working for the Order, we never received a paycheck. Our money went onto our statement, and at the end of every month, we would get a copy of that statement at church. We also weren't paid in normal dollars. The Order invented a currency called the Unit to purchase goods from Order stores and businesses. We weren't allowed to shop at stores outside what the Order owned. In fact, one of our memory gems states, "If the Order doesn't have it, we don't need it." I never saw a paycheck and I had no idea how much money I had. It didn't really matter, though, because I wasn't allowed to spend it anyway. My new job also put me in the position where I was expected to live consecration. I was given a form called, "The Ten Percent Form," which legally allowed them to take ten percent of everything I earned and consecrate it to the Order. They were taking all my money anyways, so ten percent of nothing didn't seem to matter. Besides, to be an Order member, this form is the most basic requirement.

With my new after school job and school, I stayed out of trouble. My father continued to take us on outings every summer, and I got close to a couple of my sisters. We bonded over Harry Potter and Lord of the Rings because my dad was a Sci-Fi nerd when he was in high school. Many families prohibited their kids from reading the books or watching the movies, because it was considered "evil" and "Satan's tools," but my dad loved that stuff. When I went into his office, he had lined up all his Star Wars collectible characters on his bookcase. I wondered how anyone could feel the need to be more conservative than the leader of the Order, but they did. It didn't matter though. For the first time in my life, I was beginning to fit in with my family.

Acting as a catalyst in the bonding of my family, was the death of my eighteen-month-old, half-sister. Sister Laney* had become the music teacher after the school was set up in the new building. Everyone still loved her, and though she was strict, she was fun. When little Rhoda was born, Laney* took her six weeks off teaching and when she came back, she brought her baby to work with her every day. Many of the teachers began to complain because they weren't allowed to bring their babies to teach. They felt like the students were spending more time holding Laney's* baby than learning music. Laney* found a babysitter.

Shortly after Laney* stopped bringing her baby to

95

work, she received a call from the woman she had entrusted her to. Michelle Michaels was a plural wife of Paul's brother and was running a daycare for many families in the community. She claimed Rhoda had fallen and hit her head.

Laney* left her music class to attend to her baby and police were called. Rhoda was rushed to Primary Children's Hospital, where she was admitted due to bleeding from her nose and mouth and had gone into cardiac arrest. The doctor's tried to stop the bleeding from her brain, but Rhoda died. The surgeon made a comment stating the girl was beaten and had not fallen, and this started an investigation into the babysitter. The doctors were certain the injury was blunt force trauma and not a fall. She had a three-inch skull fracture.

The babysitter was arrested on a Tuesday and released on bail on a Thursday. My father bailed out his daughter's murderer, but our family bonded over the loss anyway. In court and the media, Paul defended the babysitter, claiming it had been a terrible accident. Laney* was heartbroken and refused to talk about it. Rumors circulated the babysitter's husband lost his temper with the baby and threw her against the wall. There were other rumors claiming the babysitter had done it. There wasn't one story in the group or out in the media that felt like it was an accident, but my father continued to protect her even though, his daughter was dead at her hands.

While Michelle was still going through court for second degree felony child abuse, everyone else moved on with the rest of the world. I was approaching twelve years old, which is the age girls start thinking about and preparing for marriage. I was particularly close to one of my sisters who was almost a year older than me, Cassie.* She already knew who she was planning to marry. He was

Justin*, our half-brother from my father's first wife. Cassie's* mother had convinced her that either him or his older brother, was the only option because a girl needed to marry a man with a higher position than herself. Paul was the leader, and because we were Paul's daughters, our only marriage choices included our half-brothers. We couldn't choose from any half-brother's because my mom was wife number five. My options were boys from wives one through four.

I didn't agree with her system and neither did most people in the community, but her mom was one of the most extreme and most misguided members in the community. When I brought the idea to my own mom, she rolled her eyes and told me to talk to Paul about it.

Justin* had already married one woman, and everyone knew he was planning to marry many just like his father. Cassie* insisted that she had direction for both of us to marry our half-brother, and at only eleven years old, I knew I liked my half-sister and we would be friends forever if we married the same man. When I expressed my plan to Jennifer*, who was my other best friend at the time, I knew she was uncomfortable. She was having problems in her own plural marriage and probably saw me being coerced into a difficult life I couldn't possibly understand. This was the beginning of my mother trying to limit my contact with Jennifer*.

Spending time with Cassie* opened me up to a new aspect of my culture. Her mom, though extreme in her spiritual beliefs, never transferred those beliefs over to her daily life. She believed her family was better than everyone because her father was a righteous man by the Order's standards, and she was married to the leader. She believed she should have more privileges than even some of Paul's other wives.

When Cassie* invited me to the Lagoon amusement park, I couldn't have been more excited. We weren't allowed to do things like that because it cost way too much money. Cassie's* mom came up with an idea to make it much cheaper. She would pay for one person to get in and ride the rides, and everyone else would pay a much cheaper entrance fee. Only the one person would get a stamp to let them ride the rides and our first stop would be the bathroom to get the stamp wet and transfer it to everyone's hand. Everyone now had a stamp, even though we had only paid for the one.

Her mom's other devious ways were to force all the kids to pass out fliers for the Order clothing store, and she would pocket all the money. My mom stopped letting us pass fliers with her after she learned this. She would drop us off at one end of a street and force us to walk miles and miles alone putting a flier on each person's door. I was about eight years old at the time.

She would rob flowers from graves and then put them on our own relative's graves or keep them and force her kids to sell them for her. My mom rarely said anything to us about Cassie's* mom, but I knew she didn't like her. Cassie's* mom's birthday was the one on Christmas Eve and prevented my mom from ever seeing her husband on Christmas. This probably didn't help.

After Rhoda's death and Maryanne's lawsuit, I began seeing the cracks in the world I was living in. David was still currently in prison, but somehow his wives were still getting pregnant. I knew some of them were going to see him, but I didn't think they would get away with letting so many women come to the prison for a conjugal visit. Rumors went around that Jesse was impregnating David's wives with a turkey baster, but I didn't believe that to be physically possible. Other rumors claimed it was okay for

Jesse to have sex with David's wife because he was replenishing the earth, and no one knew how long David would be in prison. He had been sentenced up to ten years, and though he only served four, no one knew how long he would be in.

My father started inviting David's daughters on our family outings. We all saw this as him taking care of his brother's family, but the way he flirted with David's older daughters made his other wives and even his own children uncomfortable. Paul's daughters didn't get along with David's daughters. David's daughters believed they were better than everyone because God had chosen their dad to be the one to make a sacrifice for the good of the community. They believed God must think more of their family, and they didn't try to conceal that fact from us. We tossed them out of the tent to go sleep with some of their mothers who had come on the trip. We wanted nothing to do with them.

On May 18th, 2001, polygamist Tom Green was convicted on four counts of bigamy and child rape because one of his wives was fourteen when they conceived one of their children together. In my young mind, Tom Green was also being persecuted for the same thing my community was being persecuted for. He must be doing God's work as well. When I asked Paul about this, his response shocked me. He believed Tom Green was living plural marriage incorrectly and this was why he was arrested. This explanation didn't make sense to me. Why was David and Daniel arrested?

As I grew older, I began to see so many holes in my father's stories. When I pointed out David was arrested for the same crime, he was quick to point out David's case was different. When I probed further about the differences, Paul went to the only response I couldn't argue with. God told David to marry Maryanne. God did not tell Tom Green to marry the fourteen-year old girl. Ironically, Tom Green joined my father's group many years later and his daughters married many of my siblings after I left the Order. Paul's responses always brought more questions than answers. Trying to get a straight answer out of Paul was like trying to find a needle in a haystack.

As I was approaching my twelfth birthday, many of my friends began going through puberty. I was not. Boys teased me because I was flat chested, though that never changed even after puberty. Boys seemed to like girls who had developed sexually, but girls were pressured to stay skinny and maintain their pre-puberty weight. Many of the girls developed eating disorders. The whole topic was so confusing. I knew I would never develop the way my sisters had, and I knew I could never be as skinny as Daniel's girls. The moms were also skinny, and I later learned most of them were starving. I tried unsuccessfully to grow my breasts, and when that didn't work, I began starving myself as well, to stay skinny.

My mom had never talked to me about puberty, sex, or any of the things you might expect a mother to explain to her daughter. Sex was to be explained by your husband on your wedding night, and the whole period thing must have slipped her mind. My first period was traumatic. I was on a scout camping trip with dozens of girls around, and I couldn't bring myself to say anything to anyone. When I saw the blood, it caused a flashback and I couldn't get out of my sleeping bag all weekend. I was nauseous and holding back tears as I fought through what I now know as panic attacks. I felt so alone. I told everyone I was feeling sick and they left me alone. One of my friends occasionally came to check on me and ask me to come out and join the activities. I could hardly walk. The cramping didn't help.

When we came back from the trip, I snuck into my mom's pads and took a couple. I never said a word to my mom and every month after that, I stole a few pads from her. I think she figured it out after a couple of months because she started buying extra, but she never said a word to me. That was a clear example of the relationship I had with my mom and most the people in the community. Real issues were not talked about.

In sixth grade, Sara* came back to the Order school and Sara*, Randy*, Anna*, and I became friends again. Cassie* and I were not in the same grade and rarely saw each other at school. Because of her mom's extreme beliefs and the fact that she was a downright awful person, most people in the community didn't like her kids either. Cassie* was nothing like her mom and even found herself being a mediator between her mom and everyone her mom made upset. It was a full-time job considering her mom seemed to make anyone she came into contact with upset.

Though I adored Cassie* and stood up for her when she was bullied, we were in different grades. I didn't get along with Gina* anymore, because she didn't like Daniel's kids. She saw my friendship with Daniel's daughters as a betrayal to her and Paul's family. I was still working at the office and had moved up in the company to the Accounts Payable department. I went from filing old invoices to entering invoices and doing everything aside from printing the actual checks. My mother had always been very fast at her work, and all her bosses always loved having her because she was able to get her work done quickly. I was flattered when my boss commented that I was like my mother in that way.

At this time in my life, I was thoroughly

brainwashed. I disagreed with the abuse and the actions of many of the members of the Order, but I had never questioned the actual religion or my dad. My dad was a person who never took responsibility for anything, and because he was the leader, everyone trusted him. No one blamed him for anything. I once heard my mom confront him about something he had said to another wife to betray her confidence and cause a fight between her and the other wife. I watched him tell her she had taken the whole thing out of context and she didn't listen very well. He was very tactful in the way he disrespected and blamed her for it.

As a young teenager, I began to study him, and I knew what he was doing. I never questioned him though. I believed he was doing whatever he needed to do to help God's work because I completely believed in the religion and the principle of plural marriage despite all the contradicting evidence. So, when my aunt Ashley* told me about her plan, I knew I had to do something.

Ashley* and I had been working together at the office for over a year and though we were in separate departments, the building we worked in was quite small. We went to lunch together and I would help with her babies whom she frequently brought to work with her. I thought nothing of it, when she told me to come with her on an errand during lunch. I didn't even ask her where we were going until we passed Wendy's, which was where we usually got lunch. I always ordered their chicken sandwich with a frosty instead of a drink. Dipping my fries in the frosty was the perfect combination of salty and sweet.

"Where are we going?" I asked.

"The bank."

"The bank?"

"That's what I said."

"Okay?"

When I asked why, she told me she was opening a bank account and I couldn't tell anyone. I didn't understand what the big deal was at first, and when we got there, they were doing a drawing for a free MP3 player. I entered the drawing and waited while they told Ashley* she needed more identification if she wanted to open an account with them. When we left, we stopped by Wendy's to grab lunch and she explained why she didn't want me to tell anyone.

If you have an outside bank account, it means you aren't living consecration. The Order is supposed to have access to all your money, and if it's in an outside bank, they don't have a way to monitor it. It's one of the most basic requirements of being in the Order to have all your money turned in to the Order bank. Ashley* made it clear that if someone found out she had an outside bank account, it was grounds for being kicked out of the Order.

I had never heard of anyone being kicked out of the Order and Ashley* never did tell me the reason why she wanted an outside bank account. I believe it was to give her some independence and a sense of identity. She had been married at fifteen to a guy she hadn't wanted to be with. Like many young girls, she had been in love with another boy, but her father told her she had to marry someone with high standing in the Order. She ended up being a plural wife to my father's oldest son.

Unsure of what to do with the information from my day, I told my mom where we had gone. She called Paul immediately and I retold the story to Paul as well. Paul called Ashley's* father Adam*, and I retold the story to him. I never heard from her husband, though. Never once did he seem to care about why she was trying to exert her independence. He left it to the parents to deal with the problems in his marriage. This was a very common tactic if the parents support your marriage. Sometimes the girls will listen to their parents better than their husbands. Most of the time the women have no one on their side. When they reach out for help, they try everyone before they give up. There is no one who cares about them.

Ashley* called me that night and began with, "Hey loser."

I could hear the hurt in her voice. My father had expressed that Ashley* was going through a hard time and that it was my responsibility to be a good friend and try to help her through it. In the Order, to be a good friend, I needed to help her do what was right. My dad had converted me to his cause and I had fallen hard. Ashely* took a week off work to repent before calling me to express how appreciative she was with me for helping her to choose the right. She expressed her love for her husband and the Order. Her words sounded empty and hollow, as though she was reading a script written for her by my father. I thought I had helped her choose the right, but I had taken away her chance at independence.

Ashley* was very upset with me for telling everyone about her attempt, and our friendship was never close again after that. I continued to stay with her to help her with her babies and we continued to work together, but I was not someone she could have a deep conversation with ever again. I betrayed her trust. I ended up winning the MP3 player from the bank drawing I had entered and because I had told everyone, and made the right decision according to my parents, they let me keep it. They value their snitches and they tend to reward them well. Ashley* never did end up leaving the community. She went on to have more than ten kids and is completely engrossed in the community.

Chapter 9
Government Conspiracies

Though I had been thoroughly brainwashed, the cracks in my beliefs started getting bigger and bigger. I continued to ditch class with Randy*, Sara*, and Anna* and hear all about their latest abuses with their dad. Sara* had decided she had enough of the abuse and was planning to leave. Randy* didn't know what she wanted and could not make a definite decision. Anna* and I, despite our disagreement with the abuse, we firmly believed in the religion. We made a pact to stay even after Sara* left.

Just like so many women, I became depressed. I didn't know why. I justified it as another one of God's tests to prepare me for marriage. I believed that after I got married my life would be wonderful and I would start to enjoy all God's blessings. I wanted to be a favorite wife, and I knew from a very young age that all the favorite wives were thin, so I stopped eating. No one seemed to notice my poor body image had advanced to a complete eating disorder for a long time. I became engrossed in my own depression and I stopped caring in general.

On September 11th, 2001 the World Trade Center in New York was bombed. Despite being extremely sheltered from most things happening in the world, our PBS shows were interrupted with footage from the bombing. Even my dad couldn't protect us from something hitting so close to home. Many people in the Order thought the end of days had come and God was destroying the wicked. Most of us weren't allowed to watch the footage of the bombing and we were instructed to turn off our televisions during this time. Some obeyed, some didn't, but it didn't matter. The can of worms had been opened. How would Paul explain this?

Paul and his lack of creativity came by the answer from his extremist wife. She had found a video by some conspiracy theorists, claiming the government had set the whole thing up as a means of putting fear in the citizens to tighten control on them. Paul called a large family meeting and forced us to watch this extremist video by some conspiracy theorists. This worked in his favor to strike even more fear in his family against the government. For years, I believed 911 was constructed by our own government. I was already afraid of the government and this didn't make me any more afraid of them. It only confirmed what my father had been telling us all along.

I continued working for the office, and Leah* had moved out of our basement into a house behind a coal company my father put her in charge of. The Order had a large mine and would bring the coal to Valley Coal where they would sell it. At twelve years old, I ran the office when Leah* had errands to run and bagged coal for twenty-five cents a bag. It kept me busy and began a relationship with Leah* I had never had while she lived with us.

When she had lived with us, there was a sense of competition between her, my mom, and all the kids between them, that knew no bounds. On my mom's birthday, my little brother Caleb had come down with a fever of 106. When Leah* tried to call my mom and let her know, my mom yelled at her for trying to ruin her birthday. My mom made it clear she would be home after she was done with her date. Leah* was upset because Caleb was extremely lethargic and had quit breathing multiple times, but every time Leah* told my mom this, she made it clear her date was not ending.

Though Leah* and my mom were not particularly close because of their age difference, the hurt feelings between them did not start until Leah* moved in and her relationship with my dad was thrown in my mother's face. Every time he spent the night down in the basement instead of with my mother, I saw my mom's heart break a little more.

Now, with Leah* living on her own, she could be sure we were never there on her nights or any time Paul would be there and my mom didn't have to see her husband with another woman. Now that she didn't directly have to compete with me for my father's attention anymore, we could have a functioning relationship. Also, now that I was approaching marriage age, my father would spend more time with me in the form of scheduling "meetings" with me. Sometimes these meetings would happen at her house because that was where I happened to be working. Now, instead of me taking her time, she was getting more time because of me. The Order culture was a game from the very beginning, and relationships are made based on winning this unbeatable game.

For my twelfth birthday, my father gave me a quad version that included the Bible, Book of Mormon, Pearl of Great Price, and the Doctrine Covenants. He bet me I couldn't read the entire book. I did end up reading it. I found some disturbing doctrine. I had always felt like the abuse in my community was wrong, but when I looked in the bible, the stories were just as bad if not worse. Men had sex with their daughters and were deceitful about how they took wives. Abraham was going to blindly murder his child because "God" had told him to. I couldn't imagine any loving God asking a parent to do something like this. I didn't care that it had been a test. After reading the Doctrine Covenants, it was difficult to believe the Order was wrong. There was no place where God took away the principle of plural marriage. I had hoped reading the bible might shine some light and give me some peace of mind, but it only made it worse. If these books are the rule books, then my father did the right thing when he protected my sister's murderer.

After finishing the long reading of my birthday present, including the very long chapter that completely consists of "So-and-so begat so-and-so begat so-and-so" I began to fast and pray. My mother had just given birth to her seventh baby, and I was home helping her more than I wasn't. I was supposed to be attending sixth grade, but my education was not a priority for anyone in my life. Nearly everyone in my grade aside from a couple of people with parents who had attended some college were failing anyways.

Paul decided to put everyone's math book a year ahead of where they were supposed to be, in hopes of bringing our scores up on the state testing so we could be considered for the school grants and such. This backfired and brought everyone's already low scores down and only a very small fraction of the students even tried anymore. He missed the fact that concepts, especially in math, build on each other and you can't just skip a year of those concepts. When this backfired, he blamed the teachers and accused them of not working hard enough to teach the kids properly. The teachers did their best and the math teacher, worked especially hard, but it wasn't enough to make up for my father's stupidity.

Chapter 10
All Downhill From Here

It hurts so badly, I can hardly breathe
It's just so painful, like when they leave
The knife feels deep inside my skin
Sometimes it feels as though I'll never win
The knife begins to turn and thrust
I can't live through this, and yet I must
My body is so torn and broke
My heart is pounding so much, I choke
The lights are so bright, I can hardly see
The screaming is so loud! Is that me?
The aching and pounding will never stop;
I hurt so badly, I can never adapt.
I want this to end, I want to be free.
I want to be heard! Can anyone hear me?

As I was approaching the age of marriage, Jennifer's* marriage was slowly falling apart. No one seemed to notice until all of a sudden, all eyes were on her and her actions, when she was caught at a single guy's apartment who was not a member of the Order. Her brother claimed she was cheating. Jennifer* claimed they were just friends. No one had known there were even problems because those things were not talked about and most of the husbands didn't even care about their wives' happiness as long as they stayed quiet. Jennifer* was more than happy to keep quiet about everything. In fact, her "spiritual" husband acted like such a nice guy, everyone viewed Jennifer* as the bad guy. In reality, he had a group of wives who fought daily for his attention and he and Jennifer* had never been close anyways.

I know Jennifer* had tried to be a good wife in the

beginning, and I don't know her whole story, but she did tell me one time he had physically grabbed her. She felt like she was tricked into marrying him in the first place. I didn't know it at the time, but most girls were tricked into marrying their husbands. Rumors also circulated that he was the one who murdered baby Rhoda. Her babysitter was married to him and it would not be a far leap of imagination to think he had a temper.

Whatever her story, it had been obvious she was not happy with him for a long time. Divorce was out of the question in the Order, especially from the immediate Kingston line. They were viewed as righteous men who could do no wrong. If there was ever a conflict between them and one of their wives, the wife was viewed as the problem. This case was no different.

My dad called an emergency meeting with my mom and me, and absolutely forbade me from ever having contact with her. I was not allowed to call her, see or, or even sit near her at church or dances. When I tried to ask if she was kicked out of the Order or what had happened, he refused to answer my questions. I was given an order and was expected to do it without questioning. I didn't understand what this would mean.

After being banned from speaking to Jennifer*, I became depressed. My grandmother's family had been very close prior to this incident, and it caused problems. Two of Jennifer's* sisters were married to Paul and though my mom and Jennifer* weren't close, Leah*, Jennifer*, and Ashley* were. Leah* couldn't break off the contact with Jennifer*. Jennifer* would show up to her house with Ashley*, who absolutely refused to cut off contact with her big sister who had always been there for her after their mom died. Leah* couldn't cut off contact with Ashley*, and the boys thought the whole thing was ridiculous and stayed out of it. Family holidays became a struggle because no one would uninvite Jennifer*, but my mom and Leah* didn't want to be left out. The boys refused to take sides or say anything against Paul about the situation.

For a long time, their dad, Adam* stayed out of it. The family I had grown up with and felt safe with was torn apart. Every time Leah* or my mom went to a family party, Paul would spend hours making them feel worthless. When Leah* tried to rebel and explain her family was there more than he was, it only gave her less time with her husband, which meant she wasn't able to get pregnant. Her kids were everything to her. My mom finally stopped going to family parties to comply with my dad's wishes, but because Jennifer* lived a five-minute drive from me, I started walking to her house every Saturday. We would do puzzles and I would brush her hair and massage her back. She would always give me her old clothes from her closet which were the only fashionable ones I owned. Jennifer* was my best friend.

The more my mom tried to prevent me from seeing Jennifer*, the harder I fought to see her. My whole relationship with my mother had turned into a battle ground. In my mind, she was the one responsible for breaking up our family. Sasqwhe was the one saying no whenever I asked to go anywhere with my family. I grew disrespectful, and instead of being the parent, my mother responded to my aggression the same way she responded to my father's aggression. She became passive and allowed me to disrespect her. When I became angry, it somehow triggered her to become very passive. She often told me I reminded her of my father. I didn't understand what she meant at the time. The one time she tried to stand up to me, I had called her a bitch and she slapped me across the face. Out of shock and anger, I hit her back

112

and made it clear it would be worse if she ever touched me again. In all my teenage years, she never touched me again.

When my dad realized the level of anger between my mom and me, he tried to intervene. He called us both to talk one Sunday after church, and I got my first dose of Paul's direct mental abuse. As I watched him start with my mom and continue to demean her, for a moment, I felt sorry for her. She had obviously been dealing with this for years and as I watched my dad continue his abuse, I could almost visibly see my mother cower in front of me. My pity for her turned to anger as I realized what was happening. She was allowing him to abuse her. My mom either didn't care about me socializing with Jennifer*, or she wasn't consistent enough to enforce this on her own. My father was playing her like a puppet.

The song on the Disney show Pinnochio started playing through my head. I wanted to explain that I got no strings to hold me down, but it didn't seem the appropriate time. When my mom looked as though she had been thoroughly mentally beaten, my dad turned to me and began. I was not going to be weak. After the first comment out of his mouth, I fought back. My mom and dad looked at me as though I was some sort of foreign creature they couldn't understand.

As I walked to the car with my sobbing mother, I knew I could stop hurting my mom. My battle wasn't with her. It was with that man who claimed to be my father. I knew he wouldn't use physical abuse because he hadn't in years. Unlike his brother Daniel, he was smart and had control over his emotions. His game was a completely different one that I was determined to figure out.

Things between my mom and I were not better, but the physical fights and disrespect had calmed down. We learned to coexist in the same space without interacting much. I had stopped eating and people started making comments when I wouldn't eat at school or at work. To satisfy them, I began eating meals and then vomiting after the meal. After a couple of months of this, I preferred it to not eating. I enjoyed food and I was always an emotional eater. Puking after meals allowed me to enjoy the emotional satisfaction of the food, without gaining any weight. I was now working in the payroll department at the office and entering and adjusting timecards. During the last week of the month, I would go to the other office to help them complete the monthly statements for the businesses and the members of the Order. At the payroll office, I helped with taxes. I was learning all the different processes of accounting at the young age of twelve years old.

My work was put on hold though, when my eight-year-old sister began complaining of her joints hurting. My mom never took it seriously, until she couldn't do anything but lay on the couch and cry in pain. When my mom tried to talk to my dad about it, he continued to tell her she was fine and was trying to get out of responsibility. When Rachel* continued to get worse, my mom wasn't sure what to do. She called her brother, who happened to be in medical school at the time. He was not in my dad's family and my dad had less control over him. He was nearly thirty and not married, though, so most people didn't think of him as having any standing in the Order and therefore was less controlled.

When my uncle heard the symptoms, he came to my mom's house to look at her. Paul hadn't even done that. He happened to be studying a condition called rheumatic fever at the time and Rachel's* symptoms fit the condition perfectly. After calling around, he learned that an aunt or an uncle at one time had the condition as well. He was sure he was right, and he instructed my mom to take Rachel* to Primary Children's Hospital immediately. My mom knew Paul would never allow it, and she declined. When my uncle checked back, my mom explained she just needed to eat better and the problem would go away. My uncle was frustrated, and explained the condition was fatal. My mom told him he could ask Paul if she could go, and finally, he got on the phone with my dad. After the conversation, Paul gave my mom permission to take my sister to the hospital.

At the hospital, my mom went with my sister, while I cared for my siblings. The hospital ran tests all night and came back with a diagnosis of pneumonia. When my mom called my uncle and explained the diagnosis, he asked to speak to her doctor. The condition is extremely rare, and none of the doctors thought it was possible for such a young girl to have it in a developed country. It turns out, it is very rare because we now have antibiotics. It's caused from untreated strep throat. My sister had gotten strep and my mother's neglect to treat it, caused the virus advance, causing swollen joints and damage to her heart. It's rare because there's no reason for strep to go untreated when penicillin is so readily available for treatment.

After the diagnosis, my mom went home and left me at the hospital with my sister for the two weeks she was hospitalized. My uncle visited his niece more than her own mother did. Rachel's* condition was very serious, and the doctors explained to my mom that she would need to take a regimen of aspirin until she was eighteen to strengthen her weak heart. My mom never bought one bottle of aspirin, and Rachel* would spend the rest of her adult life with poor health, paying for my mom's neglect.

My mom's neglect for her kids didn't seem to give her second thoughts to having more. She gave birth to her eighth child, a baby girl, soon after I became a teenager. My eating disorder was getting much worse, to a point, where I had difficulty keeping anything down. I had also started very heavy workouts to avoid vomiting as much, and my periods stopped. David was released from prison after serving four years of a ten-year sentence, and a month after he was released, my cousin Jeremy Kingston was arrested for the same crime.

Our community celebrated July twenty-fourth religiously every year at the home place where my mom was still living. It's the day the Mormons founded Utah and settled here to achieve religious freedom. This holiday is even bigger than July fourth, Independence Day. The whole community will go to the home place for swimming, basketball, and a huge potluck dinner to celebrate our Mormon history.

Luanne knew her husband Jeremy would be at this celebration, so on July 24th 2003, officers showed up to the celebration to arrest Jeremy because of Luanne's accusations of sexual contact with him. She was his first cousin and she was fifteen when they were married, while he was twenty-four. He was sentenced to a year in prison for third degree felony incest.

With so many arrests in such a short period of time, our community became more and more chaotic. Parents were becoming afraid to discipline their children because they didn't know any way to discipline that didn't involve abuse. I was turning fourteen and going into the eighth grade and my mom completely stopped disciplining her kids in any way. She had tried spanking us off and on throughout our childhood and had even used wooden spoons on occasion. Especially with my headstrong attitude, she knew there was no way to discipline me and while she sometimes tried to discipline the other kids, I either undermined her, or the kids would feel like I was the favorite because she didn't do anything to me. I believe my mother was afraid of me. I don't think there was ever a time I was her favorite child.

My depression was getting worse, but with my extreme workout plan, I was able to get my eating disorder under control. Vomiting became painful for my throat and I stopped doing it. Eighth grade was not any different than seventh grade, except that I had changed. I had stopped caring about anything in general. I asked Paul if I could go to public high school after eighth grade. In my novels, I had learned about public high school and had dreams of being on the debate team and cheerleading squad. I knew I would thrive in a public-school system like I had in the past and I knew the Order did not have a high school and wouldn't have one before I was old enough to go. The only options I saw was either no schooling after eighth grade or public high school.

I needed a change, but unfortunately, my father didn't care what I needed. I came back to school with the same girls and we did the same things. We ditched class and talked about our abuses. Now that we were getting closer to the age of marriage, this became our new topic of conversation. Somehow, the abuse still didn't change. Instead of hearing about girls who had been beaten by their fathers, our new topic was of the girls being beaten by their husbands. I had a half-sister, I never knew personally, marry one of Daniel's boys, and then leave suddenly. I never knew what had happened. The husband had three wives and according to her full sister, her husband had beaten her and caused her miscarriage. This was the reason she had left the Order. The first wife would wear long sleeves all summer to hide bruises from his extreme abuse. Many of the girls had heard some of the men make the comment, "Sometimes you need to slap your wife around a little bit to keep them in line." Marriage was sounding less and less appealing to me.

I was in school for the first three months of eighth grade before one of my teachers suspended me for the first time. I gave him attitude and made it clear how much I did not care. My suspension turned into a full expulsion after I flipped off my teacher and made a nasty comment about his disability. He had been in a major car accident and lost the ability to walk. He was now in a wheelchair. Most of the students hated Ensign Learning Center and I knew they admired me for standing up to the teachers. When I was expelled, all the students clapped as I took my last walk down the hall to my mom's classroom. She was a teacher at the school for a younger grade, which made it easier for the teachers to talk to her about my behavioral problems. Fortunately for everyone, my time at Ensign Learning Center came to a close. I was proud of the way I went out.

I had not received an answer from my dad about a public high school, and I knew it was not a good time to ask because I had just been expelled from his school. I felt like the man was a somewhat reasonable guy and if I asked to go to high school and pursue an education, he wouldn't deny me that. I planned to work full time and lay low until the eighth-grade year ended, before I brought up the public-school idea again. I felt like I was finally learning his game. Unfortunately, I was still green in manipulation and he threw me a curveball.

When my mom said Paul wanted to have a meeting with me about school, I tried hard to hide my excitement. Maybe he had come around to the public-school option on his own. If he planned on me quitting school, he would just ignore the conversation. Calling a meeting meant he had a change in mind. I didn't even mind waiting the usual two hours before he finally finished his last meeting. When he brought up the option of an online distance learning high school program, I couldn't hide my surprise.

"I was thinking I would like to go to public school," I answered, trying to regain my footing in the conversation.

"You were just kicked out of school," he explained thoroughly enjoying shooting me down. "You really think I'm going to let you go out into the public?"

"I promise I'll get good grades and take it seriously."

"No." he quickly told me as though the rest of the conversation was pointless. "You need to work and build up your savings, so you can support your family after you are married."

"I'll work on weekends."

"Your mom had a great savings built up when she got married," he began. "And that's the only reason she has been able to have money up to this point."

I didn't think it would help to tell him that I didn't want to get married, so I stayed quiet. He gave my mom the information to sign me up for online high school and sent us on our way.

I was devastated. I had all these visions of a public high school and being popular and joining the debate team and being a cheerleader. I knew that would never happen if I signed up for this internet school. Maybe I could talk Paul into it later, but my credits would never transfer and being held back a year in high school sounded so embarrassing. I knew I didn't have enough time to try to change his mind even if I could change it. He promised to give me a dollar raise if I graduated. My mom had started making me pay for all my clothes, most of my food, and any personal products I needed. A raise sounded pretty good.

My hours at the payroll office moved from part time to full time and I was given more responsibilities. We owned a vending company with all the employees outside the Order, which meant they all received regular paychecks from our office. I was responsible for completing their whole payroll process and printing their paychecks every week. I didn't have a driver's license at the time and I wasn't supposed to be dropping off checks, but my co-worker, Evelynne was pregnant and often sick. She was supposed to pick up time cards and drop off checks for me, but there were times she would send me by myself. Kiona, the manager at the company, made the comment of how strange it was that his payroll girl kept getting younger and younger. There were times the Law Office was short staffed, and I often filled in for the secretary. I enjoyed that job, because it sometimes included some law research. I enjoyed working with the lawyers because they were always happy to answer questions, and I learned a lot about the law.

Working full time at the office, took me out of the childish environment of Ensign Learning Center, and put me in an environment where other adults treated me as an adult, despite me being only thirteen years old. They never censored the things they talked about as far as sex, marriage, or childbirth, and those were things they all had in common and talked about frequently. Despite my young age, I learned about being a woman from the women I worked with.

This was also the time I met Jonathon*. He was my eighteen-year-old, half-brother from Paul's sixth wife. He was cocky and annoying, but what bothered me most was his confidence. He knew who he was and didn't care what anyone else thought of him, which made him a natural leader. Unlike Daniel's family, Paul's family had cliques.

There were the cool kids and the not cool kids. Jonathon*
was one of the cool kids.

When I first met Jonathon*, I hated him. I had heard
from Jennifer* that he was rude and dishonest, or at least
that was what she said. I knew they didn't like each other,
though I had never seen them interact. I knew he had done
sexual things with our other half-sister, whom I hated. I
didn't want anything to do with him. I didn't like the cool
kids or Paul's family in general for the most part. I made a
rude comment to him the first time we ever interacted, and
from that time forward, he put forth effort to talk to me
whenever he could. I don't know if he had just finally found
someone who didn't worship the ground he walked on and
found that entertaining, or if he was attracted to me.

Even though half-brothers and sisters married all
the time, I knew I would never marry him. He was not one
of Paul's righteous sons, and he wasn't "good enough" to
marry any of Paul's daughters, despite the fact he would
become sexual with at least three of them. His mom was
the head of the payroll department and he worked at the
Order's auto shop close by, so he came to the office to eat
lunch every day.

At first, he came to talk to Claire*. She was blue-
eyed, and blonde hair with a very large chest and very
pretty. Her and I became close while I was working in
payroll, partly because we were the only ones who weren't
married. She was eighteen, which was old for a girl to not
be married. She knew who she was planning to marry, and
they were waiting for his current wife to come around and
accept the plural lifestyle. The other complication to her
matrimony was the fact she had an outside sister who was
still close to her family. This made everyone nervous about
her getting married. She was planning to marry her first
cousin and with a lot of the men going to jail for the crime,

they made her wait. I didn't realize her and Jonathon* were friends until she asked me why I didn't like him. I realized I couldn't give her a straight answer. He made me uncomfortable, but maybe I should give him a chance.

Jonathon* and I talked a couple of times at the office during lunch, because he didn't want to go back to work, and I would study in the kitchen during my lunch hour. I wanted to graduate high school in as little time as possible to get my raise and be done with school. We would talk about everything from school, to work, and our goals in life. He wanted to get married and have as many kids as possible. I pitied the girl he would marry. I wanted to go to college, have a couple of kids, and have a career. I didn't know what career I wanted, but I was interested in going into the medical field. My uncle had gone to medical school and I loved reading his anatomy textbooks and looking at the bones in his office. He once showed me a dead baby online that he wanted to buy. They were expensive, because India had just made it illegal to sell dead bodies because people were killing other people to sell their bodies to people in other countries. This made them only available on the black market and raised the prices astronomically.

While Jonathon* and I were starting to get along, Jennifer* and I were drifting apart. She didn't like my new friendship with Jonathon*, and she was growing tired of being in trouble every time she talked to me. We were still banned from each other technically, and although I still called her and tried to spend whatever time with her that I could, my mom never made it easy. Jennifer* had stopped having a relationship with her "spiritual" husband for years and was trying to move on with her life alone. She saw me becoming more and more involved with Paul's family and the cult mindset she was clearly trying to get as far away from as possible. Our phone calls became fights as we both moved forward with life, and I could see myself losing someone who meant so much to me. What made it worse, was the fact that it had nothing to do with anything Paul or my mom had done at this point. She was pulling away because of her choice. My life felt like one long list of people who had abandoned me, and here was another one.

One afternoon, I was feeling particularly sad about the situation with Jennifer*, when Jonathon* came into the lunchroom. I had been in there by myself and he noticed I was upset. He stayed with me to cheer me up and make me laugh. For once in my life, I felt like someone had finally done something for me. Even Jennifer* would use me for something or another. Any time we would spend time together it included me doing something for her. She did a lot for me as well, but that was more of the relationship we had. Jonathon* stayed and cheered me up because I was sad. He didn't ask me for anything, in fact, he offered to take me to the gas station and buy me a soda, which I took him up on. From then on, we became good friends. I knew he was going through things as well. He was trying to get married to a girl who seemed to think he wasn't good enough. We bonded over the fact that we were both going through a difficult situation. The fact that he was the one guy who didn't have an interest in me helped me to feel safe around him.

After Jennifer* and I drifted apart, I was lonely. Paul's twenty-seventh wife, Jenna* was young and we had a lot of fun together. She was about ten years older than me, but our maturity levels were very close. She lived down the street from the office where I worked, and started making lunch for everyone every day as a source of income. She had two kids at the time, a toddler and an infant, whom I loved. They were my half-brothers, but they felt like close family. I had hundreds of brothers and sisters, some of which I had never met, but because I was there for her kids so often, they sometimes felt like my own.

I started staying overnight with Jenna* on occasion, and we would talk for hours. Paul saw this as an opportunity for her to encourage me to get married. He knew my mom and I were on such bad terms that my mom would never be able to convince me of anything. Paul suggested I move in with Jenna* and nobody objected. I hoped my mom missed me, but she didn't act like she did. Jenna* assured me it was only because she knew I was happy, but I suspected Jenna* didn't really care about my mom's feelings. Paul trusted her with one of his daughters in that prime time when they were being groomed for marriage. She knew it was a high honor from my father.

Jenna* was a sweet person and I didn't want to be the one to tell her how bad things were between my mom and me. I moved in with her, except when Paul came home. She asked me to go back to my mom's whenever it was her night with Paul because she didn't have a lot of time with him. I understood her wishes and appreciated she had at least had the decency to ask me instead of demand.

Moving in with Jenna* was eye opening in so many ways. She really was in love with my dad and though she didn't enjoy the idea of sharing him, she didn't fall apart about it like other women I had talked to. I seemed to be more of an inconvenience to her because she had less time with him than she would have liked.

Because I had been very young, I didn't remember any of my dad's engagements with his wives. Those things were kept quiet anyways, but I had no idea. As soon as I realized my dad was living polygamy, he was already married to Jenna*, who was the last wife to marry him at this time as number twenty-five. Jenna* told me stories of when she was engaged and some of the wives didn't want her to marry my dad. One of his wives, had tried to run her over with her van at church when she found out they were getting married. I couldn't understand why she would want to come into such a hostile environment, but she completely loved him and believed it was what God had wanted her to do.

"Dumpster diving" or "dumpster hopping" was something many people in the Order participated in. We would drive around to grocery stores late at night, usually after closing to avoid getting caught, and rummage through the store's food dumpsters to find expired food and things to feed our families. Some of the women set up with the stores, claiming they had small farms and were looking for food to feed their animals. They were feeding their kids and their families. I went with Jenna* every weekend to go dumpster hopping. Sometimes we found good stuff and sometimes we didn't. When we got caught, the owners would generally just ask us to leave. Some of the stores started locking their dumpsters because we were taking so much from them.

Jenna* and I would get home about midnight and spend all night rummaging through the goods we had collected. Because Jenna* only had a car, we would borrow Leah's* van to be able to load more stuff and sometimes Leah* would come with us. One night, we stopped at a Smith's in a more dangerous neighborhood. We watched a car park and drop a large bag in the dumpster and then drive away quickly. We waited to see if they would come back, and they didn't so we continued our dumpster journey. When we looked in the bag, there was a blood-stained tee shirt, jeans, and a dragon sweater. We didn't know what had happened and we tried not to think about it. I still own the dragon sweater to this day. Many times, we waited for drug dealers to finish their drug deals and leave before we were able to take our turn behind the dumpster.

Living with Jenna* also encouraged other married women to be able to be open with me. It gave me an advantage that many girls in the community don't have when they are single. I learned about marriage before I ever had to take the plunge, and I didn't like the reality I was seeing more and more of. Most of the women who were married did not find sex enjoyable. They had sex with the lights out and their description was tragic. I didn't have any pre-existing knowledge other than my trauma, and these women were describing a situation very similar to some of my abuses. Most of the women were raped on their wedding night. None of them understood what sex was before they were married. It was something a husband was supposed to explain to his wife. I couldn't find one girl who enjoyed sex on the first time, or any time after that. It was either brutally painful or emotionally dead. Sometimes the guys would have sex with one wife and then go to another wife and have sex without a shower in between. Every time a new wife would come into the family, someone would warn her that she should be prepared to have yeast infections often because he didn't clean himself. Sometimes the guy couldn't get completely hard enough to even allow the girl any stimulation and Viagra was not an option because drugs like birth control and Viagra were strictly forbidden. The more I learned about what marriage in the Order was really like, the less I wanted anything to do with it.

In February 2004, I was working full time at the

payroll office, which was also the office that distributed cash to the members of the community. If any member needed cash, they had to request it from the office I was working. One day, Anna* came in to request cash. She was still attending her last year at Ensign Learning Center, and I asked her why she wasn't in school in the middle of the day. She withdrew her cash and asked me to walk with her. We left the building together and when we were safely out of earshot, she explained her plan to me.

Daniel and Heidi were out of town in Vegas and had left Megan*, who was sixteen at the time, in charge of the house and the kids. Megan*and Anna* were going to the mall to get their ears pierced while the other kids were at school. Pierced ears were strictly forbidden in the Order. We were even discouraged from wearing clip on or magnetic earrings because it showed vanity. There was no way Daniel would have allowed this and I feared for their safety when Daniel found out. They invited me to come with them.

As much as I wanted to skip work, I knew I had a deadline. Checks were due tomorrow and if I went with them, I would not get them finished in time. I knew my boss would assign someone else to do them, but I didn't want her to have to do that. I declined the offer and wished the two girls luck. After they drove away, I instantly regretted my decision, but there was nothing to do about it at this point. We didn't have cell phones and there was no way to get back in touch with them. I finished my work and went home to Jenna's* house.

The next night was a Saturday and there was a community dance. Megan* and Anna* showed up in the prettiest dresses I had ever seen, and their new pierced ears were gleaming. New earrings were obviously not the only things they had gotten from the mall. I couldn't believe they were even walking. Apparently, Daniel hadn't gotten back to see them yet. On Sunday, Megan* promised to dye my hair for me, but she told me it would have to be after their meeting with Daniel. I set up the appointment more as a plan to make sure they would be okay after the meeting. I wanted my hair to get done, but I was more afraid for what Anna* was about to go through. I knew the idea had been Megan's* idea and Anna* had just gone along with it. I knew Anna* had been abused, but nothing compared to what she was about to experience. Megan* had been selfish in putting Anna* in the line of danger. She should have known better.

When Sunday came and went, I heard nothing from either of them. I didn't have their phone numbers or any knowledge about where they were staying. Often, when a child is abused, they are sent out of town to let the bruises heal before anyone can see them again. When I went to work the next day, the office was buzzing with rumors. Apparently, during their meeting, Daniel commanded Megan* to take the earrings out. When she refused, he told her he would rip them out. She excused herself to use the bathroom and called her aunt who had left the Order years ago. Her aunt had been standing by in case they needed to get out of the situation quickly. Megan* had prepared their getaway just in case. Anyone who knew Daniel, knew they would need it.

Megan* and Anna* went with their aunt, who then took them to the police department. They filed protective orders and started the biggest child custody case the Order had ever seen. Eventually, both girls were put in foster care, and all Heidi's children were taken from her because of her past abuses and neglect already on file with DCFS. They couldn't ignore it at this point.

I knew Heidi's children were abused, but so many

more things came out in court I hadn't known details about. Daniel had forced them to eat their own vomit and hit them with a 2 by 4. Everyone in the community was forced to eat food dug out of the garbage due to lack of resources. When that came out in the court records I wasn't surprised and quite honestly didn't think that was abuse.

Of course, everyone in the community claimed Megan* was lying. When judge Valdez made a ruling to take all the kids from Heidi, suddenly there was a bomb threat and he excused himself from the case. The community banded together and for once, we were excused from work to go to the courthouse and rally against the persecution against polygamy. The Order was so far removed from the reality of what was going on in the world, they stood behind a freedom of religion and didn't once apologize or even acknowledge the long term abuse they had been inflicting on their children. This wasn't a religious war. This was the state finally trying to do something to end the years of abuse this man had been inflicting on not just Heidi's kids, but all his kids and even some of Paul's. When he was a Sunday school teacher and one of my brothers made a comment he didn't like, he kicked everyone out of the classroom and beat him. In the span of Heidi's three-year trial, I didn't hear one person who was trying to take Heidi's kids once mention anything about polygamy, except when they were talking about the dynamics of the family.

Megan* especially, had been through so many years of extreme abuse, and I hoped that this would finally be the time she would be able to get out. Things would only get much worse for her if she came back. I would never wish that upon anyone. I knew it would mean Anna* would probably be gone too, though, and that made me sad. I would lose one more best friend. Unfortunately, just like Maryanne's case, Megan's* and Anna's* case made positive and negative changes within the community.

After three years in court, Judge Valdez finally released all Heidi's younger children back to her and closed the case. Megan* and Anna* chose to go into the state foster care system to be adopted into another family. They cut off all contact with anyone from the Order and we never saw or heard from them again. Megan* later legally changed her name to shed any part of her past life and pursued a bachelor's degree in social work. Anna* moved to Washington to pursue law school.

Back in the Order, men started abusing their wives and children less, and women were being matched up in marriages at much younger ages. Girls were now being betrothed to men when they were as young as thirteen or fourteen, but to keep them from being child brides, they would not actually be married until they were sixteen. The community also went from trying to hide from the outside to cover their crimes to blatantly lying to the outside to cover their crimes.

Heidi went public as a victim of the government being persecuted for her religion. She put on the fake persona of a polygamous wife who was happy in her marriage, and many of the other obedient wives followed suit. To all the pro-polygamy groups who were banding together to try to legalize polygamy, my community was just one more group being persecuted for their religious beliefs. Even Paul made a statement claiming he would no longer allow "spiritual" marriages for any girls under the age of eighteen. Two weeks later, my fifteen-year-old niece was married. Paul had gone from a guy who twisted the truth to fit his agenda, to a man who blatantly lied and didn't have any remorse for it. He was now asking his followers to lie for him as well. Heidi and Daniel had abused and neglected their children. No one protected the victims.

Chapter 11
Rock Bottom

After Anna* and Megan* were gone, Sara* was in a public school, and Jennifer* and I were no longer close. Jonathon* and I were friends, but we were both dealing with very separate struggles. I found myself incredibly alone. I started cutting myself to numb away the pain of my existence and I stopped causing trouble simply because I was done fighting. I went to work and studied. I hated who I was becoming. I was breaking. As I looked at myself in the mirror every day, I hated who I saw. One day while I was at my mom's, I punched the mirror. As I watched the blood pour out of the cuts, it was comforting. When my mom saw what had happened, she took me to see my dad for stitches. He tried to make jokes, but I wouldn't crack a smile.

After my dad stitched me up, my mom drove me to Jenna's* house without a word. I had the sinking feeling that she didn't want me anymore. When I went in the house, Jenna* yelled at me because Paul yelled at her for not keeping better tabs on me. Her true colors came out. Her helping me was motivated by her need to be my dad's bitch. It had nothing to do with her wanting to help me. My depression worsened, and I didn't want to be at Jenna's*. She took my depression personally and made it about her. She tried to make me feel guilty for being depressed because of how much she had done for me. Even though my mom wasn't emotionally there for me, she didn't try to manipulate or play mind games as much as Jenna*. I don't think she ever really learned how. She was just dead inside. At least we finally had something in common.

When I told my parents, I wanted to move home, Paul said no. My mom stayed quiet, but I saw her perk up.

Even though we didn't like each other, I think some part of her was hurt when I didn't want to be with her anymore. Maybe a part of her was still my mom. Though, she seemed surprised by my dad's answer, she didn't say a word. Once again, she didn't stand up for me or protect me. I really didn't care at this point though. She wasn't consistent in any other way, but in this area, I knew what to expect from her. When Jenna* found out I had asked to move, once again, she made it about her and took it personally. Any closeness we had in the past seemed to be gone.

I loved Jenna*, but she was becoming more and more self-centered. When she found out she was pregnant, she wanted to make it a surprise for Paul and she asked me to be there to throw him off. When he spent the meeting talking to me, she became angry at me for taking his time away from her. Never once did she put the blame on Paul who didn't seem to care about becoming a new father. The toxin that is polygamy had eaten away at the fun, outgoing friend Jenna* had been when I had moved in with her. Maybe having me around sped up the process the way it did when Leah* moved in with my mom because she was forced to work so closely with my mom, who was also Paul's wife. Either way, Jenna* and I were no longer close, despite being forced to live in the same house together.

When I finally had the chance to go back to my mom's house, I knew I was done. Paul was coming to Jenna's* house and I was allowed to go back to stay at my mom's house. After everyone had gone to sleep, I lit a candle, took a large butcher knife, and started cutting my wrist. I took the whole bottle of tylenol and through the tears, did my best to cut away. I thought about my mom who I hoped would be the one to find me. Maybe she would finally wake up to the horror she was living in. Maybe she would finally get out, though deep down, I knew that was impossible. I thought about Jenna*, who I felt betrayed by. She would blame me of course. I thought about Paul, and nearly stopped. This knife belonged at his throat, not mine. He was the one responsible for so much pain. He had destroyed my family. He had destroyed my mom. He had destroyed me.

My arm was nearly numb as a sharp pain started from the wound I had made and shot up through my arm to my shoulder. After that, my world went black. It happened so quickly, there were no final thoughts. I was met with a darkness.

When I opened my eyes the next morning, I saw the puddle of blood below my wrist and saw the vomit all over the bathroom floor. I had the quick flashback to the movie Ghost and wondered if I was a spirit. I felt pain. From all the talks with my dad, spirits don't feel pain. My wrist was throbbing, and my head was pounding. I heard movement upstairs and quickly cleaned up the mess I had made. I bandaged my wrist and continued to get ready for school. I had to get up. I wasn't dead.

After my suicide attempt, the world was different. It seemed that once I had hit the bottom, there really was nowhere to go but up. I could stay at rock bottom or I could go back up. God had spared me for a reason and I was determined to find out what that reason was. I began questioning my reality. Why am I so unhappy? Is my life really worse than death? I knew I was probably going to hell if I killed myself, but I realized nothing could be worse than the hell I was living in. For the first time, I began questioning the very religion I was living in. I couldn't keep blaming everything on the people. I knew the religion was condoning it. I began asking the question of the difference between an "insider" and an "outsider" and how you become one or the other. Without being obvious, I began learning the difference between the Order and the church to help me make the decision of where I wanted to be. What will make me happy?

An "insider" is simply someone who has been born in the Order and hasn't made the decision to leave or has married into the Order and hasn't made the decision to leave. The difference between the church and the Order is the difference between the business and the religion. A person can be part of the Order without being part of the church, but they cannot be a part of the church without being part of the Order. The requirements to be an Order member require you to turn in your money, work for the Order, and give them all your earthly possessions. The church is the religious part. The requirements to be a part of the church require you to go to church and live their religious teachings such as the Word of Wisdom, which comes from the LDS Doctrine Covenants which prohibits any tobacco, strong drink, which they have taken to mean alcohol, and no hot drinks, which prohibits coffee and tea.

Marriage is also something that decides your place in the community. For a man, his standing in the church is dependent on his obedience to the leader and if he is part of the Kingston bloodline. For a woman, her standing is with her husband. She cannot have a standing on her own. If she leaves her husband, it is extremely rare for her to be able to remarry unless she was in a marriage to a man of very low standing. If she is deemed worthy, she may leave her husband and marry someone with high standing. At fourteen years old, I was learning quickly, but not quickly enough.

Jenna* began pushing me to pray for my direction in marriage. Marriage was the last thing on my mind, but her and I were no longer close, so she didn't know that.

When she asked me, "Are you waiting for God to come down and strike you with lightning to tell you who you are supposed to marry?"

My honest response was, "It might be helpful."

I knew she was pushing marriage more to get back in my father's good graces after so many mistakes on my part, rather than her being worried about my impending marriage. She wasn't worried about my happiness. Getting one of my dad's wayward children married off would be a way for her to make up for all my past sins.

She had a man in mind who lived down in Huntington and already had one wife. He seemed to be a nice enough guy, and my aunt was married to his brother. His wife was not from the Order and I didn't see her loving the idea of sharing her husband. I didn't want to be the homewrecker who just moved in. Their kids were adorable, and they were obviously in love with each other. The thought of ruining something so good made me cringe. Why couldn't Jenna* find another guy who wasn't married, or at least someone who wasn't as happily married. I never wanted to be the second wife. The second wife is the one who steals the first wife's husband. The other wives were just added on to the damage.

Against my wishes, Jenna* had her sights set on Joey*. Her family reunion was coming up and she explained her matchmaking plan to Paul and asked if I could go to her reunion with her. After all the years of trying to get a trip to go to the mine to visit my aunt, I was finally able to go down there. The reunion was fine. Joey* and his wife were nice. There were no sparks between us, but I did know he was a great guy and would be a good husband. I didn't know his wife, but knew I didn't want to do that to her. They were not currently living polygamy and I had seen firsthand the damage of the lifestyle. I didn't want to be the one to bring that toxin into their beautiful family. Jenna* kept pushing for us to talk. He must have sensed something was off as well, but he was kind about it. We didn't have anything to talk about because of our age difference. I was fourteen and he was in his early thirties. I told him his wife was beautiful, which was true. After the first day, I was tired of Jenna's manipulative matchmaking tactics, and I just wanted to go home.

Jonathon* happened to be at the reunion and was leaving early with a couple of other people to get back for the community dance. I told Jenna* I wasn't feeling well, and she let me go back with Jonathon*. I hadn't seen him for months because he had started working at the mine and wasn't at the office so much. He was trying to be good enough to be able to get married and talking to other girls at all was not appropriate. It usually started all kinds of rumors. On the way back home, he became my big brother and friend again. Conversation was easy, and it involved everyone in the car. I had no reason to be concerned about where I was.

When we got back to Jonathon's* house, everyone else was still at the reunion. We planned to get ready for the dance on opposite sides of the house and Katy*, one of Patricia's* daughters, would take us to the dance. Patricia* was Paul's first wife. When I went into the house and dropped my things in the kitchen. I started looking for something to wear, when I noticed Jonathon* in the doorway watching me. When I asked him what he was looking at, he used a cheesy line he must have thought was pretty smooth. I had never seen this side of him. At one time, when we first became friends, I had a crush on him, but it was short and had ended over a year ago. We hadn't even been talking much over the last six months or so because he was working out of town. I brushed off the comment, thinking he was only making jokes.

When he suggested we change in front of each other I didn't know how to respond. I walked away without giving an answer, hoping he would let it go. He followed me though, and I said no. He wouldn't leave. I said no again, and he continued to argue with me about it. Once again, I had no control over my body or my life. When he touched me, I shut down. I had been violated so many times in my life and here was another. After saying no a few more times and being completely ignored, he tried to kiss me. It was odd, though I tried to enjoy the kiss. It was technically my first kiss. I felt ashamed because it wasn't on my wedding day with my husband the way it was supposed to be. After what felt like an eternity of him fondling and groping me, we finally heard Katy's* car horn outside.

Jonathon* ran around trying to finish dressing for the dance. I numbly put the rest of my clothes back on and zipped up my bag. When Katy* came inside after waiting so long for us, she saw me in the kitchen. I must have looked as bad as I felt. I didn't respond to her when she asked me what was wrong. I couldn't breathe, and I couldn't stop shaking.

We went to the dance, and Jonathon* couldn't look me in the eye. I couldn't have been more confused. Wishing we could just pretend it never happened, I tried to make light of it. I was in shock from the experience and the whole night passed as a blur. Katy* gave me a ride home to Jenna's* who was thankfully still at the reunion. On any other night, I would have been afraid to be here all alone, and if anyone knew, they would never let me be here alone. Tonight, I welcomed the silence and the idea of death didn't really bother me. I wanted to be alone more than anything.

The next morning, I went to church and tried to pretend everything was normal, but it wasn't. Jonathon* wasn't at church and I knew he was planning to go back to the mine on Monday to start a graveyard shift Monday night. I wasn't sure why he had even bothered to come to Salt Lake in the first place. I knew he was trying to marry a girl, and it wasn't unusual for guys to make special trips to Salt Lake to dance with a girl he thought he might have a chance of marrying.

I came back home to Jenna's* after church and realized she had come back from the reunion. I rushed to my room to avoid her questions or any conversation. Why wasn't he at church? I did something I had never done before and I called him. When Jenna* asked me who I was talking to, I made up a reason about him fixing my computer. Hopefully, it would make the phone call a lesser crime. It was against Order standards to call a boy on the phone unless it was for business purposes.

When Jonathan* answered the phone, he wasn't his usual chipper self. He couldn't get off the phone with me fast enough and he wouldn't give me any clear answers. I listened to him apologize for ruining my life and when he was done, he asked me not to tell anyone. Still completely confused about the whole situation, he explained to me that he was going to the mine and not coming back for a long time, so I wasn't going to see him.

"What about me?" I asked unsure of what this meant or what to do next. Was I even going to be allowed to marry anyone else after what we had done?

"Did you ever think we would get married?" he asked me.

I wasn't sure of the right answer to this question.

"No," I answered him honestly. I knew Paul would

never let it happen and I really didn't have those kinds of feelings for him. The thought of us together just felt so wrong. It didn't feel like there was any love or any mutual feelings for each other. It was then that I realized he never really cared for me at all. I didn't know if I was a distraction or a weakness, but I knew we didn't even have a friendship at that point.

Before I knew it, he ended the conversation. He wouldn't answer the phone when I tried to call back.

I thought I could hide everything from Jenna*, but when she asked me how my weekend was and tried again to talk to me about Joey*, I broke down in tears. I couldn't even explain what had happened or how. I didn't even understand my feelings about it. Not only had I been violated again, but it was by one of the very few people in my life I thought I could trust. He was supposed to be my big brother and my friend.

Somehow, after Jenna* heard my story, she turned the story around that I had purposefully come up to Salt Lake to do sexual things with Jonathon* instead of getting to know Joey*, who was supposed to be my future husband. I went from confused about what happened with Jonathon*, to confusion about reality in general. To make matters worse, before I had time to process my trauma and what had happened, she took me straight to the home place where Paul was conducting baptisms. I was too numb and confused to be scared of Paul, but I definitely wasn't ready to be confronted.

When we came to the home place, I went inside my mom's house. I just wanted my mom. I wanted someone to hold me and tell me everything was going to be okay. I had just been destroyed by Jonathon's* betrayal and I needed someone on my side. When my mom saw me, she asked me what was going on. Jenna* walked in moments later before I could offer my mom any explanation. I didn't know what to tell her with Jenna* standing right there. Did I purposefully come back to Salt Lake in hopes of something happening with Jonathon*? My world was spinning, and I didn't know how to make it stop.

Fortunately, I didn't have time to say anything to either of them, because Paul picked that moment to walk in the house. I couldn't help but find it ironic. The one time I didn't mind waiting for Paul, he was right on time. My mom kept asking anyone who would listen what was going on, and Paul completely ignored her and told me to go outside to talk privately. As I walked out the door, I heard Jenna* start to explain the situation to my mom. I almost wanted to stay and listen because I wasn't quite sure what was going on either.

Just as he always did, Paul said a lot of bullshit, most of which I don't remember. He blamed me for the whole situation and made it clear that I would no longer be able to live with Jenna*. I wasn't sad about that part. I was not allowed to go to dances unless my mom went, and I was not allowed to be out of her sight. I was essentially on house arrest except to go to work. Dances and church were the last places in the world I wanted to be, so the whole thing was fine with me.

Jonathon* didn't end up marrying the girl he was pursuing, but as far as I know, his life was not negatively affected in any other way. He did apologize to me again a year after everything happened, and I forgave him until I found out he molested another half-sister when she was twelve, only a year or so after he molested me. He obviously had no remorse for what he had done. He was just another good liar and manipulator just like his father.

Chapter 12
Betrayed

"I hate myself for trusting him. I will never make that mistake again. I will never trust anyone again. I will never let anyone be in a position to hurt me. I don't care anymore. I will be alone. That's the best way. No friends. No men. No people. No one will hurt me again. Jonathon* will think I have forgotten about this, but I will never forget. I'm not even sure I can forgive. Why was I so stupid? Why didn't I see? I let my heart get the best of me, and it got broke. Never again. Never, never again."

Three months after Jonathon* molested me, I tried again to put the past behind us, but when I tried to talk to him, he refused. I didn't think he could hurt me any more than he already had, but I was proven wrong. His rejection hurt. As I stood outside in the rain during a dance one night, I let the tears flow freely. I love the rain. It feels like a time to let everything be washed away. Before that night, I had been so broken for so long, and the realization hit me like a ton of bricks. I kept waiting for a prince charming to come rescue me. Even as I stood out in the rain, I hoped Jonathon*, or my mom, or someone who was supposed to be there for me would. But I realized no one was going to save me and there was no easy way out. If I wanted to make it and have the life I wanted, I was going to have to fight for it. I realized then and there, to make it in the Order, I was going to have to fight.

About six months after being molested, my mom had started catering for the weddings within the community. She was working as a cook in the private school my dad had started, and she realized she had a passion for cooking. She had never cooked for her kids in the past, so I found it odd she was suddenly so passionate about this domestic task. On occasion, she might make us pancakes, or cook some rice to feed us rice, honey, cinnamon, and milk, but for the most part, my brother or I would make dinner. Even when she started catering for the weddings, we were not allowed to have any. She would spend all day making a huge meal for the wedding, and then leave at lunchtime to take it to the event. When I asked what we were supposed to eat, she told me to eat some oats. She had never been great with taking care of us, and when she started focusing on her new job, her neglect became just a little bit worse.

When I found myself getting short of breath and feeling light headed, my mom began accusing me of trying to get attention. I would pass out for about five minutes or so, before I would regain consciousness and seem completely fine. The first time it happened, my mom called Paul and because it took her so long to call her back, I had regained consciousness. Paul asked my mom a series of questions before he came back with a peanut allergy as his diagnosis. I stayed away from peanuts, but it happened again. My dad assumed I had peanuts and had just not realized it. He stayed firm in his diagnosis. When the episodes continued to happen, my dad told me to go on a cleanse. It took me years before I realized these were panic attacks, so I followed my dad's cleanse instructions.

For the first day, I was told to completely dry fast. I was not allowed to eat anything or drink anything, including water. On the second day, I could have as much apple juice as I wanted from six in the morning until noon. At noon, I could not eat or drink anything until six in the evening. I would then take an epsom salt mixture at six and eight in the evening and then I would take a large amount of grapefruit juice and olive oil at ten in the evening before bed. We were told to lay down and go to bed directly after drinking the olive oil because if you didn't, chances were high that you might vomit and then you would have to take it again. On the third day, I would have to get up and do the epsom salts mixture at six and eight in the morning and then at ten in the morning I could eat fresh fruit. After completing the cleanse, we were told to only eat raw fruits and vegetable for ten days and then slowly start eating normal foods after that. Everyone in the Order did slightly different variations of this cleanse, but these were the basic instructions.

Finally, at the age of fourteen, I graduated high school. I finally got my dollar raise, which was great because my mom had started charging me rent after I moved back in with her from Jenna's* house. I had been working full time at the office, while doing part time hours at Valley Coal and the Law office. I thought nothing of it, when Leah* asked me to take over Valley Coal for her one day while she went out. It was strange when my mom was the one who picked me up from my office to take me to Valley Coal, and then my mom and Leah* left together. I figured it was probably a secret wedding and I really didn't care who it was at that point. The marriage talk was getting old.

When they came back from the wedding, they both looked at me like I was stupid. I knew it was a wedding and I just didn't care.

"Guess who got married?" they both taunted me with information they felt privileged to have even though everyone was always getting married.

"It's someone close to you," they both continued. I saw the hurt on my mom's face, but I didn't understand it, so I guessed a few people that I knew were getting close.

"It's Paul!" Leah* who was obviously taking the

news much better than my mom finally blurted out. She was never good with surprises. After many years of not taking more wives, my dad finally married one of David's eighteen-year-old daughters. I nearly puked as I remembered him flirting with her on our outings while her dad was in prison. She was only two years older than me and my dad was forty-four years old. If I had any respect for my dad before that point, it was gone. He was taking away any chance she had at happiness. I knew the way my mom's sister wives treated each other.

Paul hadn't asked any of them for permission to take another wife. Most of the wives didn't even know the wedding was happening until an hour before the ceremony when my dad called everyone and told them they needed to drop everything and be there. I was told many of the wives were crying during the ceremony and that it was the farthest thing from a happy wedding that a person could get.

To make matters worse, Paul married the young girl's younger sister as well, shortly after and she was only a year older than me. I was disgusted as I watched them dance together. She looked like a little girl standing next to the disgusting old man who had taken her innocence. There was nothing righteous about Paul in my mind from that point forward. He was a dirty old pedophile.

Shortly after Paul's marriage, he called a meeting with a group of the older girls and his two new wives who were also our age. Because they were so much younger than Paul's other wives, they got along much better with his older teenage daughters. I found the whole thing disgusting, and the baby wife was a bitch. I liked her older sister though. I felt badly about the damage she had married into. But our meeting was not what any of us expected. Paul had selected these girls to begin college at

Salt Lake Community College in a couple of weeks. He called us the trail blazers because our group would show him if college for his kids was a good idea. We were only allowed to take classes with two or more of the girls and we were all going for a business degree. No exception.

I couldn't believe I was going to college. I hid my excitement and pretended I didn't care either way. If Paul thought I was too excited, he might get suspicious and change his mind. It turned out that allowing his girls to go to college wasn't the only change in Paul's family. He allowed a group of his boys to go to High School as well. He realized his businesses, especially the accounting offices, needed people who knew what they were doing. They had been getting audited on business and personal taxes and he needed someone who understood the system.

Despite not having a driver's license, Jenna* wanted to help her dad get rid of his old car he had parked in her yard, and tried to convince me to buy it. It was an ugly white Pontiac GrandAM that hadn't been driven in about five years. We didn't even know if it was currently running. Jenna* wanted it out of her yard. She knew her dad wouldn't move it unless she sold it, so she asked Paul if I could buy it. He drove it once around the block to test drive it, and signed off on it. Six months before I got my driver's license, I bought my first car. It moved from Jenna's* yard to my mom's driveway where it would lay dormant until I got my license. Cassie* lived close to me and we were in a lot of the same college classes together, so I carpooled with her and another of our half-sisters.

I started college three months before my sixteenth birthday, and my mom realized the hassle it was to have the kids going to different schools especially so early in the morning. We carpooled for three months until my birthday,

146

and then as soon as I turned sixteen, I drove my own car to drop off Daniel to his carpool ride, but I was not allowed to drive by myself to the college, so I parked my car at my half-sister's house and rode to school with her. Paul claimed he was trying to save money on parking passes, but he just wanted to make sure there was always someone to spy on us. The parking passes were twenty dollars per semester.

College was the most amazing thing I had ever experienced at this time in my life. Even walking on campus, there were so many new and different people. Everyone in the Order looked the same. Despite my dad's strict rules for attending college, it was worth it. When I found myself in my first business class, doing my first group project with none of my sisters, I couldn't be happier. I had purposefully sat at a different table than them, and I made the excuse that I had come in late and didn't want to be disruptive by trying to get all the way into the back to their table.

My group consisted of a young guy from Bosnia, an LDS girl who was waiting for her boyfriend to return from his LDS mission, and on overweight guy who didn't talk much. My mind was opened during this semester and though I didn't focus much on the business lessons, I learned so much from my team members. I wanted to know everything they would tell me about their life. I had been searching for something different, and I knew I was on the right path.

The month after I started college, my mom gave birth to her ninth baby. She was a large twelve-pound baby. My dad had been in China on a business trip, and though she had tried to wait for him, he was thirty minutes late to the birth. This birth was different for a lot of reasons. For the first time in all her nine children, Paul stayed at my mom's house after the birth. My sister had weighed twelve pounds when she born, and she was my mom's most painful birth. Paul took the baby downstairs to watch television while my mom rested. I happened to be awake, and I sat down beside him. We watched I Am Legend, with Will Smith, and Paul started with his usual comments of how lucky we are that we will never have to marry a black person. I thought Will Smith was attractive and I told Paul what I thought. He didn't seem to know how to respond. When he pressed it and asked if I would want to have black kids, I didn't see a problem with it. He held my baby sister up for me to see and asked how I would feel if she was black. I told him she would be cute both ways. Though I had won the battle, I didn't realize I had just started a war.

Chapter 13
Getting Back Up

Every morning, my brother would wake me up to take him to his carpool ride around five in the morning. This morning didn't seem any different. After he urgently commanded me to wake up, I dragged myself to a sitting position. When I opened my eyes, my brother was nowhere to be found. Figuring he must have gone back upstairs, I figured I had better follow. When my eyes finally fought the grogginess and opened, my bedside alarm clock showed it was only two in the morning.

"It must have been a dream," I said to myself as I finished waking up.

When I stood up and opened my eyes, I felt a rush of adrenaline as I registered what was happening. The room next to mine was on fire. There was a small doorway where I could not see actual fire that was supposed to be my exit to get to the rest of the family. I took my chances.

As I ran past the fire through smoke and flames, I found the stairway to be full of smoke and could not see my way through as I made my way upstairs. There was smoke on the main floor, and I knew I had to hurry to make it up to where my mom and all my siblings were sleeping.

My first stop was my mom's room. I shoved her as hard as I could and told her the house was on fire. She was immediately awake and running downstairs. I called 911 for help and then one by one, I pulled each of the kids out of bed and directed them to get in the van. I didn't know where we were going, or if were going anywhere, but it was cold and I knew we couldn't stay here.

Before anyone could get out the door, my mom returned from downstairs.

"Where are you going?"

"Out to the van," I told her. "It's too smoky to stay in the house."

"I put the fire out with the fire extinguisher," she explained. "Tell everyone go back to bed."

"The smoke could make so the kids can't breathe," I explained, knowing my mom had not talked to the fire marshal in kindergarten like I had.

"There's no fire!" she argued. "Go to bed!"

"I called 911," I admitted waiting for her to be mad.

"Why?!"

"Because the house was on fire," I explained as though I was speaking to a child. I assumed my response would carry enough logic to make my point, but it did not.

"Call them back and tell them we don't need them."

Confused, I picked up the phone and untangled the chord to reach it to my ear. Just then, I heard the fire truck. I guess we could just tell them when they got here.

When the firemen came to the door, my mom tried to stop them. She kept saying everything was fine and there was only a small fire. She had used the fire extinguisher to put it out. A couple of firemen went downstairs to check it out and they came running back instructing everyone to get out now. The fire was not out. Again, I began instructing the kids to get in the van. The firemen couldn't believe how many children were in the house. As the last one came out, he asked me to count to make sure everyone had made it out. Dustin* was missing.

Just then, he came out wrapped in a blanket. Apparently, he had gone back inside to get it because it was cold. Many kids would have been frightened in the situation, but the kids were all calm and annoyed about being pulled out of their beds. Even the baby slept through it all. In our chaotic life, this was not scary or abnormal. It was just the tragedy of the day.

Finally, as we all sat in the van, my mom was by far the most upset. As difficult as it was to not say "I told you so" I held my tongue. My mom's eyes were wild as she watched the situation get so far out of control. I knew our safety was not what she was worried about. Paul would be very upset with her for nearly burning down the home place. It was the first house in the Order, and she was often told she didn't deserve it. In hopes of calming her down, I offered to say a prayer. It worked. She seemed more peaceful as we saw our neighbor running down to our house to ask if she could help. My mom and all the other kids went to sleep at her house.

Dustin* refused to go to the neighbors to sleep and insisted on sleeping in his own house. I was not going to leave him alone and I knew everyone else would be safe next door. My brother and I opened all the windows and doors and curled up on the couch under some blankets. It was freezing cold and I probably would have been much more comfortable at the neighbor's house on the floor, but I couldn't leave my brother, and for whatever reason, he wasn't leaving. We fell asleep.

My sixteenth birthday was approaching quickly. I was excited because it meant legal driving privileges, but I also knew the expectation of marriage would be stronger as well. I was sixteen and marriage was the furthest thing from my mind. Unfortunately, it was the first thing on everyone else's. One of my half-mom's decided she was going to take me shopping to find some clothing that would make me more appealing for guys. She had the reputation of dressing like a slut, but when I pointed this out, she was quick to point out how much more time she had with Paul and how many trips she went on compared to the other wives. She had a valid point and I couldn't argue with her.

Finally, my birthday was here. Paul usually made it

to my birthday's late at night and enjoyed some cake and ice cream before everyone went to bed. My birthday was the only one of my siblings whose birthdays he made it to. I guess it happened to be at a convenient time of the year when nothing else from a more important wife was going on. This special treatment could have been a positive thing in my life, but all my siblings resented me because once again, they felt like I was the favorite.

This year was different even from my normal special treatment. Paul told me I could invite whomever I wanted, and he took us all out bowling. All my friends told me how lucky I was to have such an amazing dad who was the leader, but also took time to be a dad. I wanted to laugh in their faces. This was the first time he had ever done anything like this and it would be the last.

Despite Paul being fake as he dazzled my friends with his stories from faraway places, he would never take me to, I enjoyed my birthday for the first time in a long time. He took each of my friends to their houses before going home to mine. On the way home, he stopped and taught me how to parallel park to be ready for my driving test that week. For some strange reason, he was acting like the dad he had never been.

When we came home, my mom had made me cinnamon rolls instead of a cake for my birthday because they were my favorite. I didn't really like cake. After dessert, my mom put all the other kids to bed, and Paul asked me to stay behind to talk before I could join them. When everyone except my mom was tucked in bed, Paul began our first serious marriage talk.

Have you thought about who you might have had direction on?" Suddenly the extravagant birthday made sense.

"I haven't had any direction," I answered honestly. I

152

was irritated to be talking about it.

"Someone has come forward to ask you to marry them."

"I think I should focus on school," I began, careful to not come across as rebellious, but also trying desperately to make my point and have him see things my way. I didn't want to get married at all, but definitely not before I was eighteen. He seemed upset by this answer.

"It's not our choice when we get married," Paul explained. "Only God knows the right time and you need to be open to whatever God has in mind."

"Well I haven't had any direction," I continued. "If God wanted me to get married right now, I feel like he would have given me some direction already."

"Maybe you haven't been open to it," he went on. "Have you been fasting and praying?"

Technically I had been starving myself, but that's probably not the same thing.

"I have been praying," I answered honestly. "But I haven't fasted since I stopped doing the cleanses for my appendix."

"I'm going to China for two weeks. I want you to fast and pray while I'm gone and come up with a list of guys that you might think are your number one choice to marry."

I did as he asked. I fasted and prayed, but I only felt more confident that I was not supposed to be thinking about marriage at sixteen.

When Paul came back from China, I had hopes that he might completely forget about the conversation. It didn't happen that way. We had our second meeting two and half weeks later.

"So, let's see your list," he began when we were both seated in his office.

"I don't have one."

"Why not?"

"I didn't have any direction in the last two weeks."

"What days did you fast?"

"Tuesday and Thursday," I said remembering how terrible the previous week had been due to lack of nutrition.

"Have you been praying?"

"Yes."

It seemed as though he was the one trying to push my marriage, while God was saying wait.

"Two weeks ago, was my first serious thought about marriage," I tried to explain. I was not ready for this step and I had no notice of it happening. "I'm not ready to talk to anyone until I'm eighteen."

"That's not your decision," Paul threatened, then corrected himself. "Only God can make that decision.

In that moment, I knew without a doubt, that I didn't have a choice.

"A man is coming forward next week to speak to you," Paul went on. "You will fast and pray and get your direction before then.

A guy was taking me on a date and I could not say no to the date or the marriage.

"Who is it?" I asked out of curiosity. Maybe God would give me a feeling when I heard his name. I had heard of women getting direction that way before.

"I'm not going to tell you," he said. "You need to fast and pray and get the name from God."

I did as I was asked, and I fasted and prayed. I nearly fainted multiple times from lack of food, and when I realized how weak I was becoming from the fasting, I stopped. Maybe Paul wanted me weak so I would do what he wanted. I continued to pray, and I still did not receive any dreams or inspirations like many people do when they receive their direction in marriage.

The night before I was supposed to go on my date, my mom asked me if I had any direction. I had not. When she asked me if I wanted to know who the guy was, I grew suspicious yet curious. This whole thing had been a game and my mom had just decided to become a player in it. I didn't know what her angle was. I shut my emotions down and did not trust her, but I played along.

When she told me it was Mark*, I thought she was kidding. We had danced together, and he was a nice enough guy, but there were no feelings on my part. He was eleven years older than me and even though I liked his family okay, there was nothing there in terms of an emotional connection or physical attraction. I told my mom this, and she explained that many girls do not love their husbands when they marry them. The love comes after marriage. I had seen too many girls become stuck in a marriage with someone they didn't love or who had abused them. I wasn't going to be one of them.

I suddenly felt like I was drowning. I was a lamb about to be slaughtered and I could see them coming. It was only a matter of time. I physically ran out the door. I could hear my mom call after me, but I didn't care. I had been athletic and there was no way my mom could have caught me, and I really don't think she tried. I'm sure she, like so many girls in our community, knew this drowning feeling well. I had heard some of the girls talk about it, but I had never felt it, and while they described it as the feeling of settling down, I felt like I was just settling. I found myself sitting on the grass at the only public school I had gone to and crying. I wasn't completely sure what I was feeling. I was overwhelmed, scared, and stuck.

When I gathered my emotions and put them all back into the box in my head they had climbed out of, I slowly walked back to my house. I couldn't run forever. They would only chase harder.

My mom came to my room where I had plopped onto my bed.

"What do you think about it?" she began as she sat down next to me on my bed.

"I don't know," I answered honestly. "I have never thought about him before."

"Are you okay?"

No! I wanted to scream.

"Yeah, just surprised."

"Do you like him?"

"I don't know."

"You have danced with him before."

"I don't plan on marrying every guy that I have danced with."

"He seems like a really nice guy."

"Can I not go?"

"You have to go."

"Why?"

"It's rude not to, for one thing, and me and your dad both think this is the right thing to do."

As she left the room, I felt like I had just received a death sentence. I didn't hate Mark.* He seemed like a nice guy and his family was nice. I didn't know him except for a couple of times I danced with him.

The next night, I awkwardly sat across from Mark* at the local Sizzler. We both ate from the salad bar, because I didn't know how to order food from a menu. The only restaurant I had ever been to was Chuck-A-Rama a couple of times for a birthday. I realized how sad my situation was. I was sixteen years old and I didn't even know how to order a steak, yet I was expected to be able to pick the person I would spend the rest of my life with.

When Mark* nervously came to the part where he told me he thought he was supposed to marry me, he nervously stopped. It was excruciatingly painful for me because I knew what he was asking, and I wished he would just say it. When I saw how nervous he was, I found some patience. He didn't seem to want to be here anymore than I did. He told me about some dreams he had. He felt like it was direction and asked if I had any direction on him.

"I haven't had any direction on anyone," I answered him honestly. "When I do, you'll be the first to know, at least besides me."

"I appreciate that," he told me softly.

"I appreciate you coming forward," I continued, rehearsing the lines my mom had gone over with me before I left. This was also a line Claire, who had multiple guys ask her to marry them, told me about. She was much calmer than I was about the whole situation and fortunately for her, her dad had died when she was young, so she would never be forced to marry someone she didn't want to.

When the date ended, Mark* drove me home. He didn't walk me to the door, there was no kiss goodnight, we hadn't even physically touched except when he shook my hand when I got into the car. Oddly enough, even before I realized marriage was just a business arrangement in my community, that's exactly what it felt like. My mom tried to talk to me about it as though it was a special moment in my life. I told her exactly what happened, and she didn't understand why I didn't want to marry him. Him and his family were nice, and I would be a first wife if I married him. I once tried to tell her that I wanted to be the only wife, but it only caused an argument. That wasn't my choice.

After my date with Mark*, I knew the walls were closing in, but I didn't know what to do about it. My parents dropped the marriage topic for the moment, but I knew it was only a matter of time. My car was having problems and I found myself broken down on the freeway every other week. The last time it broke down on the freeway, I was done. A nice Mexican guy with his girlfriend stopped to help me. He asked if I wanted him to look at my car. After a look, he told me what was wrong, but I didn't listen. I really didn't care. I asked him if he was heading north. He said he was, and I gave him an address close to the freeway and close to my house. I asked him to take me there. I appreciated him helping me and didn't want to put him out of his way, and I was taught that outsiders weren't trustworthy, so I didn't ask him to take me all the way home.

When my mom came home later that night, she asked me where my car was.

"On the freeway."

"Why is it there?"

"It broke."

"Are you going to go get it?"

"Nope."

"Why not?"

"I don't care anymore."

Jenna* had talked me into buying a lemon car to help her dad and once again, I was screwed over in the process. My mom called some of my half-brothers to get the car and I don't know what happened to it after that. When my mom was upset with me for getting a ride with a stranger, I pointed out the fact that he had done something nice for me. Just because she was comfortable being a bitch to people who helped her out, I was not. She didn't say anything more about it.

Turning sixteen brought more than just marriage pressures. My mom had been charging me for my clothes

158

and any items I wanted, as well as food for the household as my way of paying rent. When I turned sixteen, the Order started taking money out of my paychecks as "child support" to be paid to my mom. I found it ironic that my own father was not paying child support for his kids, but I was. When I confronted my mom about this change, she informed me that it would be better for me because I would pay less in taxes and get a bigger tax return at the end of the year. Because I was only being paid just over five dollars an hour, I wasn't earning much, which kept me from being required to pay taxes anyways. My larger tax return was given to my mom to support my siblings. When I tried to explain this to my mom, her defense was that it was time for me to start paying my own way. I was old enough to be an adult.

Though I had never been extremely close with my half-brother Josh*, everyone knew he was planning to leave the Order. When he finally did, no one tried to stop him. His two older siblings had left, and his mom had been moved to a new ranch away from everyone else in the family. Many people claimed it was exile, but Paul never actually said this to my knowledge. Most people who left in the past, never tried to come back. They were told they were cutting all ties and they were not welcome back. Josh* didn't care. He knew where the dance was being held and he showed up. I asked him to dance, because I wanted to know if he had regrets about leaving. The thoughts were in my mind as the walls of marriage began closing in. Josh* was in tears when he talked to me. He didn't know how his own brothers who he had grown up with could turn their backs on him and not even acknowledge his existence. I had my first glimpse into what I would be losing if I left. Was it worth it?

I was still working and going to college, but I had

stopped showing up and trying in my classes. I was forced to take classes for a degree I didn't want to go for, and the marriage pressures were growing. There were little things to give me courage every now and then. A teacher required we read Maya Angelou in one of her classes, and I read her book, "I Know Why the Caged Bird Sings," over and over.

One day my dad asked my sister and I to go to his car for a book of some sort. When we went through his gym bag that fit his description of where the book was located, we found three porn magazines. This solidified my father's depravities in my mind, and I would not trust him to be the mouth of God. At least we now knew why my dad favored the wives he did. All the girls in the magazines were blonde. Apparently, my dad had a thing for blonde hair and large breasts. I was disgusted to know that all his wives were desperate for his love of any kind, and here he was looking at porn stars. The hypocrisy of it wasn't the worst of his crimes in my mind.

I was still having my episodes, and Paul's diagnosis was still appendicitis. I was doing a cleanse every two weeks and I felt worse than before Paul decided to play doctor. The next marriage meeting with my dad was not as secretive. He must have seen how damaging his games were with the first guy who came forward to marry me. It obviously did not work. My mom and her sisters really liked the second guy and pushed me to say yes before I had even talked to him. He was nineteen and I was almost seventeen and he was not married yet. My mom and Ashley* loved him. Jennifer* pointed out that he was my first cousin and that he was Daniel's son. I didn't really care about any of their input. I didn't want to get married to someone I didn't love, and I had never met the guy.

My date with Joseph* was more enjoyable than

with Mark*. I was older, and less awkward, and I had already done it before. Joseph* and I were closer in age and we both had outgoing personalities. He took me to dinner at a Hawaiian restaurant and then we went to Fast Kart to race go-carts with his brothers. I had a good time, and I knew he felt pretty good about himself, but I was still not ready to say yes. We talked about our goals for the future and where we saw ourselves going with our careers and such. He told me he was fine with me finishing school and having a career. When I asked him about polygamy, he would do whatever God wanted him to. Because I liked him better than Mark*, my mom and my friends were all sure I would be engaged soon. I nearly agreed to marry him because I was so tired of fighting.

One night as I was driving to the community dance, I prayed to God and made a deal with him. If I was supposed to marry Joseph*, he would make the next three lights that I drove through green. As I hit the first light, it was green, and my heart sank. I was devastated. Right then and there, I knew that if Joseph* was the right one, my heart would not be so heavy. Maybe God had given me these feelings for a reason.

Fortunately for me, Paul became preoccupied with a pending incest charge against him. Because he had married three of his half-sisters and Daniel had married two half-sisters they were being investigated by the Attorney General's office. The Attorney General, Mark Shurtleff, had given Paul a head's up. He needed DNA from them and those specific wives and their children. When Mark Shurtleff gave them the heads up, those wives were sent into hiding across the border in Colorado while those warrants expired. The officers had thirty days to collect the specimens before they expired. Jenna* was one of the wives who was sent away because she was Paul's full niece. This was fine because we were no longer close, but I knew I was leaving the Order soon and I wanted to be able to tell her goodbye when I left. Unfortunately, that never happened.

In May 2006, one of Daniel's wives, Lana*, had decided to become a lawyer. She was upset by what had happened in Heidi's case and wanted to be able to do something for the women in the future. She had finished law school and applied for a court internship in Utah. She was denied because she was Daniel's wife. The Order had even more ammo against the state of Utah for the persecution of religion stance. Lana* ended up moving to California during the week for a few years while she continued her law education. Her kids were shuffled between the remaining wives in Utah, and Lana* came back to see them some weekends. May 2006 is also when Warren Jeffs of the FLDS was put on America's most wanted list. When I read the charges against him, I laughed. Paul and Warren were exactly the same. The only difference between the two was the fact that Warren physically isolated his community and made them wear prairie dresses. Warren was later arrested in August driving a red car, even after he had banned red from the community. They were two sides of the same coin.

By this time, I knew I was on the path to leaving the Order. I had too many dreams and goals I just couldn't give up. I just didn't know how I would get there or when. Kristine*, Sara's* younger, more rebellious sister and I ditched church to pierce my ears in a KFC bathroom with a pin and a piece of ice. I was rebelling and trying to get some control, even though I knew I had none. Under the surface, I didn't realize just how much my dad and Joseph's* dad were trying to manipulate my life.

One day, one of my half-sisters and I were talking,

and she began telling me about our honeymoon that our parents were planning and booking tickets for. She had assumed I had said yes or at least was close to it because they were already planning the honeymoon. I had no intention of taking that trip, but I had no idea how to get out of it. I failed my spring semester of college because of all the stress and even though I wanted to go back for the summer to try again, I knew it would probably not happen unless I accepted Joseph's* marriage proposal and even then, the chances were slim. I was not ready to give up on my life just yet.

After Paul pulled me out of college, my world didn't make sense. College gave me a place to think critically about the world I was living in. Without college, I felt like I was drowning again. I needed a lifeline. One Saturday, I pulled out the phone book and opened it. It landed on a section for karate classes and there was a huge ad for a nearby school. I copied down the address, closed the phone book, and sneaked out the back door. It took thirty minutes to walk to the studio for classes four days a week. Because I no longer had a car, walking was my only option. The classes were the most expensive of any other studio around, but that didn't bother me either. I would use all my clothes money to pay for them.

After a month or so of sneaking to classes, my mom began to realize I was missing. After a Saturday class, I came home. My mom had her wild eyes again. When she demanded to know where I was, I finally told her. When she tried to tell me I was dropping the classes, I refused. When they told me they would cut off my money to pay for them, I told her I would stop working for the Order and get a job where I could actually keep my paychecks. She called Paul immediately and handed the phone to me. When he asked me about it, I told him I needed something to do after I quit college. He agreed that I could go to class, but my mom was required to go to every class with me.

As embarrassing as it was to have my mom sit and watch every class, I knew it was only a matter of time before she would grow tired of spending four days a week at the studio with me. After a week, she tried to talk to the sensei and ask him to kick me out. He was confused. She was the mother. If she wanted me to quit, then she could tell me to quit. When he pointed this out, she stomped out of his office.

My sensei, James*, called me into his office to talk to me about my first belt test after about a month of attending classes. I was shocked. I hadn't been doing this to get better at martial arts. I needed something outside of my community to survive the time I was forced to spend inside the community. I grew excited that I was doing well at something. I advanced two belts before the end of the summer, and Paul had agreed to let me go back to college for the fall. I think he planned on me quitting karate because I wouldn't have enough time. I went to college classes with my half-sisters in the morning, worked at the office in the afternoon, and jumped on the city bus to get to karate in time for classes. I missed some of the classes during the week because my bus ride was an hour to get to class from where I worked in Salt Lake City, but I was there every Saturday.

After a couple of months, I found myself wanting to be at the dojo all the time. I would sit on the floor and do homework while James* taught private lessons, and eventually, I was able to talk to him about my family just a little bit. I told him we were from a polygamous group in Salt Lake, but I never told him which one. He smiled when I told him because he had already figured it out. When I

164

asked him what gave it away, he told me it was my mom. She just had a look about her. To this day, I'm not entirely sure what he meant. Maybe her brokenness really was that obvious.

Opening up to James*, gave me an outlet to be able to figure things out in my head. He questioned everything I thought and asked me why I felt that way. I had never had someone make me think about my thought process. I had never been so self-aware. One day, James and I were talking, and he mentioned the idea of being a martial arts instructor.

"I'll be married in the next year," I told him matter-of-factly. My husband wouldn't let me pursue that dream.

"People shouldn't get married until they are at least twenty-five," he told me as though he knew something I didn't.

"I don't have a choice," I told him sadly.

"Everyone has a choice."

"I don't."

"Whose choice is it?" he asked me, probably thinking I was not serious.

"My parents," I answered. The conversation was making me uncomfortable and I was no longer able to look him in the eye.

It was then that he seemed to understand. My mom was evasive and uncomfortable around outsiders. She was a walking advertisement to our lifestyle.

The longer I stayed single, the more they pressured me to get married. They were only allowing me to go to college to keep me away from the people in karate. Somehow, I was still single when my seventeenth birthday came and went. I was beginning to accept the fact that I would probably leave the Order, though I tried not to focus on that thought. It was too overwhelming to think about everything I would lose, but I began making plans for my escape. One of my instructors at the dojo cosigned on a bank account for me to start stashing money for my escape. I had eleven months until my eighteenth birthday, and when I told James* my plans, he helped me think about all the things I would need to move out on my own.

Chapter 14
Planning My Escape

Should I Stay In The Order?

Pro's
I have a responsibility to my family
I can take care of my family
I can do what I want before I am 18
I will be stable
I can have my kids
I will be assured to have someone there for me
My father will be proud

Con's
I'm so not ready
I don't know Joseph* (staying the Order means marrying him eventually)
I don't love Joseph*
I will be stuck
I have have to worry about pregnancy
I may never go to Europe
I may never finish school
I may never be a karate instructor
I will have to readjust all my goals and dreams
Financial issues
Can't afford a wedding, house, etc.
Will have to live off my family
Karate will be much harder
I'll be talking time off karate whenever I may be pregnant
I won't be who I want to be in 20 years

After James* helped me make a list of everything I needed to do to prepare to leave the Order, I began figuring out how to accomplish each thing on the list. First thing I needed, was to find a job outside the Order and save as much money as I could as a cushion in case I lost the job. I had no idea how to find an outside job. In the past, when I wanted a job, I went to my dad and he told me where I would be working. I would start the next day. James* taught me how to do a resume and showed me some websites to apply for a job. Being under eighteen disqualified me from a lot of employment options. I had a high school diploma and some college, which would help.

Chris* was another sensei at the dojo, and he was a little more involved in my situation than James*. James* did his best to help me but also keep our relationship professional. He was aware of the laws against me and didn't want to find himself in trouble for helping an underage girl known as "jail bait" or get in trouble with my family for harboring a runaway. He knew he would be the first one my mom would come to if they wanted to hurt someone, and he kept my mom chasing him while Chris helped me. Another student, Kevin*, was one of Chris's* students, and he agreed to help me get a job. Chris* had told him about my situation, and Kevin* told me he could get me a job waiting tables at the Denny's in Bountiful. There wasn't a bus that went too close to that particular store. Now I found myself needing a car.

James* had an old car sitting parked at the studio. He had bought it for another instructor and he had no use for it after the instructor took off to California with her boyfriend. James* offered to sell it to me for a great deal. I agreed to buy the car, and promised to have the money to him by the end of the week. I just needed to figure out how to convince Paul to let me take eight hundred dollars from my Order account.

When I met with Paul after family meeting that

Thursday, his first response was no. He did not think I needed a car.

"It's my money," I argued. "I want to use it to buy a car."

"You don't need a car."

"I do need a car, and I'm going to buy it. You are welcome to test drive it if you want, but I am going to buy this car."

"If you want to play that game, little missy, we can go down to the Driver's License Division and get your license revoked until you are eighteen."

I held my ground.

"Fine, while we are down there, I'll go ahead and let them know you are Paul Kingston, wanted by the federal government. I don't think they will care much about my driver's license at that point."

A dark, threatening look came over my dad's face, but I was determined to win this. "Don't make threats," he said in a low tone I had never heard him use before.

"It's not a threat," I pressed on. "A threat is something you have no intention to follow through with, and you can be sure this is not a threat."

I could see the twitch in his upper lip as he processed my words. I didn't know if he was going to yell, hit me, or threaten me again. I held eye contact. I was not going to be bullied by him this time. To my surprise, he did none of those things. He dismissed me and told me he would talk to mom about it. The next day, we test drove the car, and I handed James* the eight hundred dollars cash for the car. I didn't trust my dad to give me a check.

Now that I had my own car, I was able to keep up with my school, work, and karate schedule much better. My dad told me I would no longer be working for the office, and I would now be working for the grocery store. I think he began seeing signs that I might leave the Order and didn't want to risk me knowing too much about his accounting operations. We both knew the damage had already been done, and if I told too many people, he would be investigated for a whole list of crimes committed by him and everyone in the accounting departments.

Paul tried to spend time with me at the grocery store and taught me the basics to managing a grocery store. I listened to everything he taught me, because I didn't know what things would come in handy and what things I wouldn't need. I enjoyed working at the grocery store. The television company National Lampoon filmed a movie called "Bag Boy" while I was there, and I met Wesley Jonathon who had been a Co-star to Amanda Bynes in the TV show "What I Like About You." The art director was cool and flirted with the cashiers. I don't think he realized I was only seventeen when he gave me his number and told me he was in town for the rest of the week after filming ended. I found it flattering, but I never called him.

While I was working at the grocery store, I became friends with Vanessa*. She was my age and we had gone to school together, but because her family was not Kingston, she was the girl me and my family teased. We never became friends despite being in the same class for five years together. I couldn't believe how naive she was to the scams the Order was playing.

Talking to her one day, she was doing her best to try to convince me of the value of the Order and the honesty we find within our community and nowhere else.

"Honesty?!" I nearly shouted. "That's a load of crap."

"You don't even know," she tried to tell me.

"I worked in payroll, honey, and trust me, you

yourself have been cheated out of at least a couple thousand dollars over your lifetime."

"It sucks to be making minimum wage," she admitted. "But they are not cheating me out it."

"You are not making minimum wage," I assured her.

"Yes, I am."

"No, you are not."

"My father is a lawyer and he would sue them if they were doing that to his family."

"Well they are, so he better open up a lawsuit," I said becoming hopeful.

"How do you figure?" she asked unsure of my confidence.

I laughed and asked for a paper and pencil where I drew out the scam. When a person works so many hours, for example, eighty hours within a pay period, the payroll office will first apply a formula they have written down to adjust the hours. For overtime, the law requires a company to pay time and a half. The Order does not pay time and a half to their Order employees. They take the extra hours and plug them into the equation to cut the hours in half. If an employee works 85 hours in a pay period, they will pay them their rate for the eighty hours and then take the extra five hours and multiply them by 3 and divide them by 2. The employee will be getting paid for 82.66 hours instead of the full 85 hours and they will never know because their timecard is adjusted, and the payroll department keeps the timecards. They don't give them back to the employee and the rest of the paper trail appears completely legitimate. They have a similar formula to pay employees less than minimum wage as well.

When I explained this to Vanessa*, her eyes grew wide with disbelief. How could they do something so illegal and not get caught? When I explained they only do it to Order members and I know they do this because I worked in payroll for years, she was not convinced. When I told her I personally figured the time cards and prepared paychecks, she still wasn't convinced.

"Pull your timecards," I told her. "Tell them you want a copy of all your timecards to save them, and they will give them to you because they know it is very difficult to find the error. Calculate them yourself and you will see I am right."

I only figured out the scam when one of my aunts was working ninety or more hours for the grocery store and was not getting time and a half for her overtime. When I asked my boss about it, she explained that the Order didn't have to follow those laws. At the time, I didn't understand it was wrong. When I was working in payroll, they explained what we were supposed to do, but never the why behind it. I was a person who always asked questions, and sometimes an unsuspecting manager accidentally answered them.

Vanessa* talked a big talk about how her dad was a lawyer and he would put a stop to it, but when she came back the next day, I asked her what he was planning to do about it.

"He doesn't want to cause problems," was her response. I shook my head in disappointment. So long as they have victims, they will keep up the scam.

As Vanessa* and I became closer, I was sad to see she was trying to follow the same path every other girl in the Order was working towards. She wanted to get married. She had known who she wanted to marry since eighth grade and had even announced it to the class. Every girl in eighth grade thought they knew who they were going to marry and no one took it serious. When I found out he had come forward to ask her to marry him, I was happy for her, but I knew our friendship would be over shortly. I was on my way out of the Order mindset and she was immersing herself deeper into it. We were temporarily in the same place for a moment, but I knew that wouldn't last long. When I finally told her my plans to leave, she asked me to wait until after her wedding. She had just gotten engaged and had just set a date. It was about three months away, so I agreed to wait.

Sara* was the last friend on my list I needed to tell. She didn't seem surprised by my decision, and she had other friends outside the community, so it wouldn't be as difficult for her. She made me promise not to ditch her, and I did. No matter what happened and no matter where life took either one of us, she could always call me. I wasn't planning on leaving until I was eighteen, which was nine months away. Unfortunately, in the Order, nothing ever works out the way you plan.

My mom had seemed more pleasant over the last month, which was abnormal considering she was heavily pregnant with her tenth child. She told my brother and I she had a surprise for us, and we climbed into her van. I had a karate test that night, and I was worried we might not make it. She promised we would. When we showed up to the home of one of my dad's wives who had gone to Colorado to escape an incest charge, I was confused as to why we were there. This was when my mom pointed out we were moving here. My brother and I were both upset and my brother Dustin* began yelling at me. It was no secret we were moving to Salt Lake to keep me away from my friends at karate. I was afraid her plan may actually work.

When I went to my karate test that night, James* reminded me to calm down and think. I was panicking. I knew what this meant, and I knew this was only the beginning of their plan. We were moved into the new place in less than a month and my mom gave birth to her new daughter in the new house. I knew I needed to act quickly before they had a chance to make their next move. James* tried to tell me I was overreacting, and I turned on him. He didn't know my family like I did and the only reason he would be telling me to calm down was if they had gotten to him. It sounded crazy even in my own head, but I knew what they were capable of. I couldn't trust anyone. Luckily, Kevin* happened to be in class that night and I asked him if he could still get me that job. He did, and I started working at Denny's the next day. Paul and my mom didn't have any idea what was going on because my mom had just had a baby and one of Paul's toddlers from another wife had a large brain tumor. He passed away that month.

It was a month before my parents realized I had quit my job at John's Market. When my mom asked me how I was planning to pay for my car, I told her I had gotten another job at Denny's. I wouldn't tell her where because I didn't want her to try to interfere. When she explained that was grounds to be kicked out of the Order, I explained that I didn't trust the Order with my money. I didn't tell her I was planning to leave the Order at that point, because I wasn't quite ready to admit that to myself or anyone else. Also, I had made a promise to Vanessa*. The wedding was a couple of months away. As soon as I boldly stated I was leaving, that was it. I stopped coming home every night and started staying at Kevin's* on occasion to avoid the drama at home. Being stuck in the middle of leaving and staying was like being stuck nowhere. Finally, during a fight with my mom, she told me that if I didn't want to be there then I should leave. I knew her words were said out of anger to hurt me, but it only showed me she had no idea where my head was at. I still wasn't ready to tell her my plan but hearing her say those words almost made it feel like permission instead of a hurtful comment.

James* and Chris* were expressing concern about my recent decisions. They felt like I was heading down a bad path and there would be no one to stop me. James* told me he felt responsible for me because I didn't have any parents. Chris* spent long nights at the local Denny's with me, keeping me company and out of trouble. Out of nowhere, James* decided to quit teaching karate to take care of his family. He didn't go into a lot of details, but he had tears in his eyes when he said goodbye. He told me family is everything and sometimes he wondered if I should completely give up on mine. All his students were sad to see him go. He had mentored so many kids in bad situations, and he had changed so many of our lives for the better. I wished him happiness but didn't have much time to dwell on his absence. I was in survival mode.

I had started quietly dating my karate instructor who had gotten me the bank account. Even though he was twenty-six and I was seventeen, he was LDS and didn't believe in sex before marriage. He never pressured me to do anything. He also knew he couldn't marry me until I was eighteen because my parents wouldn't consent. Being in a relationship with him was a safe place for me to be. We were in a comfortable dating space we both knew couldn't go forward until I was eighteen.

We only dated two months before he told me he was leaving for Alaska to work for three months and he would call me when he came back to see if I still wanted to be in a relationship with him. It was quite sudden, but he let me keep my bank account and didn't do anything vindictive, even though he could have because he was the cosigner on the bank account with all the money I had saved. He was taking a leap of faith on me for cosigning on the account. If I had racked up any charges, he would be responsible. We never ended up getting back together when he got back. In fact, I never heard from him again until my birthday when I called him and asked him to take his name off my bank account. He told me he had already done so and wished me well. He had met an LDS girl and was engaged to her. I was happy for him and I thanked him for everything he had done for me. I think we both knew I could never join his church after what my own had put me through, and he respected that. I appreciated him for everything he had done for me.

One night while everyone in my house was sleeping, I knew it was time. I had packed up my box of journals and picture books and put them in my car earlier that day, and now at 2am, it was time for me to go. I would not be safe if I stayed here. I would be married before my eighteenth birthday and maybe pregnant. I would never be able to leave if I stayed till I was eighteen. It was now or never. I opened my bedroom window and stood in front of it. I didn't know what was on the other side of this choice, but I knew what was on this side, and I knew it wasn't what I wanted. I loved my brothers and sisters with all my heart, but I knew I couldn't help them if I stayed in the Order. I climbed out the bedroom window. As I ran as quietly as I could with nothing but my small backpack full of some clothes, a toothbrush, and some deodorant, I realized I really wasn't leaving too much stuff behind, because I didn't really have much to begin with.

I couldn't help but look back at the dark windows. Behind each window, I was leaving someone behind. My eyes filled with tears as I opened my car door. I closed it as quietly as I could. The whole neighborhood seemed way too quiet. When my car started, I thought for sure I had been caught. My engine was loud because my car needed a new muffler, but somehow the house stayed silent. I carefully put the car in reverse and drove out slowly and quietly. As I drove away from my mom's house, I didn't really know where I was going. I just knew I wasn't staying there.

Chapter 15
On the Run

To my family,

I am not exactly sure how you feel about me right now, but if you're listening to our parents, it's probably not good. I'm not going to apologize for anything because I'm not ashamed of what I have done, and judging from the way our family works, it's probably not what you think.

I just want to tell you that no matter what happens, I love you and I'm still your big sister. Situations don't change the fact that we are family. I wish I knew what to say to make things easier on everyone, but I don't. Sometimes life puts you in crappy situations and you just have to make the best of it.

No matter what anyone says, I didn't ditch you. You can call or email me anytime you want. I'm still here for all you kids. I hope this letter is of some comfort to you, I write it from the bottom of my heart.

I love you. Follow your dreams. It's scary sometimes, but I think it will all be worth it in the end. It seems I can't say, "I love you" enough times.

Good luck with everything and remember, I'm just a phone call or an email away.

Best Wishes,
Nicole

The next morning, I woke up in the Denny's parking lot. I was freezing, because I had kept my car off all night not wanting to waste gas. My reality suddenly hit me. I was homeless. My plan had been to wait until I was eighteen, get an apartment, have a job, and live a normal life like everyone from my karate class. Why did my life have to be so damn hard? I didn't know where to go or what to do. I couldn't call anyone. James* had always told me to calm down and think. If I stay calm, there wasn't a situation I couldn't get myself out of. I pulled out my list of things to prepare to leave. I had already gotten a job and built up some savings. I had a car as well. I was enrolled in classes at the Salt Lake Community College, and I planned to continue those classes. Without telling anyone, I had switched campuses to avoid seeing people from my community. The only thing I was missing was a place to live. Maybe this wouldn't be so bad.

After living in my car for a week, I realized I needed a phone. If ever anyone from my work needed to communicate with me or there was ever an emergency, I needed to be able to call someone and people needed to call me. I didn't want anyone to know about my situation, and not having a phone was drawing attention to myself. Kevin*, who had gotten me the job at Denny's was now currently my coworker. We were spending time together, but neither of us had any sexual feelings for the other. I think he knew I was in a bad place, even though he didn't know the extent, and he sincerely wanted to help me. When I asked him how to get a cell phone, at first, he thought I was kidding. I was seventeen years old and had never used a cell phone, let alone owned one. I didn't know the first thing about getting one.

He told me to go to the nearest Cricket store and get on a pay as you go phone. It was unlimited texting and calls, but no internet. I did my best to talk to the store's clerk, but I think he could see I was way out of my league. He was kind though and walked me through the plan and the way it all worked. I walked out with the cheapest flip phone in the store. When I got in my car, the first person I called was Kevin*. I was so excited to own my first cell phone that he must have thought my excitement was sarcasm, but I didn't care. I kept putting one foot in front of the other, I would be fine. I left the Cricket store smiling and went to my college class, and then off to work my serving shift. This was a good day.

As the month went on, and the nights were cold, I was growing tired of sleeping in my car every night. I had found the Sapp Brothers a couple of miles from the Salt Lake Community College and realized it was a truck stop with showers. I didn't go too early in the morning, or too late in the evening. I found the best hours to shower without too many truck drivers waiting around. I was cautious about my surroundings. I had read about self-defense and being aware of my surroundings as a woman to avoid being attacked and I followed the advice. There was one sales clerk I became friends with, and I tried to only shower when he was there, because I knew he would watch out for me. I was still attending karate in Bountiful, Salt Lake Community College in Salt Lake, and working as many shifts as possible at Denny's, which was also in Bountiful. I knew I didn't want to be doing this until I was eighteen and could sign my own lease, so I started looking at other options.

My half-brother Josh* and I got in touch shortly after I had run away, and he told me of his plans to go to Las Vegas to find mechanic work. I didn't see another option if I stayed in Salt Lake other than living in my car until I turned eighteen. That was seven months away. I finally came clean to Kevin* about my problem of being homeless and told him my plan of moving to Vegas with my brother. He seemed surprised. He hadn't even known I was homeless. As he washed his truck one night, he began questioning my plans.

"How old is he?" he asked referring to my brother.

"About six months younger than me."

"I don't think that's a good idea."

"Why?" I asked completely naive to any dangers in the outside. I was fully prepared for anything in the Order, but the outside world presented a completely different set of challenges that my upbringing had not prepared me for.

"Vegas is not the place for a young girl to go by herself, especially as naive as you are."

"I'm not naive!" I shouted offended. "And besides, I won't be by myself."

"Your brother will be doing his own thing. Who is going to watch out for you?"

"I can take care of myself." That, I was sure of.

"Not in Vegas, you can't."

"Well living in my car sucks."

"Don't live in your car," he said as though it was the simplest explanation in the world. "My sister is moving out of our apartment at the end of the month to move in with her boyfriend. I'll have an extra room and you can move in with me."

"And pay rent and everything?"

"No one lives for free out here." He seemed offended.

"I didn't mean I don't want to pay rent," I explained. "I just don't know how."

"Just pay me half the rent before the end of the month," he explained. "I can't really put you on the lease because you are underage, so you can just pay me."

I had started getting excited about the Vegas idea, so I told him I would let him know in a couple of days.

Turns out, Josh* was going to be staying with a bunch of other guys, and I wouldn't really have a place to stay anyways if I went with him. I called Kevin* immediately and asked if his offer was still available. After a month of living in my car, I moved into his apartment. I hadn't called my family while I had been running and I was starting to miss my mom and my siblings. I didn't have any furniture in my new place and I knew my mom would never let me have my furniture anyways, but I started to come up with a plan. If I agreed to meet with my mom, I could find out a time when no one would be in my mom's house and I would be able to sneak in and take my furniture back. I had bought some blankets and pillows from the secondhand store, but I didn't want to risk not making rent, so I didn't buy any furniture. I just wanted to sleep in a bed and feel like I had a place of my own.

I went to the college and called my mom from the courtesy phone. I didn't want her to know I had a cell phone or where I had been staying. When I asked her to meet me at Village Inn to talk, she seemed excited at the idea.

She was already there when I walked in, and she seemed to have aged dramatically since the last time I saw her. Her roots were showing where she had obviously not kept her dye job up on her hair. She seemed to have put on some weight as well. I had always thought she was pretty in the past. I hoped her obvious decline wasn't entirely my fault. We talked, and she was obviously trying to get as much information from me as possible. I told her I didn't trust her, and I wouldn't give her any information.

She sincerely seemed confused by my obvious distrust of the Order in general. I told her I didn't want to get married and Paul made it clear to me that I was getting married. Running was my only option. Instead of denying my accusations, she told me I should feel lucky that Paul cares enough about me to want me to get married and have a successful life in the Order. After being out of the brainwashing for about two months, the words out of her mouth were just so sad for me to hear. She believed everything she was saying. How could I be angry with someone who really didn't know the damage they were causing. Once again, my heart softened towards my mother. I almost felt bad about what I was about to do. After I got the information I needed, I promised my mom I would think about what she had said and be in touch with her. The community dance was in two days, though, and I needed to be prepared.

I called Kevin* after I met with my mom and asked him for a favor. I needed to borrow his truck, but I knew it was a stick shift and I couldn't drive a stick shift. He loved his truck and probably wouldn't have let me drive it anyways. I could use the extra hands as well. I asked him to help me break into my mom's house while they were at the dance to get my furniture, and though he hesitated, he agreed. I assured him they would all be gone and that they wouldn't call the cops anyways because that wasn't something they would do. They wanted to draw as little attention to themselves and their community as possible.

When we pulled up to my mom's house that night, every window was completely dark and lifeless. Everyone was gone. He thought it would be smarter to park on the street in case we needed to leave quickly, but I told him we would be better off in the driveway. It wouldn't cause any suspicion with the neighbors and we would be there for less time. He saw my point and pulled into the driveway. He stopped by a window thinking we were going to need to break in, but I just went to the back. The sliding glass door wasn't locked. I opened it. My mom was from Bountiful and we never locked the door. Half the time, the lock didn't work anyways. We had never really had anything of value worth stealing.

As we walked into my mom's new house she had

only lived in for five months or so, the smell of rotten milk filled the air. When Kevin* looked over to the counters and saw gallons of rotten milk on the counter, I could see the disgust in his face. I thought nothing of it. This was how we lived. Mice and roaches were common in my houses growing up and our house was never clean. As much as my mom didn't like to admit it, a new house wasn't going to change her bad habits. As we walked into the main living room, he pointed to the large picture of my dad on the wall.

"Is that your dad?"

"Yeah, why?" I asked. "How did you know?"

"It's the largest picture on the wall. It makes sense to have a large picture of the prophet on your wall."

I wasn't quite sure what he was getting at, and when I asked for an explanation, his only response was, "It just makes sense."

We stepped over the mattresses and garbage all over the floor in my little sister's rooms and carried out my small white desk I had gotten for Christmas one year and my daybed I had paid for a year ago when I had started working. My dresser was broken in the corner, so I took one of my sister's small ones we had gotten from a second hand store many years before. We loaded everything into the truck and drove away without a second look. Kevin* asked tons of questions on the way home.

"You lived there?"

"Yeah," I answered, more preoccupied with checking behind us to be sure we weren't being followed.

As we drove away, Kevin* shook his head.

"That's a sad place to live."

"Why?" I asked keeping conversation. I hadn't known any other lifestyle and hadn't realized what a shock it must have been for someone who had never lived that way.

184

"There's rotten milk on the counter and the whole place was unsanitary."

"My mom's busy," I said, trying to make excuses. "She hasn't been home all day."

He dropped the conversation, but I knew he wasn't satisfied with my answer. I think it was the first time he had a small idea about what I was dealing with.

As I had promised, I called my mom the following week. I had settled into my new routine of working and going to school, and I tried to stop by karate every now and then whenever Kevin* went to classes. Things were going well for me, but I missed my family. I had never been away from them for so long and mornings were especially difficult.

In my mom's house, I would wake up to kids laughing or fighting and my mom yelling at people to do something or other. In my new apartment, I woke up to silence every single morning. It was maddening. My mom told me that Joseph* wanted to talk to me and asked if I would be willing to meet with him. I felt bad for the guy because everyone had planned on us getting married and I just disappeared without a word. I felt like I owed him some sort of explanation or something. I had never even told him no to his proposal. I agreed to meet with him.

I told Kevin where I was going just in case they tried to do something to me. I was in new territory and didn't know how far they would go.

"I'm going to meet Joseph*," I said to Kevin*

"Why?"

"I don't know," I answered honestly. "I just don't know."

"Are you coming back?"

"I'll be back in about an hour."

"Good luck."

"Thanks."

Not wanting to be followed or to give my family any clue as to where I was living, I agreed to meet him at the office where I had worked throughout my childhood. It was a place we both knew well. When I pulled my car into the parking lot, he pulled in shortly afterwards. I got out of my car and got into his. I didn't want to go inside to see anyone, and I didn't want to run into any old friends. Leaving everyone behind was difficult. I didn't need it thrown in my face.

Joseph* seemed nervous to be meeting with me. He obviously didn't know what to say and I didn't know how to help him. I didn't know how much he knew or why he wanted to meet me, so I couldn't help him out. Even when he spoke, he seemed to trip over his words and had a difficult time forming complete sentences.

"Did you have any more direction?" he asked after we had driven around in silence for about fifteen minutes. I didn't know if he was playing dumb or if he didn't know I had left the Order. There was no way he had missed that piece of gossip.

"I honestly don't know what I'm supposed to do. I don't know who I want to marry or if I'm even going to stay in the Order." There was no point in beating around the bush. He deserved to know.

"I see."

"I don't want you to wait for me," I continued. "If you find something else, don't feel like you have to wait for me. I don't know how long this will take.

I knew Joseph* was in a hurry to be married. I was not. I was okay with being alone. He was not.

"Okay," he answered after what seemed like hours. There were tears in his eyes. I waited for him to say more, but he didn't. We drove back to my car in silence. Though few words had been spoken, I was shaking when I got back into my car. I drove away as quickly as possible. I didn't need anyone from the Order to see me when I broke down and cried moments later. I was overwhelmed. Did I just make a huge mistake? Should I go back and just marry him? He promised he would let me go to school and have a career. Maybe he wouldn't be abusive like his dad and a lot of his brothers. I could hardly see through the tears as I drove back to my apartment and I went into my room to cry.

Kevin* came in. "Are you okay?"

I was crying too hard to speak.

"What happened?" he asked and seemed to prepare himself for the worst.

"He felt so bad!" I sobbed. "I didn't mean to hurt him."

"You weren't obligated to marry him," Kevin* tried to reason. "He shouldn't have put so much feeling into a girl he didn't even know."

"But he did," I argued.

"That's not your fault."

Kevin* would never understand and this argument was going nowhere. What I didn't understand, was that I was groomed to please everyone except myself and I was struggling so hard to finally do what I wanted instead of what my religion wanted.

"Let's go watch movies," I told Kevin* to end the conversation.

The meeting with Joseph* wasn't the end of my parent's manipulation to try to get me back. I had hoped they would just give up and let me go on in peace, but that never happened. Being underage I wondered why they didn't call the cops on Kevin* for harboring a runaway, but then I had a friend point out there was no way they could prove I was living with him. They knew I spent time with him, but I had never actually told anyone where I was living or who I was living with. I had opened a PO Box to receive mail and my name wasn't on the lease or any of the utilities. As far as anyone was concerned, both in and out of the Order, I was untraceable. They did call the cops on Kevin* one time and claimed he had drugs on the premises. When the cops showed up to search the house, there were no drugs on the property. He and his friends smoked weed recreationally, and one of his friends was a dealer, but they never had anything to do with any hard drugs. I smoked weed a couple of times and enjoyed it. I've always been a very energetic person whose mind works very quickly. Marijuana calmed me down.

Living with Kevin*, I also tried alcohol for my first time. I told him I was going to try drinking and there was nothing he could do to stop me. He told me that if I was going to do it anyways, he was going to make sure I did it safely. He called his friends over, who brought the alcohol and I called Sara*. She was on the fence about staying in the Order or leaving, and we missed each other. She came over and we played drinking games. The guys ended up taking care of us as we stumbled around the apartment and cut us off before we had too much. They put us in bed where we passed out at the end of the night, and I had never felt safer in my life. This was where I met my future husband.

I started down the party road with Kevin*, Alan*, and their friends. I knew I was safe to drink with them and that they would never hurt me or take advantage of me. It wasn't long before I realized I was using alcohol to numb the pain of losing my family, though, and eventually even the alcohol wasn't enough.

I was still attending college, and kept a 3.7 GPA

during all my partying and living in my car. No matter how much I had drank the night before, I was always in class and at work when I was supposed to be. I got my first tattoo the morning after a night of drinking in Wendover.

Fortunately, a college ID doesn't have a date of birth on it, and my tattoo artist didn't believe a seventeen-year-old could be in college. Alan* sat with me for my first tattoo. I was a little self-conscious because the tattoo was on my rib cage, and I was in only a bikini top for hours while two grown men looked at my bare midsection. I had never had anyone see this much of my body except during my sexual abuse.

I finally gave my mom my cell phone number, and it wasn't until many years later before I realized this was a huge mistake. She began calling me frequently, and I started receiving death threats. I was told that if I didn't stop talking to all the kids in the Order, then they would "bury some rounds in me." I called them out and dared them to try anything. I repeatedly asked for their name and when they wouldn't tell me, I called them a "Coward." I was done being bullied. My friends told me I was crazy for egging them on and they wanted me to file a police report because they were afraid for me. I knew it was just the same intimidation the Order always used. There were a couple of members who were crazy enough to do something, but most of them just talked a big talk. Thankfully, this person happened to be one of them that talked the big talk, because I never heard from them again.

It wasn't long before I found myself in the same Order mind game again. I was physically gone, but mentally, they still had a hold on me, and they weren't letting go. They were slowly getting stronger as I started to let my guard down. I missed my siblings and my mom continued to remind me of my sins. I was growing depressed again, and suicide was on my mind again. My mom must have seen this as her opportune time to wear me down. It nearly destroyed me when she made the comment, "You might as well kill yourself, because you are dead to me and your brothers and sisters, anyways."

Sara's* brother kept trying to talk to my mom and tell her that if I came back, he would marry me. Guys from the Order were suddenly all very interested in coming forward and trying to get me to come back and marry them. I seemed to have grown quite a fan club. Later, I learned, my dad was sending anyone who I may have any connection with to get me to come back. When that didn't work, my dad sent my two best friends.

One day while I was working, Sara* and Mandy*, who were my best friends from our childhood, showed up to Denny's. I was happy to see them. It had been months since I had even seen Mandy*, and Sara* had drank with me only recently. I knew she was the one who told Mandy* where I was working. I went on break and sat down to talk to my old friends.

They were going on a road trip and wanted me to come with them for old time's sake. Mandy* had been trying to get married to my half-brother and she wanted to go to his ranch to visit him. She reasoned that it wouldn't be inappropriate if his sister was there, and then we would go on to Idaho to visit her aunt and spend some time with her. A road trip sounded great. I could miss a week of school and hopefully get my shifts covered at work. I told my boss I had a family emergency and that I needed to go out of town. He told me it was fine, and I packed a bag to leave that weekend.

On our way to the ranch, everyone was quiet. This was not the fun road trip I had envisioned when I agreed to go. When we got to the ranch, we stayed in a trailer that was too hot and did not have enough room. There was no internet, no animals, and nothing to do. I was happy to leave to her aunts the next day. Susan was Sara's* and Mandy's* aunt, and had lived in Idaho for as long as I could remember. I really didn't know her well, but when we came to her house, she acted like she knew me. She was a kind host, but all our talks were about the bible and doing what God wants you to. She tried to bond with me by telling me she knew everything my father had done was not right, but she knew the Order was the work of God and it was our responsibility to change the negative things. I liked Susan, but the lectures were old, and I just wanted to go back to my apartment. Finally, the road trip was over. There had been no karaoke songs in the car, no fun adventures, just lots and lots of preaching and long silences.

On the way back to Salt Lake, Mandy* turned the car off to head to Boise instead of Salt Lake. When I asked where we were going, she explained we were stopping back at the ranch to stay the night before heading home. I didn't complain. The trip was almost over and changed plans was something to get used to in my inconsistent community. It was late when we pulled up next to the trailer, but we ended up talking late into the night. This was the part I had missed about my family. It was nearly dawn when we finally fell asleep.

The next morning, I gathered my things to prepare for the long trip home, but no one else seemed to be doing the same. When I asked when we were leaving, Mandy* told me we would be leaving the next day. I pointed out that I needed to get back to work, when she finally told me that she was told not to bring me home until I was ready to drop school and get my direction in marriage. She hinted that Joseph* was the one they wanted me to marry. I was angry. I had literally been kidnapped and held hostage until I did what they wanted. Instead of showing anger I stayed calm. I knew their game. If I became angry they would know it would take me longer to calm down. I needed to be humbled and pray. I went through the motions. I prayed and pretended to be searching. Finally, a couple of days later, I put on the same sad, resigned face I knew from hundreds of girls who had been forced into their marriages and agreed to marry Joseph*. We left for Salt Lake that day.

Mandy* seemed excited as we drove home, and it finally clicked in my mind. If she helped me find my place, she would be good enough to marry my half-brother. The whole thing was sad. Despite what she had done to me, I wanted her to be happy. I went along with the whole charade while she got her gold star for converting me. She was engaged soon after and I left again. I went back to Denny's, but I had missed so much work and had been fired for not showing up. I was angry and defeated.

After learning I was fired, I got in my car and called Kevin* in tears. He told me to calm down and go get another job. People lose jobs all the time. It's not the end of the world. I calmed down and went to the Village Inn close to the Denny's where I had worked. I was hired on the spot and started work the following day. I was upset with Mandy* for what she had done and didn't want a relationship with her. She was getting married anyways, and had no need for our friendship anymore. Sara* was still sitting on the fence about knowing if she wanted to stay in the Order. I didn't know how much she was told about the purpose of our little road trip, but she couldn't have done anything about it if she had wanted to. My mom began promising me whatever she thought I wanted if I would only come back. I was lost and confused.

192

Chapter 16
Giving Up

I can't really talk to anyone about it because every time I try, then I start crying and can't even finish sentences. I can't even get the words out clearly. Have you ever been so sad that your thoughts aren't words anymore? So you really can't say what you are thinking because there are no words to describe it, or maybe I'm so sad that I can't even think. My thoughts on my family are not even words, but emotions; lots and lots of emotions. Sometimes it hurts so bad that I can't breathe and sometimes I go numb and can't feel any emotions at all.

My heart is bleeding and aching as I try to hold back the tears that threaten to spill over my cheeks every ten minutes. I think it's time for me to move on. It looks like there is nothing here for me now. It's time to move on. Those words are so hard for me to write. I feel so horrible, like I am being torn up from the inside out.

Finally, after six long months of running, I was mentally and emotionally exhausted. My family was held as a carrot in front of me, and I was the dumbass who kept chasing it. My mom was all but begging me to come back and give it another chance. She had promised I didn't have to get married and I could stay in college if I came back. Our relationship had improved dramatically because for once in her life, she stood by me. I knew it was because she didn't want me to leave the Order. She would be looked at as a failure as a mother if one of her kids left. My father would blame it on her. Out of a combination of guilt and missing my siblings, I agreed to come back.

After the decision had been made, and moving day

was set, I hadn't even come back before the first manipulative move was made. I wasn't moving into my mom's house. One of my half-sisters Emma*, had agreed to let me move in with her. I was required to quit my job to come back, and I would be working at their restaurant supply company for Mark*. I hoped it wouldn't be awkward because he had proposed to me two years previously and he was still unmarried. At first, I thought they wanted me to work at Standard to get me closer to Mark*, but when they forced me to go on weekly dates with Joseph* as a stipulation of coming back, I chalked my working arrangement up to a coincidence. Maybe they were trying to get me from all angles?

Living with Emma* was calmer than any other place in the Order had been. Emma* had become a plural wife to one of Daniel's sons and was not in the competition for my dad's attention. She obviously wanted to make my dad proud, but I didn't realize how much of a factor this was at the time. She was about six months pregnant with her second child, but her first baby girl had died at birth. When I asked her about it, the story broke my heart. She was about seven months pregnant, and the pregnancy had been going completely fine and normal. She was feeling movement and had no reason to be alarmed.

One night, contractions started. Instead of going to the hospital, like most pregnant women, she called her husband. The contractions were getting stronger. She told me there was a point they both knew the baby was coming out. Because she was so early, there was no way she would survive. Sure enough, the baby came out. Emma* didn't know if she was dead when she came out because she couldn't look at her child, knowing she wouldn't watch her grow up. She asked her husband to just take her and go. She didn't name her, because she believed she would be sent that same child in a future pregnancy. She didn't know what her husband did with her daughter's dead body, and she didn't want to.

Because I could see the pain in Emma's* face as she told me about her experience, I didn't tell her what I was thinking. How could a man sit there and watch his wife labor in pain, knowing their baby was going to die? Why didn't he take her to the hospital and do everything he could to save his daughter? Why didn't Emma* fight for her daughter's life? On a different subject, what happened to her daughter's body? I learned later, that most miscarriages or babies who didn't live long enough to get a birth certificate were simply buried in the backyard to be forgotten. The mothers believed they would give birth to that child in a future pregnancy and there was no need to name or mourn their lost child. God had taken their child because of either their sin or someone close to them and they would only be given that child when they were worthy of them.

My heart broke for my half-sister because I knew why she did what she did. Going to the hospital was not even an option to be brought up. Her husband was the head of her household and he made those decisions. I realized all the reasons I left were still there. I couldn't deny that nothing had changed. I was still being forced to date Joseph* until I finally agreed to marry him. I realized nothing had changed, they were just picking their battles carefully and giving a little before they took everything from me. My eighteenth birthday had quietly come and gone, and it seemed no one noticed. I think they didn't want to accept the fact, they legally no longer had any power over me. Unfortunately, I was so caught up in the games again, I hadn't even thought about it.

I had started dating Thomas*, a boy from karate,

before I had left the Order, and had never broken up with him when I came back. There were times we would break up for a week and I would explore things physically with other people, namely some guys from the Order who I considered marrying and coming back to the Order to be with. Thomas* was almost two years younger than me, which was abnormal for me to be interested in a younger guy. He had a close family and that was what I craved at the time. Also, I knew he had his own damage. His mother had battled severe depression throughout his childhood. He had watched her try to kill herself more than once. When she finally passed away they learned she had lupus and it was probably the cause of most of her other problems.

I went to Vegas with my karate class and though I should have figured it out by this time, I had hope my family was not as damaging as I was learning. Thomas*, whom I was still dating went to Vegas as well. His dad had talked to a chaperone to make sure we were going to be staying in separate bedrooms and that we would not have the opportunity to do what young teenagers do when they are alone. We were both still virgins and aside from making out every now and then, we hadn't become physical with each other.

It wasn't until we got home from Vegas that I lost my virginity to Thomas* a month and a half after my eighteenth birthday. Because I was so disassociated, it wasn't a special moment. My sexual abuse prevented me from emotionally or mentally connecting with him or the experience and it was as though I was standing in the corner, watching my body experience something that I wouldn't allow myself to try to understand. After that, I used sex the way I was taught. Though the physical sensation was enjoyable, sex was a tool that I used to control my boyfriend the way I had always been taught.

One of the stipulations for coming back to the Order was to go to all the Order events. This meant, I was required to go to every single community dance. I was surprised to find Josh* at the dance again, this time he was much happier. It had been almost a year since I had asked him to dance the last time, which was right after he had left, and it was as though he was a completely different person. He had stayed out of the Order. When I asked him how he was doing, he sincerely told me how good he was doing. He had heard that I had left and didn't know I had decided to come back.

When he found out I came back to the Order, his eyes went wide. He couldn't understand why, after knowing the outside, would I ever come back. I couldn't give him a good reason. He shook his head and we had a little heart to heart. If you want to leave, then leave. Don't make excuses and don't let anyone make you feel guilty for it. If your siblings want you in their life, they will make it happen. Some of his sisters continued to reach out to him after he left, and he had other siblings who ended up leaving after him as well. He told me there is so much more to life out there than there will ever be in the Order. He was disappointed in me for coming back.

When he left that night, I realized he said everything I had already known. I wasn't happy in the Order and I would never be happy here. It was only a matter of time before I would either live their lifestyle or I would leave. I couldn't have it both ways. Jennifer* had somehow made it work to live on the fence for years, but she was miserable. Sitting on the fence was like being stuck in limbo and it was impossible to move forward with your life. It's like putting on a mask and living a double life. There's nothing more freeing than standing up and being authentic. For years I had been jealous of Jennifer* for being able to sit on the fence and have both. I finally realized I was done being cut in two.

One night, while I was sleeping in my bed at Emma's*, my phone rang. I realized it was four in the morning and I couldn't imagine why my mom would be calling me at this hour. I quickly answered it, and my mom told me she would be there to pick me up in about five minutes. She would explain when we met. I jumped up and grabbed some clothes and my purse and went outside to wait for her. It wasn't more than five minutes before she pulled in. The sun hadn't come up yet, and it didn't feel like morning, though I was completely awake. Something had happened. I would not be in her van right now if it hadn't.

It took my mom only moments before the truth started pouring out of her. The cops had just called her because Dustin* had been arrested for vandalizing cars with some of his friends. I almost started laughing. He was my mom's pride and joy. He believed in Paul and the Order with all his heart and he was angry with me for leaving. I wasn't sure why.

When I saw the police lights flashing up ahead, I wondered if more had happened. As I watched my mom's face, she had the same look she had the night our house was on fire. Her life was completely out of control and had been for as long as I could remember. While we waited for the officer to release my brother, I hugged my mom. We had never hugged when I was a child, but I knew she needed someone who loved her, and I was beginning to understand her damage. I didn't feel like all her years of neglect were justified, but I just wanted the pain to end for both of us. I drove my brother's car home that night, and my mother drove Dustin* home.

The next day at church, I listened as Paul explained

the financial crises the Order was now going through. We were told we could not take cash from the office anymore unless it was an emergency, and we actually had to disclose the emergency to Ramona* at the main office. She had always been the keeper of money and the one to help the members budget. They had come up with a carding system to decide how much control you had over your own money. About ninety-five percent of the Order members were on a green card. This meant they had less than seven thousand dollars in savings and didn't make more than they spent. This included all the women with more children than they could support, all the teenagers who didn't save money well, and even a couple of the men who tried to help their wives support their families. These people had almost no control over their money before the financial crises. After the financial crises, many of them were declined when they asked to get utilities paid or have things they felt like their families needed. They were required to get authorization from Ramona* to spend money.

If a person had at least seven thousand in savings and usually made more than they spent, they received a yellow card. They were only allowed to spend up to about five hundred dollars without authorization, but any more than that required approval. If a person had more than ten thousand in savings, they were on a blue card. These members were not regulated by Ramona,* and they were allowed to spend their money as they saw fit. Some of them were even allowed to get a credit card from another bank if they needed it for work or if they were running a business that required frequent money transactions, which was often if they were able to have that much money. Most people were working for minimum wage or less. Saving up ten thousand dollars was not easy on that salary. Even on a blue card, they were still required to give all the banking information, including pin numbers to the office so they always knew the standing of that bank account. When the financial crisis hit, everyone's money was tied up, though blue card holders had first priority to their money.

The mine had been receiving fines and lawsuits because they continued to stay out of compliance with safety regulations, and the government was on the verge of simply shutting down the mine. My own grandfather had died in a mining accident at thirty-two years old, and I knew plenty of other men who had also died in those accidents. There were funerals every few years or so, from someone dying in a mining accident or in a car accident driving back and forth to Huntington for work. The mine seemed to be a death trap of sorts, but my father saw it as the Order's greatest asset. It was the most successful of the businesses and it hit the Order the hardest when they lost it.

Before I left the Order, I had been on a yellow card. I had been working since I was eleven years old and had been full time since I was fourteen. I had received financial aid for college every semester and had never needed to take out student loans. I knew I was getting ready to leave the Order for the final time, and I could see no reason I wouldn't be able to take my money with me. Paul had always taught honesty, and I thought he might have some integrity.

Before I could start planning for my final departure, Emma* and her husband beat me to it. They sat me down on a Friday night and explained I had plenty of time to come back, and they were now giving me a deadline. When Monday came around, I had the option to either completely close my outside bank account and turn all my money over to the Order and completely cut off all my friends outside the Order, or I needed to find another place to live. I knew they were betting on the fact I had nowhere else to go, and it was a weekend, so I wouldn't be able to start looking for a lease until Monday at the very soonest. They were trying to force me into staying. When I asked for more time, my suspicions were confirmed.

I left the conversation unsure of what to do. If I closed my outside bank account and gave them all my money, I wouldn't have money to be able to pay rent to another place without everyone knowing about it. They would make it impossible to leave. I called my boyfriend, and he was calm as he listened to me. He suddenly told me he had to go and asked if he could call me right back. I was livid. I was going having a crisis! I was going to be homeless again. What could be more important?

When he called me back, he told me his grandmother was willing to let me move in with her. I had met his grandmother, Anne* a handful of times, and she was a very sweet lady. I didn't know what else to do, so we began to make plans for me to move out on Monday while Emma was at work. Throughout the weekend, I began packing small things up that wouldn't be noticed if someone walked into my room. I had already gotten rid of all my things that were unimportant in my last moves so I didn't have much. When Monday came around, Emma* went off to work as usual, and I worked like a madwoman to finish packing as quickly as possible. An hour before Thomas* and his parents were supposed to show up with the truck, Emma* came home unexpectedly. She saw me packing and didn't say anything as she headed to her room. I had finished packing and figured the least I could do was thank her for letting me stay with her. I followed her to her room.

She had just had her daughter she had been

pregnant with when I moved in. She was a beautiful little girl with dark black hair and she looked like her mother's side of the family. I had known I would never watch that little girl grow up because I would either marry into a family of my own and Emma* and I would never be close or I would leave. Either way, I knew better than to get attached. Emma* was sitting on her bed changing her baby when I walked in.

"Hey," I said, breaking the ice.

"Hey."

We both stayed silent before she finally asked the question neither of us wanted to bring up.

"Did you make your decision?"

"Yeah," I told her. "I'll be out before noon."

She glanced over at the clock on her night table and read 11:33. The truth didn't appear to surprise her much, and I think she had been expecting it since they gave me the ultimatum.

"Thank you for everything," I told her sincerely. Staying with her had been a nice change from the drama I had come to expect in the Order, but it was time for me to move on and find where I was supposed to be. I knew that place was not in the Order.

"I only wish I could do more."

"What do you mean?" I asked.

"Paul depended on me to help you and I failed."

"Don't blame yourself for this. None of it was your fault and you were simply a bystander to suffer in this whole mess."

I knew she must feel guilty because that was the emotion everyone always felt in my community. It was the emotion the leaders fed off.

"I just wish I could have done more."

Knowing I could not change her feelings on this, I

changed the subject.

"I really hope you are happy, Emma*."

I knew her first baby's death still weighed on her, though the birth of her second baby seemed to help.

"I am," she said as she looked down at her daughter. With that, I excused myself and asked if she wanted me to call her again.

"You already know the answer to that," she said growing defensive.

"Yeah, I thought I would try. I am going to miss you."

"I'll miss you too," she said as her eyes suddenly filled with tears. "I really like having you here and having help with everything."

"It's been my pleasure," I told her.

I told her I would leave her key on the counter and lock up before I left. Her lunch hour had ended, and she was heading back to work. The tears were gone by the time she had gathered her baby and diaper bag to head back to work. If she had been heartbroken by my leaving, she seemed fine now.

Less than an hour later, Thomas's* parents showed up with their truck and car. Thomas* was in school, so he was unable to come help, but I didn't have much. We finished loading up quickly. I locked up Emma's* house, left her key on the counter as I had promised, and I was gone. I wasn't familiar with Thomas's* parents on a personal level, and as much as I wanted to, I wasn't about to cry in front of them. I didn't want them to feel obligated to try to make me feel better. There was really nothing they could do anyways. I knew I was leaving for good this time. The drive to Bountiful looked the same but felt so different. I had been terrified the first time I left the Order, but this time I was just sad. I knew I was losing my whole family again, though I had never really gotten them back in the short time I had decided to go back to the Order.

I had stopped dating Joseph* shortly before I started dating Thomas*, after I found out he had lied about everything he had told me. He had promised I could go to school and have a career, and then turned around and told his brothers it shouldn't take long to wear me down and get me pregnant. I wouldn't be able to go to school if I was home with kids. He was now courting a fourteen-year-old girl who was much more submissive than I had ever been. They are currently married and last I heard he had at least two very young wives.

When we came to Thomas's* grandmother's house, it didn't take long to move my things into her spare bedroom. Her home was decorated beautifully in light colors and a sixties style with some modern touches. Her only rules for me were to keep my room and my bathroom clean and to clean up after myself. She was a firm believer in the LDS religion and asked that I not have alcohol, cigarettes, or coffee in her home. I didn't have any of those habits, so her rules were easy to comply with. I was still attending the Salt Lake Community College and I was getting close to an Associates' degree in Biology. I was planning to become a doctor and fight cancer. Maybe if my grandmother had survived her cancer, my life would have gone differently.

My first night in this strange, foreign house was unlike Kevin's* had been. I had learned so much in the past year and I was now eighteen. I was legally free, and I knew it. My life was finally mine to do with whatever I chose. But because the fear was now gone, the sadness came on at full force. I knew my brothers and sisters felt like I had abandoned them, and in a way, maybe I had. But I knew I could never be happy there. My brother Dustin* secretly sent me the song "Where'd you go?" by Fort Minor, and I couldn't stop sobbing for days. The song still brings tears to my eyes. Nothing hurt me more than the pain I knew my siblings were feeling. None of them understood what I had been through or why I needed to leave, and my parents did everything in their power to make sure I never told them. I was cut off from everyone I had known and loved. But I was finally free.

Chapter 17
Where'd You Go?
-Fort Minor (Mike Shinoda)

Where'd you go?
I miss you so,
Seems like it's been forever,
That you've been gone.

She said, "Some days I feel like shit,
Some days I wanna quit, and just be normal for a bit,"
I don't understand why you have to always be gone,
I get along but the trips always feel so long,
And, I find myself trying to stay by the phone,
'Cause your voice always helps me to not feel so alone,
But I feel like an idiot, workin' my day around the call,
But when I pick up I don't have much to say,
So, I want you to know it's a little fucked up,
That I'm stuck here waitin' at times debatin',
Tellin' you that I've had it with you and your career,
Me and the rest of the family here singing
"Where'd you go?"

I miss you so,
Seems like it's been forever,
That you've been gone.
Where'd you go?
I miss you so,
Seems like it's been forever,
That you've been gone,
Please come back home…

You know the place where you used to live,
Used to barbecue up burgers and ribs,

*Used to have a little party every Halloween with candy by
the pile,
But now, you only stop by every once and awhile,
Shit, I find myself just fillin' my time,
With anything to keep the thought of you from my mind.
I'm doing fine, and I'm plannin' to keep it that way,
You can call me if you find that you have something to say,
And I'll tell you, I want you to know it's a little fucked up,
That I'm stuck here waitin', at times debatin',
Tellin' you that I've had it with you and your career,
Me and the rest of the family here singing "Where'd you
go?"*

*I miss you so,
Seems like it's been forever,
That you've been gone.
Where'd you go?
I miss you so,
Seems like it's been forever,
That you've been gone,
Please come back home…*

*I want you to know it's a little fucked up,
That I'm stuck here waitin', no longer debatin',
Tired of sittin' and hatin' and makin' these excuses,
For why you're not around, and feeling so useless,
It seems one thing has been true all along,
You don't really know what you've got 'til it's gone,
I guess I've had it with you and your career,
When you come back I won't be here and you can sing it…*

*Where'd you go?
I miss you so,
Seems like it's been forever,*

That you've been gone.
Where'd you go?
I miss you so,
Seems like it's been forever,
That you've been gone,
Please come back home…
Please come back home…
Please come back home…
Please come back home…
Please come back home...

Because I was now back in Bountiful, I was thirty minutes away from college, work, and the dance classes I had begun. My car had broken down shortly before I had gone back to the Order, and I was now walking or taking the city bus everywhere I went. Now, living out in Bountiful again, I would have to be to the bus stop by six-twenty in the morning to go to class at seven and then I would go to work at about ten in the morning. I was still working at Standard for the Order, because this was the one business where they hired people outside the Order. I think Mark* secretly hoped I would come back to the Order if he kept me on at Standard. He hadn't moved on to find another wife yet, and him and I had a comfortable relationship. After work, I would either take the bus to Bountiful for karate lessons or to the dance studio where I was taking dance classes. I would get home about ten or eleven at night and crash before I got up to do it again.

Thomas* insisted I get home earlier a couple of nights a week to have dinner at his house with his parents. I complied, though it was tough to make it happen. I appreciated everything he had done for me, but I was at a point where I wanted to pursue my own dreams. He had obviously had other plans about me being the attentive

209

girlfriend. I never filled that role well. I was getting along fine in my new life, though I did miss my siblings. I later found out my two sisters got married. Rachel* invited me to her wedding and then uninvited me when all the drama surrounding my attendance came up. I didn't understand the drama until months later, when Sara* invited me to her wedding.

I knew she had men coming forward for her, but I didn't know she had seriously been thinking about taking that step. I had always thought she would leave. Ever since our talk in eighth grade, she had always wanted to leave the Order because of her dad. I couldn't believe she was taking the step of marriage. They had broken her.

After I was invited to the wedding, her dad objected to having me there, so I was shortly uninvited to the wedding, but Sara* asked me to come to the reception. Order weddings weren't anything special and they happened all the time. A wedding in the Order was nothing but a long, drawn out meeting where instead of toasting the bride and groom, the topic of the speeches were more along the lines of a church sermon or having numbered men talk about how great they are and how much they love God and the Order. They were usually the worst day of a girl's life because of everything involved. No one cared about the bride's wishes, so bridesmaids showed up late or not at all, ceremonies never started on time, and nothing ever went the way the bride wanted. Most brides had high expectations for their big days, but by the end of the engagement and the nightmare that turned out to be the ceremony, they were just glad when it was over. They justified that one day didn't matter in comparison to the amazing life they would have for the rest of their lives. Little did they know, it only went downhill from there.

When I showed up to Sara's* reception, I hugged

her and wished her congratulations. She had a sad smile on her face, and it wasn't until later that I learned what a mess her wedding day had turned out to be. Things always go wrong in weddings, but in Order weddings, everything goes wrong. She appeared to be exhausted, but she was beautiful in her wedding dress. After the reception, I asked one of her brothers to give me a ride home. When her dad found out, he tried to intimidate me and told me never to speak to his kids again. I told him his kids were adults and if they wanted to make that decision, it was up to them. When his intimidation didn't work, he tried the guilt trip. My mom must be so sad I had left the Order. She was not as sad as I was for staying there for as long as I did.

Like so many people in and out of the Order, I hated Daniel. He was an abusive piece of shit who didn't have the ability to control his temper. Instead of fighting someone equally matched, he took his anger out on the weaker women and children. I knew he was just a big bully. Even Sara's* brother, who had once respected Daniel, began to see the problems in the Order. I was surprised to learn later, that he had come out as being gay and ended up leaving the community. Last I knew, he bought his own house, works crazy hours, and is doing great.

After I had made the final decision that I would never go back to the Order, I figured it was time to take my money and close my account with the Order. I had never been told how this works and I wasn't sure who to ask about it. I asked my mom, but she had no idea and it was difficult for her to talk about the topic. To spare her the pain, I dropped it with her and scheduled a meeting with my dad. I expected to leave with about five thousand dollars. I had seven thousand a year ago, but I hadn't kept track of how much more I should have. I hadn't been allowed to spend a lot of money over the year because I had low standing in the Order, so I had stopped putting my money in the Order.

When I sat down with Paul I was disgusted with him. According to his calculations, I somehow owed the Order two thousand dollars. When I asked him to show me where he figured this, he didn't have that information and told me there was no way to get it. I knew I would be unable to take him to court because I had no physical statement of how much I had accumulated. I didn't even know exactly how much money I was supposed to have. They had stolen from me and had set it up to make it so easy.

When you work for the Order, you are never given a paycheck. They put the money on a statement and you are given that statement at the end of every month. It shows the monthly incoming and outgoing transactions and whether or not you are ahead or behind for the year. At the end of the year, your total account balance goes to zero and you start all over. What is supposed to happen, is your money from the year is supposed to go into your account, which is saved for you like a traditional bank and the Order is supposed to pay you interest like a traditional bank would. The problem is they never issue statements for this savings account and the only way to find out the balance is to call the office and give them twenty-four hours to find out the number. They then tell you this number over the phone. They will not issue a statement for this number. For years I had felt as though this number was a random number pulled out of thin air. After my meeting with Paul, my suspicions seemed confirmed.

After Paul disclosed he felt like I owed him money, he could clearly see I was angry. Where had my money gone? I had given them all my financial aid money for years and was working full time. Even working at a rate less than minimum wage I should have had well over my original amount at seven thousand dollars. Paul offered to give me five hundred dollars as a favor to me when he could see I would not be walking out of the office completely empty handed. I couldn't believe the level of dishonesty, and I numbly I accepted the check. I was done with his games. This was the final straw. I took the money and never looked back. I would never deal with that crook again.

Wanting distance from the Order and everyone in it, I quit my job at Standard and started nannying for a rich couple who lived on the hill. It was closer to where I was living, and it made it much easier for me to get more hours. Standard had never raised my pay rate, which meant I was still being paid less than minimum wage. The couple was an older LDS couple with a drug problem. The husband did meth on weekends to unwind, and the wife was constantly medicated for bipolar and anxiety. They had three of their five kids living at home because their oldest was on an LDS mission and their thirteen-year-old son was in a detention facility for touching a four year old girl inappropriately. The drama was something I knew well and didn't bother me. They had gone through four or five nannies throughout the past year, but the wife, was very nice and motherly towards me. She tried to act seventeen despite being well over forty.

I was trying to continue a relationship with my siblings somehow, and I knew my dad was the only way that would happen. When I met with him, I had high hopes that maybe he would see that I wasn't coming back and that there was no point in using my family against me anymore. I was told to meet at Adam's* house one night, and the irony of the situation was not lost on me. My first memories in the Order were of Adam's* second wives' house. My last memories were at his first wives' house.

"How are you doing?" Paul asked as he climbed into my mom's front seat. Apparently, this conversation was taking place in the car. Was I so bad I couldn't even enter the Order homes?

"I'm fine," I answered.

"How is school?" he asked. Some things never change.

"It's good," I said wondering if he ever really cared how school was. "I want to be able to see the kids for birthdays and holidays."

I paused to see his expression, and when he gave nothing away, I continued. "I'll stop by for five minutes and just give them a hug. Mom can be there the whole time."

"That's not going to happen."

"That's not fair."

"You made your choice."

"Why can't I see them?"

"We already talked about this."

"You never told me why."

"I don't want to raise questions in the kids minds and I don't think you do either," he said as his tone grew threatening. "I don't want to go into detail about the things you have done. Do you want them to think badly of you?"

"I don't care what you tell them as long as it's the truth. I want them to know I still care for them."

"You're being selfish," he argued and for the first time, he began to lose his cool. "If you really cared about them, you wouldn't have left."

"That makes two of us," I retorted growing angry.

"What do you mean by that?" he asked.

"You aren't there any more than I'm not."

"Care to elaborate?"

214

"Instead of running from the government, why not go home and see your family from time to time?"

He stared at me for a minute as though he didn't have a response to that.

"You have a point," he said quietly, and for a moment, for the first time, I felt some humanity coming from this man.

"Do we have a deal then?" I asked with a glimmer of hope.

"I don't want there to be any contact," he said sternly, and just as quickly as it had appeared, the humanity was gone. "If you want to talk to mom and I, we will always do what we can to help you, but I don't want the kids to be around that kind of influence."

"What kind of influence?" I asked sincerely confused.

"I want the kids to grow up in the Order and be firm members. Having you around only detracts from that."

I realized the conversation was going nowhere and my eyes welled with tears. My parents weren't going to play fair here. We ended the conversation with neither of us giving anything, and Paul seemed to be annoyed that I had wasted his time.

Sara's* younger sister, Kristine*, had been contacting me, and she would sneak out with me after school from time to time. One day she called me, and because I had full access to the vehicle for the kids I was nannying, I was able to pick her up from school. When she got into the car, she told me she was done with the Order and she wanted to leave. She asked me to find her a place to stay and let me know that either I would do this, or she would go crash with a school friend. I knew her school friends and knew they were bad news, so I did what I could. I had an aunt from my mom's side of the family who had left before I was even born who had recently come into my life. I called her to see if it would be a good fit. She was happy to help a young girl get out of the Order and the only step now, would be to convince her mom. I called her mom and explained the situation to her. I knew her mom was one of the few moms in the Order who would occasionally stand up for her kids, and I didn't want to ruin their chance at a relationship the way my relationship with my mom was ruined. I agreed to take Kristine* to Standard, where her mom was working, to talk.

When I showed up to talk, there were police waiting for me. I hadn't expected her to try to pull something, but I should have. The women in the Order were brainwashed and I should have known the first person her mom would call when we hung up was Daniel. She was taught to tie back to her husband and even though sometimes she would have moments of clarity when she was pushed too far, she was still in the Order for a reason.

I stayed calm as the police officers asked me questions. I knew I had done nothing wrong and had only picked Kristine* up from school. I had called her mom immediately to tell her, and then even brought her daughter to her. I knew I couldn't be charged with kidnapping. She had not been called in as a runaway and even if she had, I had eight hours before I had to report her. I had not broken any laws and I knew it. Besides the fact that a harboring a runaway charge was a misdemeaner. It came with a two hundred dollar fine and potentially thirty days in jail, but in all the cases I had researched, I never found one with a jail sentence. It was a petty charge that most prosecutors wouldn't even bother to prosecute.

Kristine's* mom did not remain calm. She yelled at me and yelled at the cop, and by the end of it, Kristine begged her mom to just stop. The officer really didn't seem to understand what he was doing there, and I agreed with him. I had brought Kristine* to her mom and I wasn't going to try to fight her to take her away. The cop left with a recommendation to stop pissing people off and I laughed as he walked away. After talking to her mom and then stepping back to let both of them talk to my aunt, everyone finally agreed to let Kristine* go live with my aunt. At that point, I was pushed out of the situation.

My aunt then turned on me and Kristine* and began forcing her to go to church and stop spending time with her friends. It seemed that my aunt had decided she was going to convert Kristine* to stick it to Paul and Daniel, and Kristine's* mom went along with the drama. Kristine* didn't like to be played and she wasn't about to leave one religion to join another. She began acting out even more. The whole situation was a disaster, but I didn't hear anything about it until months later when Kristine* managed to text me from her mom's phone because she was being kidnapped. I tried to call her mom's phone, but it went straight to voicemail. There was nothing I could do, because I knew she was being kidnapped by her own mother. If I called the cops they couldn't do anything. I felt helpless as I continued to try to call someone. I called Sara*, but she was deep into her abusive marriage at the time and had been forbidden to even talk to me. I hadn't known her marriage was abusive at the time, but I fully expected her to not be able to be friends with me.

Finally, her mother called me back to tell me Kristine* had been sent to Idaho to stay with her aunt Susan because it wasn't working out with her current situation. When I called my aunt, she had been in on the whole thing. I don't think she realized what she had done. She was just tired of putting up with a rebellious teenager.

I was powerless to do anything for Kristine.* She was only fifteen and her mother could ruin her life as much as she wanted. No one could do anything to help her.

Months later, Kristine* came back to Salt Lake and asked to meet with me. I met her in a group of girls. No one would let her be alone with me. I asked her how she was doing, and her eyes darted around as though hoping no one would hear her. She had found the person she was going to be married to, and they were getting engaged. Now I knew why they allowed her to even come back to Salt Lake. He was a boy from Idaho and I didn't know much about him. She would be getting married a month after her sixteenth birthday. I was shocked. Her and her sisters were so determined to leave when they were growing up. They had watched their friends and siblings be abused and neglected and it spilled over into their lives as well. They had been to public school and hadn't been as brainwashed as the rest of us. How had none of them managed to get out?

My life had presented its own problems though, and Kristine*'s wedding was no longer on my mind. She had promised to invite me, but after Sara's* wedding, I knew her dad wouldn't even let me come to the reception. I was right. After her wedding, Kristine* was moved to Idaho to be with her husband. She had always had big dreams of being a model and doing something with makeup. The small-town farm life was never something that would work for her, but she tried. Her marriage lasted a couple of years before she came to me and asked me to help her leave again. I was in a better position and I was able to let her stay with me before we found her a more permanent host home through a non-profit that was designed to help people leaving polygamy. Her host home ended up becoming her second family and she stayed with them for years. She had finally gotten her happy ending.

Chapter 18
All Grown Up

In my own life, I was a week late for my period, and had been using the pullout method, which I knew wasn't very effective from my research online. Unfortunately, Thomas* didn't like condoms and I refused to take hormones. I should have pushed condoms harder, but I had never been told anything about safe sex. I let him have all the power and make the decisions when I should have. As a girl, I had a responsibility to respect myself and my body, and by letting him make that decision, I was not.

When I told my boss that I may be pregnant, she was happy for me. She would let me live with her and she would help me with the baby. I think she really wanted a new baby and was too old to have one of her own. When I told Thomas* about the possible pregnancy, he was the opposite of happy. We were too young to have a baby and he didn't want that kind of responsibility. He told me my options were either to have an abortion or to give up the baby to let his parents raise it. They would legally adopt my baby.

I wasn't ready to be a mother, and I knew Thomas* wasn't anywhere close to being ready to be a father. When I thought about our future, I didn't really see kids in it. I knew without a doubt, his parents were the last people in the world that I wanted to raise my baby. His dad didn't value college or education. He ran a horse stud farm and they did shows. He believed hard work was what made you successful. He often pushed Thomas to work at his business instead of pursuing an education after high school. It was no secret Thomas* would work for him after high school instead of going to college.

College had been my savior. It was the thing to

help me grow and get out of a bad situation. My kids were going to college if I had to pay for it myself. Fortunately, I wasn't pregnant, but I began to resent my boyfriend for his complete disregard for me or what I wanted. I knew it would always be a struggle to accomplish my goals with him, but my pregnancy scare put it in perspective. He had learning disabilities that made it difficult for him to read. He would put himself down because he felt stupid, and he expected me to pander to his putdowns and bring him up. While I built him up, he tore me down. He would tell me I was getting fat and I needed to start going to the gym. He wanted his girlfriend to look like a model.

After the pregnancy scare, the abuse and control only got worse. I never saw his dad hit his stepmom, but he did hit me. When I tried to tell him it wasn't okay, he justified it by saying that since we were about the same size and we took karate together, it wasn't abuse because I could defend myself. When Thomas* proposed, I should have said no, but I didn't. Instead, I bought our promise rings because he didn't have a job.

I continued to keep contact with Kevin* and a couple of his friends, and when Alan* finally came back from California, they were all going to Wendover. They offered to pick me up, and I was excited to go. I needed to get some space, because Thomas* was crowding me more and more. His dad had told him that I needed to stop salsa dancing because it wasn't appropriate for his future wife to be dancing with other guys. If I was going to be his wife, I needed to start acting like it. When I told my fiance I was going to Wendover, he told me I couldn't go. I told him I needed space and he didn't have a say in the matter. He hung up on me and I hurried out the door to meet my friends.

Hanging out with Alan*, was a breath of fresh air,

Despite the fact, a guy who had liked me in the past and had actually tried to force himself on me was going to be there, in Wendover, I went anyways. I knew if Alan* was there, I would be safe. Alan* drove, and we enjoyed a night of drinking and gambling. At the end of the night, we got a hotel to stay in because no one was safe to drive. We were all very intoxicated. One of the other guys had tried to get me to share a bed with him, but thankfully, Alan* stepped in and asked me to share his bed. As we lay next to each other, I could hear the guys in the other bed snoring soundly. Alan* began talking to me, and it was the first time I understood why he had come back to Utah.

His ex-girlfriend had given birth to his daughter and he was trying to figure out the situation. The mom wouldn't let him see his daughter unless they got back together and when they were together, all they did was fight. It wasn't a good situation for either of them and especially his new baby girl. I did my best to be a friend. I had begun developing feelings for him, but I couldn't be the one to take a dad away from a little girl. I told him to do whatever it took to fight for his daughter. All a little girl wants is her daddy.

At the start of my new college semester, my mom gave birth to her eleventh and final baby. She was just shy of her forty-first birthday, and having babies was getting harder and harder on her aging body. I was allowed to come see my new baby brother, and because every time may be the last time I'm allowed at my mom's, I took lots of pictures. My relationship with Thomas* was growing more strained as we were growing apart, and I was spending more time with Alan* since he had come back from California and this only made things worse with my fiance. I was spending time with my dance teacher, Eddie, who had also become a good friend in the past few months. He

222

was married and him and his wife ran a dance studio together.

A month into my fall semester, I had started putting my life together, and was finally doing well for myself. I was hoping to be able to rent my own place soon, because Thomas's* grandmother needed her extra bedroom for her son who was blind and needed some extra help. They were moving down from out of state in three months. I had begun looking at places and had found one. I would move in at the end of the month.

About two weeks before I was set to move in, I was spending the day with Eddie. We were friends and there was nothing abnormal about the day as we went to lunch and then to run some errands for the dance studio. I had helped him run errands a hundred times before and had even helped him paint his studio. When he asked if we could stop by a hotel room, so he could take a nap, I thought nothing of it. It wouldn't be the first time we had been in a hotel room together and nothing had ever happened. He was married to a beautiful, successful woman. I had no reason to suspect he would want anything with me.

As we went into the hotel room, I plopped on the bed and flipped on the television while he climbed in under the covers for his nap. After about five minutes, he turned over and looked at me with a look I hadn't seen before. Before I knew it, he was moving closer. When he started kissing me, I thought he was joking at first. I tried to push him off, and explained him being married, but he wouldn't budge. Before I knew it, he had my pants off and was inside me, raping me. Tears streamed down my face as I realized what was happening, and he finally stopped.

After he finally got off me, I went into the bathroom and slammed the door. I hardly noticed my tear stained face as I looked at myself in the mirror. The only thing I could focus on was my cold, dead eyes. Once again, I had been violated and I wasn't anywhere near the Order. How does this keep happening to me? Was it my fault?

When I came out of the bathroom, Eddie was on the phone with his wife. I wanted to start shouting at him, so she would know I was there, but I couldn't. I couldn't speak. I could hardly breathe. He gathered his things and gestured to the door. He asked me what I was thinking, and I couldn't respond. When he asked if I wanted him to take me back to work, I could barely mumble, "yes".

I needed to get as far away from him as possible. We worked together, but I figured he could explain to his wife why I wasn't there. I went home and stayed in bed the rest of the day. I didn't cry very much, though some tears did seep out. I was numb. I couldn't even comprehend what had just happened. I went from shock, to anger, to sadness, to a feeling I could only describe as empty. If Jonathon's* abuse took me to a dark place, this place was a whole new level of dark.

The day after being raped, I called Thomas*. I told him I needed to talk to him but couldn't give details over the phone. When he came over, he could clearly see something was wrong. I told him I was going to tell him something, and I didn't want him to say anything until I had finished. I would only tell him once and it would be difficult for me to do even that. I could see the panic on his face as the possibilities rushed through his mind. I calmly told him the whole story of what happened. Everything from the errands to him holding me down as I sobbed, to him calling his wife afterwards. I was so emotionally withdrawn from the situation that my voice didn't crack once.

I think his wife had been the one to call him after the ordeal, but I didn't think this detail was important to the whole story. When I had finished, I was numb and was successfully holding in the tears. Thomas* told me he needed to hurry home because his dad hadn't known he had left. He hurried over because he thought it was emergency. Apparently, the emergency was over. He needed to hurry home. He hugged me and promised to talk about it more tonight when I came over for dinner and then he left.

I spent the rest of the day alone in bed going through the roller coaster of emotions again and again. The ride never changed, it never got better. I never felt better. I wanted to cancel dinner plans that night but fighting with Thomas* seemed an even worse option than dealing with his family. I went to dinner.

We went to his room to talk and he insisted I press charges against Eddie. Pressing charges had crossed my mind while I had been in the anger emotion, but I couldn't stay there long enough to form a decision about the matter. I told my fiance I honestly didn't know what I wanted to do. I was so confused. He was supposed to be my friend.

As Thomas* listened to me, I could see him growing angry, though I didn't know why, and I definitely didn't think it should be directed at me. When I asked him why he was angry, he told me he didn't think it was really rape if I didn't want to press charges. He thought it was an excuse for cheating on him. I was in shock. I couldn't even respond to his accusation. To add insult to injury, he told me how he felt betrayed. I was the only girl he had ever slept with and now he couldn't say that he was the only guy I had ever slept with. Somehow, he thought rape and sex were the same thing in this situation. Thankfully, his stepmom interrupted the conversation to tell us dinner was ready.

We sat quietly at our dinner and his parents and brother commented on the fact we were fighting. They assured us that whatever it was, we would work it out. When the meal ended, Thomas's* dad insisted on him walking me home. Neither me nor my fiance wanted to be anywhere near each other, but we didn't want to explain why we were fighting either. When he tried to talk to me on the walk home, I wouldn't respond. I told him not to speak to me. I had never been so angry, and he knew it. When I came home, I was in a rage. I was angry at my childhood, Eddie for what he had done, Thomas* for not believing me, and myself for everything that had happened to me.

When I moved into my own place as planned, a couple of weeks later, I was suddenly glad I had chosen a place in Salt Lake instead of Bountiful. I had argued with Thomas* for weeks about it and had finally decided on it because it was closer to everything I had in my life except for my fiance. I had quit karate and I was spending most of my time in Salt Lake anyways. Thomas* had less going on in his life and would be able to come see me more than I would be able to see him. When he helped me move into my new place, he promised me he would come whenever he could before he kissed me goodbye.

Since being raped, I had not been able to talk to anyone about it since the conversation with Thomas* and it seemed to remain a gaping hole inside of me I couldn't fill. He had not brought it up again, though it was a huge thorn in the side of our relationship. I continued working for my rapist and his wife and dancing on the team, but I tried to avoid Eddie when possible. He kept trying to talk to me and during some of my low points, talked me into having sex with him. I had met a guy from school and we also began a friendship with sexual benefits. I couldn't figure out how to fill the void that my assault had left, and because of my upbringing, I didn't understand the difference between sex and love.

Alan* and I had been getting closer, and I finally opened up to him. I didn't want to be accused of anything, so I simply told him the story of what happened, to hear his thoughts on it. When I finished telling him, his response shocked me.

"You know that's rape, right?"

His words hit me like a blow to the chest and I couldn't breathe. I had never heard anyone else say the words out loud and I had not been able to validate the experience. I seemed to be suspended in a state of confusion. Hearing him say those words gave me the validation I needed to be able to process what had happened. I was not crazy for feeling violated and hurt and I certainly didn't do it to justify cheating. I knew then and there Thomas* and I were over. Unfortunately, I was so intertwined with his family and his world, it felt impossible to break it off.

One of my dance teammates was living in a ski resort with an older woman and since she was going on vacation with her husband, the resort would be available for me to have a birthday bash for my nineteenth birthday. I danced my performance and then invited all my friends to the resort for my birthday. Most of the guys didn't realize all my friends were male during that time, and I think some of them had shown up hoping to hang out with some attractive girls. They were sadly disappointed when there were only a couple of girls in the resort that night. At the end of the night, Alan* was the guy I slept next to.

When we woke up the next morning, he seemed confused that we may have done something, and he just didn't remember, though I remembered the whole thing. He was the one I felt safe with, and he was the one I wanted to sleep next to after a night of drinking and partying. Thinking we had already done something sexual, he initiated things the next morning. I stopped him. I didn't want to start a relationship with him while I still had other men in my life, and I didn't want him to just be a fling.

To confirm my trust in him, once again, he stopped. He had been the only guy in my life who respected me and didn't ever try to hurt or control me. I started spending every free moment I could with him. The other guys in my life kept calling me, but I was usually busy. I knew I needed to end things with them, but I didn't want to think about it. Finally, one night after a night of drinking with Alan*, I was the one to initiate our first time. At first, he declined because I had been drinking, but I assured him over and over again, he was the only one I had ever wanted. I felt safe when I was with him. My first time with him was like the first time ever. I had never emotionally or mentally connected during any sexual acts. When he hugged me, I didn't want him to let go. When he touched me, my body wanted more of him. I had never been so head over heels in love. Even the sound of his voice made me want him.

My love for Alan* gave me the courage to break things off with every other guy in my life. I wanted to be everything for him. I told Eddie's wife that he had been cheating on her, though I didn't tell her he raped me. I didn't see a reason to put that on her. My other sex friend had a girlfriend at the time, and our breakup didn't seem to affect him much, though he called me about six months later. His girlfriend had caught him cheating with someone else and broke up with him. I was so in love with Alan* and had never wanted anything more with other guys anyways. Thomas* was the only one who seemed to keep hanging on despite my constantly trying to tell him it was over. We had been together a year when I had been raped, and I was his first serious relationship. I had been engaged a couple of times apparently, but he was my longest relationship.

Christmas was coming up, and Alan* and I had just started dating. To avoid the Christmas drama with the Order, Thomas*, and everything else in my life, I made plans to go to China during the whole Christmas holiday. Thomas* was angry. I had clearly broken up with him, but he had hoped that I would spend Christmas with his family and we would get back together. I didn't tell him that I was already with Alan* and though it had been such a short time, I had never been more serious about anyone. Thomas* and I were not getting back together.

When I told Alan* I was going to China, he was the only one who was happy for me. I asked him to come with, but he told me I needed some time alone to figure out what I really wanted. He knew I was still struggling with my rape and that had been the reason I had booked the trip in the first place. I told him I was scared he wouldn't wait for me. I would only be gone six weeks, but that may be enough to make his love for me fade. He laughed and assured me that wouldn't happen and promised to pick me up from the airport in six weeks.

China was beautiful. Mark* had worked out for me to take the trip when he thought it might get me away from my outside friends. I think he figured it was one last shot to get me to come back from the Order. Standard had a warehouse in China, and Mark* dangled the idea of maybe me managing the warehouse in China. That was the reason he justified sending me. I enjoyed the trip. I met a couple of nice Chinese girls and learned so much about the culture. I fell in love with the food from the southern part of China. In northern China, they eat a lot of duck, which is too sweet. I don't like my meat to be sweet. In southern China they eat more fish, bok choy, and rice. I lost about ten pounds in China even though I ate whatever I wanted. None of their food was fattening or sugary, and most of it was caught out of the lake next to the building I was staying in. Some of it was grown in the orchards surrounding the lake. Partially out of boredom, I started running around the lake every day. I realized I was getting stronger and stronger and my head was getting clearer. I knew I wanted to be with Alan*.

After a week or so of being in China, I was finally able to get a computer to instant message Alan.* I had promised other people I would email them as soon as I could as well, but I wanted to wait as long as possible before I opened those floodgates. Because China doesn't really celebrate Christmas Day, the twenty-fifth of December just felt like another day. It wasn't so hard to be away from my family for the holidays, though I did miss Alan* like crazy. Finally, two weeks before I was scheduled to come home from China, I emailed everyone while my head was finally clear. I told Thomas* we were broken up and that I had decided to be with Alan*. I told my mom I was not coming back to the Order and I had fallen in love with Alan*. I had a couple of other friends who were asking when I would come back to the Order. I emailed them as well. My heart had found where it belonged.

Unfortunately, I hadn't planned on the consequences of my newfound clarity and all the questions it would raise. Thomas* was angry at me for never even telling him about Alan*, and my mother called him nothing but a fling. She told me that at least Thomas* had some morals because he was LDS, but Alan* would only lead me down a path of heartache. I laughed because though Thomas's* parents were LDS, he was an atheist. Alan* was an atheist as well, but I didn't know it at the time, and while Thomas* tried to shove his beliefs down my throat, that was never something Alan* did. I knew her biggest distaste for Alan* was because he was not white. His mother was white, but his father was Tongan.

My mom was right about one thing. I had a path of heartache in front of me, but it would be because of the damage from the Order. It had nothing to do with anything Alan* did, and it would have been much worse had I tried to take that path alone instead of with Alan*.

Alan* and I talked online through instant messenger for hours every single day while I was away. Our first, "I love you," was a typed conversation while he was playing Dota. A week before I was schedule to come home, I decided I didn't want to be away from him for another minute. I had my clarity, and I was never one to waste time. I had gotten what I wanted from China, so I emailed Mark* and told him I was ready to come home. He worked out the plane tickets, and I was in the car heading to the airport the next day.

The flight to China is about twenty-eight hours long with multiple connecting flights. To get back to Salt Lake, I had to fly from HaiNaan, China, to Guangjhou, China, to Seoule, Korea, To Los Angeles, California, to Salt Lake City, Utah. After I got off the flight to Guangjhou, my cell phone rang. It was Mark's* contact from China calling me very panicked. When he asked why I had left HaiNaan, I explained what Mark* had told me. He continued to tell me Mark* was an idiot and he had been told him multiple times that there was not a flight from Korea to the United States. If I left China, I would be stuck in Korea for a week and I could be picked up by a sex trafficker or at the very least I could starve in a Korean airport for a week. He booked me a flight to head back to HaiNaan.

When I tried to ask Mark* about it, he shrugged it

off. I began to suspect that he may want me to get stuck in Korea to teach me a lesson for leaving the Order, or he really was just stupid and naive that things just might work out despite his friend's warnings. Either way, I told him I wanted nothing to do with him booking my flights and I worked with his friend from then on. A week later, I took my regularly scheduled flight home.

When I finally touched down at Salt Lake, I tried to call Alan*. He didn't pick up. I tried again, but he didn't pick up. Maybe he forgot me? My heart broke a little until I saw him on the caller ID when my phone started ringing. I asked him if he could come get me, and he said he was all the way out in Bountiful, so it might take a little. I was a little sad because I thought he would be more excited to see me. I was nice, but then he said just kidding and he was already waiting for me in baggage claim. I couldn't stop smiling as I got off the plane. Sometimes his sense of humor was too much for my sensitivity.

Being the tallest person in most groups at 6"3, Alan* doesn't hide well in groups, and I immediately spotted him standing by the baggage claim waiting for me. I couldn't wait to be in his arms again and I ran to him. In all my youth I had always wanted my movie moment, and this was the best one I could have hoped for. He was happy to see me, and we grabbed my bags and went home. We didn't leave my apartment all weekend except to get food. A month later, we moved in together. When my family found out, I was fired from their company. A month before, I had been promised a promotion in China and had an all-expenses paid trip to visit the country. I was supposed to pay for the plane ticket, but I figured my dad had never paid a dime in child support as I was growing up. This would be his small way of doing something. I knew the whole trip was to get me away from my boyfriend, but their plan completely backfired. I was completely head over heels in love with Alan* and our relationship and future, was the only thing I saw when I came back from my trip. He was living with a friend at the time and paid rent on both places.

Two months after I returned, we were lying in bed together one night, and I asked him if he wanted to get married.

"Sure," was his response. I thought he was kidding and I assured him that I would be fine with it if he wanted to wait. He said he wanted to get married and we were engaged. Two weeks later, I found out I was pregnant with our baby. I'm not sure who was more excited between the two of us. Four months after I came back from China, we were married. Unlike all the girls in the Order, my wedding day was one of the happiest days of my life. We had a very small ceremony of only about forty people. We had planned to use his mom's pastor to marry us, but after a couple of couple's sessions to prepare for marriage, he told us he wouldn't marry us because our marriage would not last. Because we did not have God in our lives or a close relationship to our parents, we did not have a chance of a lasting marriage.

I was much happier with the cool blonde lady I found in the phone book. In my religion, a woman could never have the authority to marry a couple. It was even more amusing when her husband was the only black person at our wedding. I was just piling on the fuck you's to my family and religion at that point. Only about five people from my side of the family showed up. I had invited my dad and mom, but they both refused to go because they didn't support the marriage. They went to some of my other sibling's weddings who had left, but they had all married white partners. My family could not accept the fact that I had not chosen a white husband. None of my full siblings were allowed to attend the wedding.

Chapter 19
Out-Of-Cult Normal

Married life wasn't the happily ever after I had imagined when I signed on. I was so in love with Alan* and I never once questioned our relationship. Many women talk about getting cold feet right before their wedding. I didn't. I knew I wanted to marry Alan*. I was nineteen years old with about fifty years of every kind of trauma under my belt, and three months into my first pregnancy, but it didn't matter. I knew we would figure it out.

Unfortunately, I was only nineteen years old with about fifty years of every kind of trauma under my belt, and little to no self-awareness about my issues. Throughout my whole life, I had always been prey, to all the predators in my childhood. Even my father had become a predator, and in my culture, there really wasn't a difference in the relationship between your father and your husband. When you were married, it was simply a transfer of ownership. Marriage didn't come with any rights for women. I had never seen a healthy relationship between a husband and wife. I took the only dynamic I knew into my own marriage.

Because I was still programmed to be prey, my husband became the predator in my mind. When he asked me to do something different, I refused. Not because I disagreed with him, but because I didn't trust him. Whenever he confronted me about something I did, I became very defensive and a huge argument erupted over the smallest things. I turned my marriage into an emotional war zone. Not knowing what else to do, Alan* became emotionally distant, which only triggered my abandonment issues, and confirmed my initial programmed suspicion. The man who had once been my best friend, became another person I couldn't trust.

I wasn't open about my past to strangers at this point, and most people didn't understand my strange behaviors or why I was so reserved. After I was fired from Standard, I got a job as a hostess at the local restaurant down the street from my house. I wanted to apply to be a waitress, but I was only nineteen and wasn't allowed to serve alcohol until I was twenty-one.

The owner was a man who had suddenly lost his life and business partner in an accident the year before. I had never closely known anyone who was openly gay. It was strange for me, but Dave was a very kind man who was happy to answer any questions I had about his sexual preferences. As I grew to know the staff, I learned that most of the servers were also gay and chose this restaurant to work in because they were able to be very open about their lifestyle. It was more than a job. It was a community and a support system. Even though I wasn't gay, they were very supportive of my past. For the first time, I was able to start opening up about my past.

One day, when I was working, two women walked in. The older woman looked to be in her sixties and the other was a much younger woman who looked to be in her forties. At first, they didn't stand out to me, but as I continued my shift, they continued to look at me as though they knew me. For some odd reason, I have a very familiar face. I can't count the number of times I've had complete strangers tell me they know me from somewhere or ask me if I know someone they are acquainted with. I prepared myself for another of these situations as I approached their table to fill their water.

Giving both ladies a warm smile, I proceeded to refill waters and the older woman looked as though she wanted to say something. Trying to make her feel comfortable, I looked at her encouragingly.

"Do you know Carlene Cannon?" she asked me hesitantly.

Carlene was a woman from my community I knew quite well. I would eat lunch at her house with her daughter who ended up being my dad's twenty-sixth wife. She had been my mom's best friend when they were growing up. She was also a spokesperson for the woman of our community who fought for freedom of religion, along with Heidi Foster, but I didn't know that yet.

I must have looked like a deer caught in the headlights as I dropped the cup I had been filling and began shaking as I struggled to clean it up. I don't know if I was more uncomfortable with the question or more embarrassed by dropping the cup. Probably a bit of both. This woman obviously knew the answer by my reaction. Just own it.

"Yes," I said as I regained my composure. "How do you know her?"

"Her and I work together in the Principal Voices group," she began. "Have you heard of it?"

"No," I honestly responded. Most of the kids and even adult members are sheltered from any outside politics inside and outside the community.

"It's a pro polygamy group," she began. "Carlene is such a sweet woman."

"Can I ask how you knew who I was?" I asked her.

She smiled and took a moment before answering. "You look just like Paul."

I was surprised by her answer. Most people thought I looked just like my mom. When we used to go to the thrift store to buy school clothes, strangers swore we looked like sisters.

She finished the meal with the woman who turned out to be her daughter and gave me her card before she left.

"My name is Ann*. Please call me for lunch, sometime," she told me as she left. "I would love to hear your story."

Later that week, we met in a Chile's about half way between our homes and she bought me lunch. Neither of us could believe each other's stories. My vision of the Order was a closed and secretive community that feared the outside world. Her version was a religious group who were calm, happy, and only trying to live their religion without persecution from the outside world. She could hardly believe my stories of years of abuse and neglect and I could not believe Carlene had a friendly relationship with a woman outside the community. It only confirmed my suspicion though. My father was manipulative and two-faced when he needed to be.

My pregnancy progressed, and I continued my friendship with Ann. We had lunch about once a month and learned more and more about each other's experiences with polygamy. Her experience had been much more positive than mine had been. She had been a second wife and had married into polygamy after her monogamous marriage had failed and all her children had grown up and left home. The first wife hadn't been happy about sharing her husband, but both Ann and her husband had convinced her it was God's plan. Her husband then died shortly afterwards, but she continued her work to fight for her newfound belief. None of her children continued the practice.

While most the other polygamous communities are at least aware of each other and occasionally will marry between each other, my group did not socialize with the other groups during my childhood. My first memory of meeting someone from another group was when I was about fifteen years old, and my father invited a boy from the Lebaron group to a dance. I didn't know if my dad was trying to entice him into joining our group for his money or his capacity to work, but I remember some of my sisters and I were used as bait to entice him. He never joined our group and I never saw him again. Two of my uncles married girls from another polygamous family, but they were not a part of another polygamous group. These were the only interactions I had with anyone outside my family. I didn't even know there were other polygamous groups until I was in my late teen years.

While Ann* was very pro polygamy, her friend Tonia, whom she later introduced me to, was very anti-polygamy, even though she could not publicly state this. She had founded a small nonprofit organization and because the victims would not trust her if she publicly criticized a religion they had grown up with their whole lives, she could not take the anti-polygamy stance despite its contradiction to her very strong Christian beliefs. Even members of her own church became upset with her because she refused to take the anti-polygamy stance. The polygamous culture was one most people didn't believe existed anymore, let alone understood.

When I met Tonia, she had only just started her organization, and had very little experience with the culture. She had done the Christian thing and helped a homeless mother who was trying to leave, get back on her feet. The children were passive and well-behaved, and the mother was a timid and sweet woman. The culture had taught them honesty, respect, and fear and the mother had been taught to work hard to care for the home. They made for very pleasant house guests and inspired Tonia to start a whole organization when she realized there were very little resources and these women had no clue how to navigate the ones available. Her pleasant house guest did nothing to prepare her for her next client.

Harmony was a pretty little blonde seventeen-year-old who was soft spoken and sweet. When I found out this little girl, who was also my half-sister, had left the community, I couldn't believe it. No one left the Order, especially in my father's family. Out of two hundred siblings I had at the time, there had only been four who had left before me, and they were all full siblings who had gone to live with their grandparents who were not in the Order. They had family outside the community, which meant they had a support system. For girls like Harmony and I, leaving the Order didn't happen. Even if those thoughts had been on her mind while we were growing up, we would have never talked to the other one about it. She was also much younger than me. I had been close to her older sister.

When Tonia received the call about working with the leader's daughter she jumped in head first without any knowledge of the culture, the laws, or any knowledge of the manipulation my father was skilled at. Her and Ann* had been good friends because of their work involving this controversial topic, and Ann* advised her to speak to me when Harmony's case came in. Tonia originally thought I was overreacting when I warned her about my father's mind games and she continued with her plans to emancipate my seventeen-year-old sister.

Emancipation is not an easy process on its own. Trying to escape a cult at the same time, makes it nearly impossible. When Harmony got her court date, everyone including law enforcement and attorneys advised Tonia to get Harmony as far away from her family as possible, or that date would never happen. They warned her that the Kingstons were notorious for tapping phones, kidnapping, and the bomb threats hadn't been completely disregarded either. Harmony was terrified, and this only added to Tonia's fear. Tonia had planned to allow Harmony to live with her until her court date and have another pleasant house guest. It soon became clear this was not an option, and Harmony was passed around many different safe houses while she waited for her court date. She was successfully emancipated.

Tonia loved telling this story over and over again. It not only gave her organization credibility as an organization that could help people successfully leave their groups, but it was something right out of a movie. Unfortunately, this movie was not as entertaining when it was your everyday life, but I knew Tonia meant well, and I did have to give her credit. She had successfully helped a youth leave and become emancipated. Harmony ended up marrying into another polygamous group, but I was told she is the only wife and her husband has no plans to remarry. Tonia, my father, and Harmony's mother all went to her wedding.

After Harmony's case was over, Tonia took an interest in me. She invited me to church, her home, and because I was no longer working due to my progressing pregnancy, I helped her run errands for her organization as well. Alan* had been my only support since I had left my group and I missed having girlfriends to talk to. She was extremely religious, and our conversations included a lot of religious talk. My husband's sister was from a Christian religion, but we had never had a conversation about it. Tonia was my first exposure to a Christian religion and I found it to be a much more forgiving religion than I had ever seen in the LDS or the fundamentalist Mormon religion. They believed you were saved by Jesus' sacrifice and not by your own actions. While it was a relief to know I could be saved no matter what, I also had a difficult time accepting a religion where your actions didn't matter. If a serial killer accepts Jesus as his Lord and Savior after killing ten people, then he can go to the same heaven as me? Not likely.

I continued to go to church every Sunday though. Not because I necessarily believed the religion, but because I was lonely. Everyone was so nice and accepting whether they knew about my past or not. Tonia had become a friend when I needed one the most. As a newly married woman, marriage had brought some challenges I had never expected. My husband didn't want to spend every waking moment talking to me and he had completely different ideas than I did. Neither of us had great childhoods and neither of us were skilled in the communication area, but through every complaint I made about my husband, Tonia reminded me that marriage is forever. She made an excellent point that even if I left my husband, I would take my baggage with me and I would have the same problems with a new person. She knew neither of us were religious and she seemed to believe that with time, my husband and I would both come around and find Jesus and live happily ever after as a Christian. She didn't realize my husband is way more stubborn than that.

Meeting Ann* in the restaurant started a domino effect that seemed to bring the right people into my life at the right time. She invited me to the support groups held by her organization, but they weren't for me. I had been out of the cult for almost a year and was in a much more stable environment than most of the women in the group. My husband was working, and I didn't have to. We had a home, food, and money to play with. We weren't exceptionally well off, but my husband had a good job, and we didn't worry about our basic necessities like many of these women, which only seemed to keep them in their depression. Some of them seemed to be comfortable in the victim role, and that bothered me. I felt some of them would have been better off staying in their cult. Leah Remini stated, "You can take the girl out of scientology, but it's much harder to take scientology out of the girl." I think this is true for most people coming out of a cult. I did meet Pat through this process though, and she became the therapist I needed to move forward with my healing process.

Pat was a kind LDS woman who seemed to understand my culture better than anyone I had ever met who had never been a part of it. She had worked with many people from different groups, including mine. I didn't know she was LDS until a year or so into our therapy. She successfully kept her faith out of her practice, which I appreciated. Her office was covered with pictures of her and her family and all the exotic places they had been. As I sat in her office, waiting for her to finish a phone call in the other room on our first visit, I remember looking at all the photos and falling in love with her instantly. She obviously had a sense of adventure and a passion for life. This was a therapist I could open up with, even though I didn't start therapy because I felt like I needed it. Everyone told me it could help me, and it was something my family frowned upon. I wanted to see what the fuss was about.

Chapter 20
Becoming A Mother

Though I was out of the Order, it hadn't been enough time to rewire most of their damage yet. I planned a homebirth with my first baby to hold on to some of the things I thought were still good about my upbringing. I had asked the midwife from the Order, who had delivered a couple of my mom's babies to be the midwife. Alan* didn't like the idea, but he respected my decision to have the birth I wanted. Two months before I was due to deliver, my midwife was delivering a baby for my uncle, who was currently in medical school. He felt like something was wrong. When he brought this to the midwife's' attention, she dismissed it. The baby started looking worse, and he insisted on bringing his baby to the hospital. His newborn died before they made it. They hadn't caught the baby's lungs which were filling with fluid with every passing moment, and she wasn't able to breathe until it was too late. My Uncle lost his first baby daughter. I immediately scheduled my appointment with my original OB doctor and continued my prenatal treatment with a licensed MD.

Two weeks before my due date, I woke up in the middle of the night with a feeling that it was time. I had always been told to sleep as much as possible in the beginning of labor, so I went back to sleep. The next morning, Alan* got ready for work, and I explained he needed to keep his phone close because I was having the baby today. His look showed disbelief. This was our first baby and I was not showing signs of pain. I was completely calm, but he agreed. I had a doctor's appointment that morning and I just knew he would send me to the hospital. My contractions were far apart, but they were regular, and they just felt different.

When I went to my appointment, my doctor told me I was having braxton hicks' contractions, and there was no way I would be having a baby today. My husband called me after my appointment and I gave him the doctor's news. I was annoyed. The doctor was wrong. I went home and took a nap and when I woke up, contractions were closer and slightly more painful. I wanted a second opinion. I texted my sister-in-law and her opinion was, "better safe than sorry" so she picked me and my husband up and we went to the hospital. Everyone planned on going back home, including me.

When we arrived at the hospital, and I was checked. I was dilated to a six, which is far enough into active labor to be admitted. Everyone was shocked, including me. The pain really didn't seem so bad. I had every intention of having a natural birth, and I made this clear with the nurses. My family never birthed in hospitals and I was still carrying a lot of fears of pushy nurses who only wanted to medicate me and my baby and poison us. I received the complete opposite care of what I had feared. The nurses were amazing. They allowed me to sit in a hot bath, and labor naturally for hours. After five hours, I had not dilated any further, and they suggested breaking my bag of waters. Growing up, I had heard many birth stories, and my father had broken plenty of water bags during labor, so I trusted this intervention. It was a natural way to speed up a labor and didn't involve any drugs.

Five minutes after my waters were broken, I began progressing very quickly. Too quickly. I soon found myself in the worst pain of my life and I begged for drugs. The nurse reminded me of my strong desire to go natural and offered some natural pain relief techniques. She massaged, pushed on my legs, and helped me get into other birthing positions to relieve pressure. This was more assistance for a natural birth than I had ever heard of any woman in my community receiving. Most birth stories involved women laboring on their own until they called their husband and a numbered man to show up in the last hours. At all the births my father attended, most of them were spent with him on the phone.

Though I appreciated the nurse's enthusiasm and her eagerness to help. It didn't matter. I was in too much pain and I was not ready for it. I don't think any woman could be ready for it unless they had already been through it. I begged the eager nurse to just give me drugs. I was exhausted and needed sleep anyways, after laboring for nearly twenty hours. She completely supported me in that birth too.

The epidural turned out to be the best decision I could have made for my birth. My son's head was stuck, and it was three and a half hours of pushing before he finally came out. I was exhausted and if I had tried to do it without pain relief, I don't think I could have done it. I hadn't wanted an episiotomy, (procedure that involves them cutting the perinium to allow more space for the baby to come out), but I ended up with a pretty large one after I spiked a fever and they were worried about my baby getting an infection. They needed to get him out quickly.

A c-section was the last thing I wanted, and the epidural probably saved me from that. Most of my labor was natural, and I was happy about that, but the epidural was an important part of my labor as well. Many home births go very well, in my experience, but you don't know that it won't go well until it doesn't. I have also seen many home births go very badly, and I know many women who have lost their babies because they weren't close enough to medical care when they needed it. So many things can happen in a birthing situation, and many times, there isn't

246

enough time to get to the hospital. A home birth would not have gone well for me and I have decided it is not worth the risk. My nurses and doctors were completely supportive of whatever birth I wanted, until I spiked a fever, and then they intervened for mine and my baby's safety. I wouldn't have wanted anything different. My beautiful baby boy was born the day before my twentieth birthday on November 6, 2009, and I was so happy with my decision to do it in a hospital.

My first thoughts after I was wheeled into my recovery room, and reflected on my experience, was that my mom had done that eleven times with no epidural. It was a miracle she was still alive, though her sanity needed to be called into question. While Alan* was bonding with our son, I called her and told her my thoughts. She only laughed at me while we shared a moment of bonding. In her eyes, according to our religion, I was officially a woman.

After coming home from the hospital, I was surprised by all the help I was offered. In my culture, after a woman has a baby, an unmarried niece or younger sister will stay in her home to help her with cooking, cleaning, and her younger children for a couple of days and then she's on her own. No one calls. No one visits. No one brings food. If the woman had stitches, their husband will show up after a couple of days to take the stitches out, but he doesn't hang around to help. My mother was often looked down upon because she would ask her help to stay for a full week to help her and would make a big fuss if they left earlier.

My birth experience was completely different. Someone from my husband's family stopped by almost every day for the first two weeks. Sometimes it was just to visit, sometimes they brought food, and sometimes they brought presents. Alan* was embarrassed because our house wasn't clean, but I couldn't care less. I was in a daze for the first two weeks after having a baby, and if they hadn't brought food and presents, my husband would have to run out for fast food every night. He didn't know how to cook, and I wasn't going to try.

My shock compounded when my mom and two of her sisters stopped by to visit. It was unheard of for a mother to keep contact with their child after they leave. To this day, I don't know why my mother stayed so close to me during the birth of my son. I was her first daughter and she had just had her last baby. I think that was hard for her. She often made comments that many women were able to come back to the Order even if they had a child with someone outside the community. I just wouldn't be able to marry someone as high in the community, but something was better than nothing. Maybe she still had hope that I would eventually come back to the Order. Whatever the reason, I appreciated having her there. She held my son the whole time and seemed to fall in love with him. Maybe this was the start of something new.

About three months after giving birth to my son, I started back in college and therapy. My husband was working full time, and this allowed me to stay home with our son full time. I would stay home and be a mom during the day, and I would go to school at night while Alan* cared for our son. I only had enough time at night to attend college part time, so that's what I did. My emotions were unstable, but I was told this was normal after having a baby. My son was an easy baby. He was on a normal sleep schedule at six weeks old and only the first two weeks of breastfeeding were difficult. He was a great eater.

About six months into my routine, I began feeling

sick. I had panic attacks and crying episodes in the past, but I had assumed it was related to pregnancy, hormones, or whatever else was going on. It was the first time in my life things had calmed down for a moment and I was able to start paying attention to what was going on with my body. I was breastfeeding, but my baby was almost nine months old and everything was going great still. What was happening to me?

When I mentioned the regression to my therapist, she explained I was finally in a safe place and I was ready to deal with my trauma. If I faced it, and worked through it, it would help me heal. If I didn't, I wouldn't move forward. I tried. Most days I was unable to function. Most nights I woke up screaming or in cold sweats. I felt like I was going crazy because I grew paranoid and constantly had the feeling that someone was watching me. Some nights, it was so bad, I swore I could see a figure watching me from my closet. I was afraid to be alone. I would cry for absolutely no reason. I started fights with my husband and did everything to push his buttons. My abandonment issues came out in full swing and subconsciously, I was testing him to see if he would leave me like everyone else in my life had.

Though my mom and I were closer than we had ever been in my life, I couldn't tell her about the emotional battle I was fighting. Sometimes I would show up at her house after a fight and stay the night. She would ask me about my fight with my husband, and I couldn't talk to her about it. Most of the time I didn't understand it myself. She would then remind me I could still come back to the Order and let me sleep on her couch. This went on until my son was about ten months old.

One day, I showed up to my mom's house like I always had, and the whole atmosphere had changed. My mom asked me to leave.

"Did I do something?" I asked, genuinely confused.

"You know Uncle Paul said you couldn't be here," she answered as though we had gone back in time to before I was married.

"I'm always here," I reminded her.

"And that's been my mistake," she answered quickly looking around as though she was waiting for someone.

"Is Paul on his way?" I asked her.

"No!" she answered too abruptly. "Why would you ask that?"

"Because you're a horrible liar," I answered as I climbed back into my car, rolling my eyes. I guess she hadn't been telling him about our visits.

When the weirdness didn't change over the next month, I questioned my little sister.

"What's going on?"

"Rachel* and Jess* are engaged," she told me.

My heart sunk. My sisters were fifteen and seventeen. Neither had ever dated anyone, gone to school outside the Order, or had even seen anything outside their community. After more details, I learned they were waiting until their sixteenth and eighteenth birthday. The older one would be a third wife, and the younger one would be marrying her first cousin as a first wife at the young age of sixteen. Her husband would be at least ten years older than her.

I called my mom on the way home.

"Getting the girls married before they can leave, huh?"

"Who told you?"

"Does it matter?"

"Yes."

"I would have found out eventually."

"Both of the guys are really great guys."

I rolled my eyes. My mother and I would never see eye to eye on this topic and I knew that. She was still the fifth wife to a man who treated her like garbage. In her eyes, it was a step up for one of her daughters to be a first wife, and my older sister was also marrying her first cousin, but his family was known for having more than most people in the Order. Not because they worked harder, but because they felt they were entitled to more, and their mother was Paul's big sister, whom he adored. My mom saw this as her daughters hitting the jackpot in marriage.

As much as it hurt, I knew this was not my choice to make. When I talked to my sisters about it, they both wanted the marriages very much. They had never seen anything different, but how could I show them that without making them feel like I didn't support their decision? If I had objected, it would have only shown them my parents were right about me. Besides, it really wasn't my choice to make.

After I knew about my sister's engagements and did nothing to try to stop them, my mother relaxed around me again and things went back to normal. I was still friends with Tonia, and my mom began asking me a lot of questions about her. I tried to be as open with my mom as I could be without giving away any confidential information about her organization. After some time, I felt like that was the information my mom was looking for. I knew she would never care about this information on her own, and I realized she was fishing for information for Paul. My suspicions changed.

Originally, I suspected my mom had been hiding our relationship from Paul, even though everyone in the Order is horrible at keeping secrets. He had to know I was seeing them. Paul seemed to have a tendency to not really care about an issue unless it directly affected him. I figured he thought as long as he let me see my family, I wouldn't try to influence them to leave. If he pretended not to know, he didn't have an obligation to his other followers to prevent it. Now, I realized he absolutely knew, whether my mom knew he did or not, and he was allowing me to be there to get information.

Paul is an intelligent man. He did well in school and received a scholarship for running, to a college out of state. His father made him turn down the scholarship because he was being groomed to run the Order and Paul went to law school instead. He passed the bar. He has the ability to listen to everything you say, and then either use it against you or use it to manipulate you in some way. Most people like to talk about themselves and Paul knows he can use it later. He loves control. By letting me continue to see my family, he still had a lot of control over me.

Chapter 21
The End of Out-Of-Cult Normal

It wasn't until one Sunday afternoon, everything changed again. Caleb, only two months away from his fifteenth birthday, was riding his bike to tell me goodbye after a long visit.

"Nicole," he stopped me before I got into my car. "Can I talk to you?"

"What's up?"

"I'm done," he told me quickly as he glanced back towards the house to be sure no one would be interrupting this conversation.

"What do you mean?" I asked. I suspected the answer, but I needed him to say it.

"Paul bashed my head into the wall," he said. "I don't want to stay here."

I immediately shut my car door and my blood boiled. I had made it clear to my father and mother that they would never abuse my siblings. They both knew I wouldn't tolerate this.

"What happened?" I asked.

He explained Paul had accused him of something, Caleb denied it, and Paul bashed his head into the wall before accusing him again. I had heard this story so many times, it was difficult to not believe it. Fortunately, I had learned by now, that it wasn't my choice anyways. As unfair as it is, kids in the Order are forced to grow up way too quickly. They are working full time as young as thirteen years old. They are married at fifteen years old. They aren't allowed to make any of their own decisions, but they are expected to fill adult roles. Little kids in the Order have to make adult decisions and Caleb was one of them.

"What do you want to do?" I asked him.

"What are my options?" he was suddenly interested.

"I can take you to file a report, which if you really want to leave, is probably your best choice," I explained. "Or you can do nothing."

"I want to file a report."

His answer was quick as though he had already thought everything through. I knew the look in his eyes. He wanted to leave. He was ready. I couldn't push him though. This would be the hardest decision of his life, and if I was the one to push, he would just come back anyways. Though I wanted him to leave, I knew I couldn't influence this decision. I was here to support whatever he decided.

After thinking about how to handle the situation, I realized I wasn't quite sure how to handle this. I would need some help. I told Caleb to secretly call me in a couple of hours and quickly gave him my phone number on a crumpled piece of paper before I left. I needed to make some calls of my own. My first call was to my therapist. She had dealt with kids from abusive homes through her own organization and I knew she had some resources. After explaining the situation to her, she gave me my options and precautions and wished me luck.

My second call was to Tonia. She made a quick call to her attorney to be sure I wouldn't be breaking any laws and to explain legal processes to remove a minor from their parents' home. She emailed me some different forms to give me a myriad of resources and options that would be available to me very quickly. In her experience, cases with minors were very delicate and many times decisions and resources need to be immediately available. You're racing against a clock. By the time my brother called, I had formulated a plan. I told him to meet me at the park down the street from my mom's house. I couldn't pick him up, because I could technically be charged with kidnapping and if this went badly, I didn't want any legal charges on my record.

When I pulled into the parking lot at the elementary school, I almost expected him to not be there. Maybe he changed his mind. But soon, I saw him riding on his bike. I pulled into the nearby parking spot, and we walked towards the large fields where there were no people around. I explained my plan to him, and why each part of it was necessary, then I explained to him if he had any doubts, he should wait. If we did what we were going to do, we could not take it back and because they had no control over me, he would be the one punished, and it would be severe. A flicker of doubt crossed his eyes before it was gone, and he said, "Let's do it."

At 11:45pm, I checked my phone to make sure I wasn't late, before I continued to my mom's house. As I drove past the front door, I saw that the house was completely dark. When I had stayed there during my fights with my husband, my siblings would sometimes be awake at two or three in the morning. My mother never enforced any type of bedtime and the kids went to sleep whenever they wanted, most of the time well after my mother had gone to sleep. Some nights when I showed up at one in the morning, my mother would be fast asleep, and I would spend time with my siblings until three in the morning. My mother wouldn't know I was there until the next morning.

This night was different though. The house was silent. One of the older kids could be watching a movie in the family room, or even in their bedrooms. After they started working, some of the kids started insisting the be allowed to buy tvs for their bedrooms. After I left, my mother seemed to give up on parenting even more than when I was there. I drove around the block a couple of times, and when I was sure the house was quiet, I parked along the fence near the backyard. If for some reason my mother looked out her bedroom window, she would not see my car. I did not park in the driveway, because I was not supposed to go onto the property. I could be considered trespassing. I couldn't help myself though. What if something happened to my brother? What if Paul had found out and hurt him?

At midnight, I left the safety of my car and quietly walked over to my brother's bedroom window. I didn't hear anything inside. Maybe he changed his mind. The sound of the window opening made me jump, and I was afraid my outburst may have woken someone.

"You scared the shit out of me!" I hissed as my brother through a small backpack out of the window before climbing out himself.

"Baby," my little brother said with a grin. He seemed to be excited by the whole thing without an ounce of fear. I didn't know if it was because he was young or naive. Probably both.

When we were safely in my car, I explained the plan to him again.

"Are you sure this is what you want?" I asked him again.

"Yes."

"Because once you make this decision you can't take it back, and I'm not sure what they will do to you, but if Paul hit you once, it will probably happen again if you come back."

"I know," Caleb replied. "I'm sure."

With that, we kept going. I relaxed after about five minutes and we found ourselves in comfortable conversation. Had we not been in such an intense situation, the whole ride would have been nothing more than a nice memory together. But the moment was cut short when we pulled into the police station in the district where the abuse had happened. My therapist had explained to me that when you file a report for abuse, you must do it in the district where the abuse happened. Fortunately, it had happened at Paul's office, which was in the same district my therapist worked in. She was familiar with the police officers at the precinct we were supposed to be in and called in ahead to notify them we were coming.

When we showed up at nearly one in the morning, there were two officers waiting for us, and they let us in the front door of the building. One officer shook my hand and explained the process to me. He would be taking Caleb into a separate room to do the interview and I would not be allowed to be present. I was fine with this. I had already told Caleb that no matter what happened, as long as he told the truth, everything would work out right. I made it clear that if he went down this road, he would need to tell his story multiple times and if he was lying, it would come out and would hurt him more in the long run. I was naive about the system and had only seen one case in which things worked out in the end.

I waited about forty-five minutes while the officer interviewed my brother. The weight of what I was doing hadn't yet begun to sink in because I was so focused in doing everything right. I didn't have time to second guess or overthink the situation. With so much time to wait, the doubts began creeping in. What would this mean for my relationship with my mom? My siblings? I believed we were family and even though most of the Order doesn't keep contact with their siblings who leave, mine did. Deep down, I knew part of it was because they secretly hoped I would leave my husband and come bac. With all the problems our first year of marriage brought, they believed our marriage would not last. The fact that we didn't have God in our marriage, didn't help our credibility either.

Finally, Caleb and the police officer came into meet me. The first officer led Caleb into another room and the officer who had done the interview sat down in front of me.

"So, I believe Caleb's story," the officer began. "I can't tell you what was said in the interview, but I don't think it's safe for Caleb to go home tonight."

I was in shock. What did he say? Wanting to protect my mom, I jumped in.

"My dad's not home," I began. "I'm trying to protect him from my dad, not my mom."

"According to Caleb, your mom hits him too."

I felt as though I had just been slapped in the face. I didn't know what to say.

"I don't know anything about that," I said honestly. I knew my mom was neglectful, but I didn't know there was abuse outside the occasional slap when my mother lost her temper. It wasn't right, but I didn't think it was grounds to take her child from her.

"It's up to you," the officer said. "We'll make the report in case anything serious happens and you'll at least have that."

"What do you mean?" I asked not knowing how this could help me.

He went on to explain that any time there's a situation of abuse, you should always report it. Even if nothing is done about that report, it starts to show a pattern of abuse in case you ever need to prove your case in court or down the road if a child needs to be removed. The state will almost never remove a child from a situation on a parent's first offense. Abuse tends to get worse and worse and if you don't report it until things are really bad, no one is going to believe you when you finally do try to get help. The officer's words were comforting to me. Even if this doesn't work, it's still a small win for the next fight.

"I do want you to take him to the Children's Justice Center though," the officer said, interrupting my thoughts. "I think he needs to be interviewed by a professional."

I agreed and at almost two in the morning, we showed up to the Justice Center. I could see Caleb growing tired from lack of sleep and the weight of what he was doing was just sinking in as well. He completed the last interview with the Justice Center and by the end, we were both exhausted. They agreed to let me take him home because Paul wasn't in the home, but they informed me that DCFS would be doing a visit in the next couple of days to check in on things. I took Caleb home, he climbed in his window, and I drove home to prepare for the next step.

The next morning, I called my mom and explained to her that I needed to speak to her and Paul together. She didn't understand my request, which was good. It meant Caleb had not said anything to her yet. After asking again and again, I gave her no answer. Her next line of defense was to let me know Paul is busy.

"I promise you, he wants to talk to me today."

I knew DCFS would be coming the following day, and I wasn't going to give that piece of information up until after I had tried to be civil with my parents and work this out in the family. At this time, I was under the impression I was part of the family and we were on the same side. I truly believed we both only wanted what was best for Caleb, and if anyone looked at the situation, my mom's house was not best for any child. I truly believed my mom loved her kids and really did want what was best for them.

Also, my dad had often said, if someone wants to leave, they have that right. I was out of the Order, but I was still very much a part of the mindset and I still believed many of the lies. My mom finally called me back and told me to be at Paul's office at seven.

When I walked into the office, Paul and my mom were waiting for me. In the past, Paul always led me back to his office when we had a meeting scheduled. I had spent more time in his office than any other room in this building, despite working in the building for a couple of summers. This time, he led us into the conference room. I had never been in a meeting in this room except during the after-school meetings where he would reprimand his kids for behavior at school. The room was way too big for three people, but I found a seat near the front of the huge boardroom table and took it. The room looked as though it hadn't been changed since I had left two years before. The carpet was falling apart and had dark stains that could have been dirt or broken pens. The glass table was severely scratched, and the chairs had the same dark stains as the carpet. Either the room had fallen apart or I was beginning to pay better attention to details.

"Honesty is the best policy," I said to myself as my parents took their seats in front of me.

"What's up?" my dad asked with the same fake smile he always used to greet me.

"Caleb wants to move in with me," I told him. While he was great at bullshit and beating around the bush, I never was.

My mom's jaw nearly visibly dropped and for a moment, I saw a look of amusement cross my dad's face.

"Really?" he asked me as he leaned back in his chair. He acted as though I just told him a joke. I reminded him of my years of abuse. Nothing was held back. I reminded him of the time he beat me with a bar, and at first, he didn't remember. My eyes welled with tears.

"How can you not remember when it ruined my life?" I asked as the tears fell.

"I did my best," he explained. "You will never understand."

"You're right," I said as my tears finally stopped. "I will never understand how you can do that to a person you love."

He finally seemed to be out of his comfort zone. For the first time in my twenty-one years, Paul did not have a response to that. I didn't care though. I continued with all the years of sexual abuse. Now it was his turn to cry.

"I didn't know Ben got to you," he said as his own eyes welled with tears.

"You knew?!"

His look of defeat changed suddenly, to a look of drowning. "I'm sorry," he sobbed as he grabbed me into a painful hug. I couldn't respond at first. Was this fake? The tears seemed real.

"Me to," was all I could say. I was very sorry it happened.

Finally, after about five minutes of tears, he let me go, wiped his glasses, and composed himself, so I went on to my mother's crimes. I told him details about her neglect for years. Throughout every accusation, my mother stayed silent. Occasionally, my father would turn to her and say, "Did you know about this?" or "Is this true?" and she would answer with a "yes" or "no" with absolutely no explanation to anything. She didn't show any remorse for what she had done. I knew in that moment I had made the right decision. My mom didn't care if Caleb stayed or left. This decision was Paul's to make.

Finally, I addressed the abuse that started this

whole situation in the first place. Of course, Paul denied it. Suddenly, the purpose of meeting in the conference room was now clear and I remembered Caleb saying to check the wall in his office. He was sure I would see the mark in the wall.

"Let me see the wall," I asked him.

A huge smile was the last thing I expected. "I just got the walls redone."

When I went into his office, there were no marks on the wall behind the chairs where Caleb had told me it happened. They had obviously been painted recently, though, and I wasn't buying this coincidence, but I couldn't prove it, so I continued with the many other arguments I had come prepared with.

After about five hours of confronting my parents about their lack of parenting and argument after argument, my dad finally agreed to allow Caleb to make the decision. We all drove separately to my mom's house. Despite the fact it was one in the morning, everyone in the house was still awake. I arrived before either of my parents and asked Caleb if he was okay. He seemed fine, until I told him Paul was going to come talk to him and if he stayed firm, he would make it out. My mom showed up only five minutes after me and hovered to be sure I couldn't have any quiet conversations with Caleb before Paul showed up. It felt as though she was his watchdog and we were the prey. It was in that moment I realized it didn't matter that we were her children. She would choose Paul instead of us every time until the day she died.

As Paul walked in, I knew this was a trap. I didn't know what they were planning or how they would manipulate the situation, but as Paul closed the door to talk to Caleb alone, I knew we had lost. Maybe not the war, but this battle was done. There wasn't even a purpose in me waiting here anymore. My mother wouldn't speak to me while we waited. I didn't know the extent of the damage, but I knew our relationship would never be the same again. As much as it hurt, I was okay with it. My mom would never choose her children over Paul, and though I saw it time and time again, this situation brought a whole new level of anger. The cop's words floated through my mind, "Caleb said your mom hits them too." My mother was no longer another of Paul's victims. She was a perpetrator.

After an hour of waiting for Paul to finish talking to Caleb, I was impatient. I knocked on the door, and explained that I had school in the morning, and he gave me permission to go. The look on my face obviously said he was out of line, and he asked me what I needed.

"Don't I get to talk to him?"

Paul smirked at me. He had won. He knew it. Caleb wasn't going to fight him, but I needed to know where Caleb was at and make sure he was okay. Paul stood up and gave Caleb a hug. Caleb's eyes were down as though he was a submissive who couldn't make eye contact as Paul walked out of the room.

"What do you want, Caleb?" I asked after the door had closed. I knew I didn't have a lot of time.

"I can't leave Jesse and Anna," he said as he finally raised his eyes to meet mine.

"You know you can't help them here," I said, completely understanding where he was coming from. Paul dangled my siblings in front of me when I was leaving. I knew this technique well. He didn't stand a chance against Paul's manipulation tactic. His look of defeat told me everything I needed to know.

"If you're going to stay, you need to tell them about DCFS coming," I explained. "It needs to come from you, so Paul thinks you're sorry. Otherwise, he will punish you more severely."

A look of panic came over Caleb's face. He had completely forgotten about DCFS and everything else in the world.

"He can't punish me," I continued. "You need to take the credit for this one."

After five minutes, Paul walked in, without knocking, and explained it was late and everyone needed to get to bed. He had never had an opposition to keeping everyone up all hours of the night as I was growing up, and I hadn't known that to change. He wanted me to leave his house.

"I need to tell you something," Caleb said. "I reported you hitting me."

"I didn't hit you," Paul said.

"I reported it."

"Did I hit you?" Paul asked.

"Yes."

The look in Paul's eyes grew cold and angry.

"Did I hit you, Caleb?" he asked in a threatening tone I had never heard before.

"No."

"Then why did you report it?"

Caleb could only shrug his shoulders.

"I helped him," I cut in hoping to take some pressure off my baby brother who was obviously terrified. "I told you not to hit my siblings."

Paul's cold and angry look turned to me. The words, "If looks could kill," crossed my mind. Not knowing if it was an intimidation method or if he really did want to kill me, I held his gaze. This man hadn't scared me for years. He was only a big bully who generally used manipulation to get his way.

Finally, he broke the stare and said, "You need to

leave."

My mom chimed in with, "Everyone needs to get to bed."

"No!" my dad nearly shouted. "You guys have a lot of work to do to get this house ready for DCFS tomorrow."

My mom shot me the most cold and angry look she could muster and said, "Bye, Nicole."

With no other choice, I went to give my brother a hug, and my mom stepped in front of me. "Bye, Nicole!" she said louder as though I hadn't heard her the first time.

"I'm giving my brother a hug," I explained. My mom looked to Paul for an answer, and he must have signaled it was okay, because she moved out of the way. I hugged my brother.

"I love you," I told him, knowing these words would be the final ones for a long time. "Please don't hesitate to call if you need something."

"I love you, too," he mumbled holding me tight. We both knew I was leaving him to the wolves and leaving my mom's house that night felt so wrong. This whole choice was so wrong. Unfortunately, it wasn't my choice to make.

The next week, Caleb was sent to my family's ranch on the border of Idaho and Utah to live with my half-brother. The neighbors are far away, and the closest town is at least twenty or so miles. The land is a hot dry desert and even fruit trees and gardens won't grow there. There's nothing but sagebrush and desert grasses for miles around. At night, the only light is from the stars above. They tried to get some cattle at the ranch, but there weren't enough wild grasses to support too many animals either, and water was scarce. I had been sent there when I was kidnapped after I left the first time. I hoped this was only a temporary punishment.

When I tried to come to my mom's house a few

weeks later, to explain my side of the story, she wouldn't hear it. When she asked me to leave, I went to the street and told my siblings they could come talk to me out there. I couldn't legally stay in the house after my mom had asked me to leave. My mom had never been successful at parenting or controlling any of her kids, and all the younger ones ran out to follow me. I learned later, my mom had sat them all down and told them I was now evil and they would never see me again. We stood on the street as they all held onto me as though their life depended on it, sobbing into me. The older ones stayed in their rooms. They were all so angry with me for disrupting their new normal after I had left and been told for the first time they would never see me again.

My mom called the police. When the two officers showed up, one talked to my mom and one talked to me. I gave each of the kids a hug and asked them to go to the house and wait. They didn't need to be involved in this any more than was possible. This was between me and their mother. They didn't need to be collateral damage. My mom didn't seem to feel that way. She made sure they were all standing there when she told the cop her side of the story.

"Why are you here?" the cop asked me, starting with the good cop routine. I was honest with him. I explained my brother's abuse. I explained reporting it. I explained the polygamous lifestyle. He didn't seem to want to get involved with that piece of information.

"If you left, doesn't it make sense to just let everyone here get on with their life?"

"I'm not leaving my siblings behind," I told him firmly. "Especially with abuse allegations."

"You know I could charge you," he said wanting to push the issue further.

"No, you can't," I was confident, and quite annoyed

by this time. "I'm standing on a public sidewalk and I'm not shouting or causing a scene. If you guys would do your jobs and keep my siblings safe, then maybe I wouldn't have to."

I wasn't trying to fight with an officer, but because of the extent my dad lied and abused his authority, it wasn't something I tolerated. The officer could not charge me. He knew it and I knew it. He went to meet his partner and explain my position.

"My partner is pretty upset with you," the other officer said with a smirk as he approached me.

"He threatened to charge me, and he has no grounds to do that," I explained. "I hate liars." The officer didn't seem to have a response for me, or he wasn't sure he could give one without laughing.

"Look," I said calmly. "I have no issue with you. I'm only here to make sure my siblings are safe. There are allegations of abuse and DCFS has been known to drop the ball where I come from. I'm really not here to cause problems."

The officer went and talked to my mom and then came back to me.

"We're going to file another report with DCFS," he told me. "I don't really have any rights to do more than that, as you probably know." I had to laugh at that one. "But here's my card. I've heard a lot about different abuses in some of these groups, so I believe you. I'll type up the report and give you a copy. From now on, every time something happens, report it. This is how you can build a case to actually help your siblings." It was the same speech the officer had given me when he had interviewed Caleb. I gave the kids a hug and took the officer's card.

The day was over, but the situation far from it. Later that day, I received a message from Caleb's facebook telling me the whole thing was a lie I had made up and forced him to tell. Because I had tried to hurt Paul and his family, he never wanted to see or hear from me again. The words were hurtful, but I knew they weren't from him. Even if he did feel that way, he would have never confronted me this way. My family doesn't handle conflict well and will do almost anything to avoid it. Caleb would not reach out to me of his own choice. Even if he was at the keyboard, he was only a mouthpiece for my half-brother.

My older siblings stopped speaking to me, and Rachel* uninvited me to her wedding. I was sure I would not be invited in the first place, but to have her uninvite me was like a knife to my heart. I had raised her and while I teased her and called her names when we were growing up, I couldn't have loved her more. I tried to explain what had happened to my older siblings, but they were confused and felt betrayed. We hadn't ever had the chance to repair our relationship when I had left the Order. It now seemed hopeless. It wasn't only my mom fighting me anymore, but my sisters as well. My brothers tried to stay out of the drama. They wouldn't defend me or fight me. Finally, not knowing what else to do, I stopped trying. I didn't call, I didn't come over. If they didn't want me there, I wasn't going to fight to be there.

Before the incident with Caleb, the cold sweats were getting better and the crying had almost stopped. Most of my PTSD symptoms were under control, though I felt emotionally dead and I lost huge chunks of time. When my husband would ask me why I would do something, I wouldn't have an answer for him. He felt like I was dishonest because I couldn't give him a good answer. I didn't understand what was happening to me. After losing my family again, my healing went backwards. I began drinking and smoking and partying with some of the servers I was working with. My husband didn't understand any more than I did. He did his best to step up and take care of our son while I fell apart, but it couldn't have been easy for him to work full time, be the primary caregiver for our son, and deal with my outbursts and mood swings as well.

Finally, it was the last straw. I don't know what it was to make him so upset, or if it was from dealing with so much instability for nearly two years but when I tried to walk out the door for my physiology final, he took my keys. He refused to spend another night caring for our son while I went out. After explaining my physiology final and getting nowhere, we began fighting. My father had used my education as a way to control me for years before I left the cult, and it was a major trigger for me. In my triggered mindset, my husband was not going to keep me from that final. The situation became physical when I tried to physically take the keys from him and to prevent things from escalating, my husband called the police.

Because I had been the one to become physical, and my husband didn't fight back, I was the one charged with domestic violence in front of a child. The officer told me if my son hadn't been there, he wouldn't have charged me. Recent studies show the severe damage domestic violence will do to a child, even if they aren't actually involved in the confrontation.

"Thanks, asshole," I responded as he left the scene. I went to my son's room and refused to speak to my husband. I was angry about losing Caleb and I was feeling more and more helpless. My nightmares were escalating, and panic attacks became a daily event.

"You need to take control of yourself regardless of your environment," Alan* told me when I had finally calmed down enough to speak to him. I wasn't angry with him for calling the police, or even hurt. It was as if I was so emotionally traumatized I no longer felt anything anymore. This was when I knew something was clearly wrong and I was not coping with anything in my life. Why couldn't I just let the abuse go? Why couldn't I just forget about it and move on? My flashbacks were so random, and I had no control over them at all.

The next month, I went to court for my domestic violence charge. When the judge asked me what I had to say for myself, I wasn't sure what to say. I was in a daze. I wasn't sad or angry to be there. I had been to court for so many speeding tickets, and this first court hearing was exactly as those had been. I didn't have an answer for the judge. I met with the prosecutor and he explained because it was my first offense and I had never had more than a traffic ticket, he was going to be lenient. If I didn't have any other charges within the next year and I complied with every court request, he would enter a plea in abeyance and my record would be clean. I was currently attending school to become a nurse. If this charge stayed on my record, it would ruin any hope I had of becoming a nurse.

They entered my plea and required me complete a drug test and come back to court in a month. I continued my therapy and my therapist was surprised to learn of my criminal charge. When we discussed it, I couldn't give her a good answer as to why the fight happened, and most of the incident was a blur to me. Finally, after a year and a half of therapy, my therapist was confident.

"Nicole, I didn't want to say this unless I was totally sure," she began. "But I believe you have a pretty severe case of dissociative disorder."

Relieved someone had an answer for me, I perked up.

"It used to be known as multiple personalities, and

270

doctors didn't like that word, so they changed it."

"I'm more than one person?"

"Sometimes when a person experiences consistent trauma such as years of sexual abuse, their mind starts leaving the situation more and more as a way of coping with the trauma. It's all you, but some parts of you are cut off in order to protect you."

She gave me a book about the disorder. She knew I enjoyed doing my own research. She asked me to think about it and we can talk about it more at our next session. I read her book and went online to find everything I could about the disorder. I read stories of other patients and found that the prognosis for such a disorder was generally not positive. Thinking about my own experiences, the disorder seemed to fit. I was losing huge chunks of time and saying and doing things I didn't remember. When I told Alan* about this diagnosis, he didn't say much. I guess he really wasn't sure what to say. He had grown distant since my charge and I didn't know if he was angry at me, felt guilty, or wasn't even sure what he felt. I didn't have much time to worry about where he was at though. I was trying to salvage my college semester, work at Mimi's cafe, and complete my court requirements. Alan* also suggested I join a support group for sexual abuse victims, but I didn't get much from the last support group I had gone to, and I didn't have a lot of spare time anyways.

My first court requirement was a drug test. Knowing I would come up clean in any drug test, I wasn't concerned when I showed up to the dirty old building with outdated offices and glass windows to separate everyone who worked in the building from everyone else who might walk into the building. As I waited for them to call me, I watched another guy walk in, grab a clipboard and begin filling it out. This guy obviously knew the drill.

When they called my name, I brought my clipboard and completed form to the front desk and watched as the lady looked me up and down. She gave me a cup and searched me before I went into the bathroom.

"Do they not allow weapons in the bathroom?" I asked her amused.

She did not find my comment funny.

"Weapons, or other people's urine," she said dryly.

She did find my expression funny.

"We will know if it's not yours," she said with a little wink and an evil smile.

I quickly peed in the cup and brought it back to her. After years of peeing in a cup for prenatal checkups, that part didn't bother me. The camera in the bathroom made me uncomfortable, and the sign below it that said, "Patron will be notified if camera is turned on." She didn't notify me, right?

After turning my urine into the front counter, she dipped her testing strip in the cup right in front of me.

"You're clean," she said and handed me my paperwork to take upstairs to my new caseworker.

"Of course, I am," I told her. "Why would someone knowingly test dirty?"

She looked at me as though she couldn't figure out why I was here. "Your caseworker is upstairs. Just follow the hall till you find her."

The upstairs hall was completely deserted, and I wondered if my caseworker had secretly left for the day. There was no one upstairs to verify her presence. There were stacks of folders just sitting on chairs in the hall. The whole hall looked like a cluttered mess from the 1950s. I thought I remembered the carpet from an old movie my grandmother used to watch.

I finally reached the only open door in the hall, and

found a sweet older woman sitting at a large wooden desk that fit in with the whole 1950s decor. She was working on a computer that looked like one I used at my dad's payroll office from the 1920s. Maybe 1950 was being generous?

"I'm Nicole," I said reaching my hand out to shake hers.

"Hi Nicole," she said taking my hand in her very tiny one. "Have a seat."

She started reading from a long list of questions from her computer, that included everything from any health problems, family problems, substance abuse problems, economic problems, and any other type of problem I could have. She asked me if I had any remorse over what had happened. What could I say to that? Honesty is the best policy.

"I've actually been working with my therapist about what happened," I explained. "I had a traumatic childhood."

Seeming surprised I had begun therapy on my own, she seemed to relax with me. "How long have you been in therapy?" she asked me.

"Almost a year and a half. We've worked through about half of my sexual abuse trauma and I felt like we were making pretty good progress. I don't know what happened."

She closed her binder and looked at me a moment before she answered.

"I'm impressed that you actually reached out for help and started therapy on your own," she began. "My recommendation to the court will be the following: five parenting classes, a fine of four hundred dollars, and twenty hours of therapy with at least ten of them directly discussing the incident that you got you here. I'm dismissing drug tests because you tested clean today and there were no drug charges filed on the night of the incident. Do you have any questions?"

"What do I do next?"

She gave me the information for the parenting classes and sent me on my way. When I showed up to another different, but equally outdated building for the classes, I wasn't sure what to expect. A couple of the parents were high or looked like they were coming down from something and many of the parents appeared to be homeless or dealing with another similar hardship. When the class started, we were asked to share our reason for being there, though it wasn't required.

"I left my two and three-year-old home alone while I went to work," began the woman sitting across from me. She appeared to be young, with dirty blonde hair, no makeup, and dirty clothes. She could have been a pretty woman, but it seemed life had beaten her down and she was unable to get up. Similar stories were shared throughout the group and when it was my turn, I declined to share. On the third class, the teacher asked to speak with me after class.

"Do you feel like you're getting anything from being here?"

"Honestly, not really," I told her. I could never hurt my child.

"Then why are you here?"

I explained the court requirement and what I had done to deserve it.

"You don't think you hurt your child?"

"Not physically," I admitted.

"You don't think your two-year-old was terrified as he watched you attack his dad?"

That was when I got it. I was the mom. It was my job to make my son feel safe and secure. In that moment, I hoped he would never remember the incident and I promised myself I would never become physical with my husband again. In the nine years we have been together, I have kept that promise.

After my parenting classes were completed, I was able to put a heavy focus into my therapy. The goal with disassociating patients is to validate the feelings of all the different "personalities" and work through each of their own separate traumas and allow them to "be heard." Eventually, the personalities will start coming together and be more of "one" person. Eventually I found myself no longer communicating with my other "selves and after about a year of working on the disorder, I stopped losing track of time. When I found myself in a confrontation, I stopped "checking out" and I was no longer having panic attacks. Things were better between my husband and me and we found ourselves pregnant with our second baby.

Chapter 22
Roller Coaster Ride

Alan* and I were both excited about my pregnancy, but nervous as well. I hadn't been emotionally stable for long and things had only recently calmed down. I hadn't seen my mother's family for almost a year. I was coming up on my one-year court date that would close my domestic violence case and I was still in school and working part time as a server. Slowing down was always difficult for me, and pregnancy didn't change that. My moods were unstable during my pregnancy, but my husband and I both chalked it up to pregnancy hormones and we dealt with it.

A month before I was scheduled to deliver, my husband and I began discussing our plans for after the baby. I had planned to continue working part time, serving, and be home with the kids while Alan* was working. Alan* didn't agree with that plan. He wanted me to quit my job at the restaurant because of so many issues of sexual harassment that seemed to be a part of every serving job I've ever had. It wouldn't make sense financially to continue working there anyways, because I didn't even make enough to cover childcare, gas, and the other extra expenses I would have if I continued to work after my baby boy was born. He wanted me to get a "real" job and I felt like being a mom was the "realest" job I could do.

I began talking to my friend, who ran a home daycare, and she offered me a job where I could bring my baby to work. I informed the restaurant I could only work there on weekends and showed up to my friend's house to work for her the next Monday. While I was there, I watched her work and we talked about how it is to run your own daycare. I knew I could do this and I felt like I could do the job on my own. After my first day, I told her I would be starting my own daycare and she gave me her blessing. I went home to tell my husband.

After crunching the numbers of what I would make and what I would save in childcare costs, it seemed the perfect solution. I could stay home with my kids and have an income. After doing the numbers, it would be a better income than I would be able to make with only a high school diploma, even without considering the extra costs for childcare. I could hardly contain my excitement with my genius idea when I brought it to Alan*.

"No."

What? Why? How could he not be on board?

"Why?"

He brought up concerns of our house being destroyed, liability if someone gets hurt, and the fact he didn't want strangers in our house every single day.

"What is your better idea?" I asked him. He didn't know. I moved forward with my daycare.

I called my friend the next day to get advice about how to get licensed, and she sent me in the right direction. After years of living off my husband and depending on him to support me, I would finally be making my own money and if my numbers were correct, I wouldn't need him to support me if anything happened. I spent all day making calls to the child care licensing division, fire department, health department, and the city for a business license. I read the ten to fifteen pages of licensing rules and called the right division on any questions.

A month before I was due to have my baby, I began the licensing procedures and began telling friends about my new business. My friend had been looking for a backup place to take her kids when her parents went out of town, and I got my first client. The month after my second baby boy was born, I had posted an ad in the online classifieds, and I had my second client. Three months later, I was a fully functioning licensed child care provider with paying clients. I was quickly making more money than I could ever hope to as a server, and I stopped taking shifts. My serving job became my outlet to being home all the time instead of a job to make money. After my business was running smoothly, I gave my serving job up. I had finally found something that was mine.

After a year into my business, I was doing very well both emotionally and financially. I was required to attend child development and training classes, and I loved them. Growing up, I had never had any positive parenting role models and I hadn't realized how even simple things were difficult to me. I didn't see a need for high chairs or tables and chairs or many other things that seem to be second nature to so many parents. My mother never parented us. This frustrated my husband, especially when I had other people's kids. Every day, I found myself getting better and better as a parent and a child care provider. My training classes were making me a better parent.

I was finally in a position to begin helping others who were trying to leave their communities and thrive, and I began working more with Tonia's organization. Tonia had received an invitation to be on the TLC tv show Sister Wives and was asked to bring a couple of ex polygamous kids along to provide a different viewpoint than the positive image the Browns had portrayed. The show was receiving some scrutiny because they were not addressing the dark side of polygamy. I had only had my baby three months ago, but I agreed to do it. I was battling crazy hormones and sleep deprivation from having a newborn and viewers made the comment that I seemed to be very passive and depressed, which was not my personality at all. I had

278

finally found some strength after starting my business and graduating with my associate's degree in college. More focus was put on my cousin, Kristine* because she was blonde, beautiful, and very outspoken. She was still on her journey of understanding there was more to this lifestyle than our terrible experience and the camera was able to capture that.

The whole experience was incredibly fun. While Kristine* was pissed off at Kody the whole weekend, I had a blast with Aspyn and Mariah. The Browns were so sweet, and the kids were so open and happy with their lifestyle. I knew they had a different experience than I had growing up and there was a huge difference. I never had a dad growing up. Despite having so many children, Kody was somehow able to connect with his kids. They were not perfect, but the polygamous lifestyle is a choice they all made as consenting adults. Many people want to put polygamy into a black or white situation, and it's just not that way. Some people really do want that lifestyle. I'm not one of them, but this is why I was never able to take an anti-polygamy stance and rally for the bills to make it illegal. We shouldn't be fighting polygamy. We should be fighting abuse and underage marriages.

Soon after the show, for the first time in years, my half-brother reached out to me. He had left the community about a year before me, and we had spoken to each other about once a year since then. Him and his brother asked to meet with me. Of course, I agreed, and I invited them over because with my business, I didn't have a lot of free time to meet them elsewhere.

Their brother, was the one living at the ranch where Caleb had been sent, but I didn't see how they would know anything about what was happening up there.

"Did you hear about Caleb?" Josh* asked me after

279

small talk was over.

"I haven't talked to my family since he was sent away," I told them sadly.

"Jacob beat him so badly, he thought he was dead."

My heart broke and the guilt set in. He was at that ranch because of me.

"How do you know?" I asked. I knew it was true without evidence, but a small part of me hoped I was wrong.

"A neighbor who saw it told me," Josh* explained. "If Caleb stays up there, he's probably going to die."

"What can I do?" I asked him and told him about the previous experience of trying to help Caleb out.

"Well obviously he has to want it," Josh* explained. "If he doesn't want to leave, you can't force him, but he can't want to stay there."

"He's been up there over a year," I explained. "I can't imagine him not finding a way back after a year."

"You know Jacob's four-year-old has seizures because he beat her so bad?"

The information didn't surprise me. Jacob had a history of torturing animals and enjoying it. I didn't know he was hurting his own kids though.

"What about Mandy*?" I asked referring to his wife who had once been my best friend growing up. She was also the same person who kidnapped me and took me to the ranch though. I wasn't sure what her values were.

"She's just as bad," Josh* said confirming my sad suspicion.

"Who can we go to?" I asked. I had tried the police and DCFS. Was there anyone who could help?

"Just go get him," Josh* said.

"I've tried taking him that way," I told him. "Paul

brainwashed him into coming back and going to Park Valley. I'm the reason he's there right now."

"Tell him he's going to die," Josh* suggested.

"What if we go to higher?" I asked. "The police and DCFS don't do anything. What if we go higher?"

"I know countless people who have gone to the Attorney General's office," Stephen explained. "They had evidence, and no one got anywhere."

I could hardly sit still after my brothers had left. I had a desperate need to do something to save my brother, but what? What could I do to protect him?

Not knowing what else to do, I started making calls. Tonia's response was, "Welcome to every day in my world."

Pat's response was, "You can't help someone who won't help themselves."

Ann* seemed to be the only one with any hope. She had recently heard the story of my half-brother's wife who labored at home for three days because Paul refused to allow her to go to the hospital. She had begun having seizures and going in and out of consciousness, but Paul continued to tell them it was a normal part of labor. Finally, the woman's husband picked up his second wife and took her to the hospital despite everyone's objections. The woman was rushed into an emergency c-section where her baby died, and she nearly lost her own life as well. Ann* couldn't believe something like this could happen. It was horrific to imagine this was happening under the guise of her religion.

"I can get you in touch with the head of the AG's office," she said. "Mark is a really great guy from what I've seen. I can't believe that he would hear your story and do nothing."

When I showed up to Ann's* home, there were

multiple cars in the driveway. I had been to her beautiful home a couple of times, in fact, it was where I had met my friend Tonia years before. When I came into her home, she led the way to her living room where she had many guests, especially in the political arena, over the years.

Utah's attorney general, Mark Shurtleff stood when I entered the room. He was a very tall man, looming over me at well over six feet. He seemed to be a soft-spoken man, with a firm handshake. He took a seat after I was comfortable, and I was impressed by his manners. I couldn't believe he had agreed to meet with me at all.

Ann* started the conversation with my introduction and Mark couldn't help but let out a little laugh. "I know your dad," he started.

"You do?"

"Yeah," he continued. "He's not very good with complying with state orders."

"You think?" was my cute response.

I couldn't help but ask him why he had never been charged with anything. He brought up the incest charges they tried to stick on him and explained how difficult it was to get proof. When he issued orders of DNA tests, everyone left the state. I had only heard my father's version of this and I remembered the situation well. The moms went to live in Colorado for about three months. Mark continued to explain the orders lasted only thirty days and they weren't exactly easy to get. He figured it would be a waste of money to keep chasing my dad.

"What if I can help you?" I asked him.

"I'll put you in touch with my investigators," he told me. "Expect one of them to call you." With that, he took down my number and we continued the conversation. He spoke fondly of his children.

282

I couldn't believe it when an investigator called me a few days later. I made an appointment to meet them at their office, and I began pulling out all the evidence I could find against my father. I had saved payroll check stubs where they had taken out child support, wedding invitations for underage children, and copies of taxes where they had illegally claimed children for tax benefits. If the only way to save my siblings would be to send my father to prison, then I was ready to do it. He couldn't intimidate them from behind bars and they could finally make their own decisions. I was confident as I walked into their office.

An angry blonde woman with too much makeup sat across from me, and a short dark-haired man with a large smile sat down next to her. Are we playing good cop/bad cop here? I thought I was a witness here.

"I'm Paul Kingston's daughter," I began. "Here's all the evidence I have against my father." I passed a large manila folder to the woman who seemed to be in charge. She opened it and quickly leafed through it before she passed it to her partner who seemed to be going through it more thoroughly.

"I have evidence of illegally collecting child support, underage marriages, and tax fraud. I could probably get evidence of even more crimes."

"Most of those are petty crimes," the blonde woman began. "We were trying to get him on an incest charge that would be a felony, but we could never find him."

"What if I help you find him?" I asked her. "I would be willing to sit outside his office and then call you when he's there and you come pick him up."

"Would you be able to set up an appointment?" the blonde woman asked me.

"Absolutely."

"You would have to wear a wire."

"Sweet."

Amused, she took down some notes and explained how the situation would work. I would set up a meeting, her team would be nearby, and when I was sure I could identify him, they would arrest him. It seemed easy enough. I left her office feeling like I was in some kind of a spy movie. The look on my dad's face as he was getting arrested would be priceless.

A week later, I had no news from the investigators. I was told they would contact me within a couple of days. Maybe they had another plan to arrest him? The thought disappointed me. I really wanted to see his face and wearing a wire sounded pretty cool. I had worn a wire when I was on the TLC show Sister Wives, but this would be way cooler. After a week, I decided to check in to see how things were going. It took a couple of times before the short, dark haired man called me back with sad news.

"It's not moving forward," he told me appearing as confused as me.

"Why?" I asked unable to hide my disappointment.

"I don't know," he told me. "We were moving forward, and then we weren't, and I was transferred to medicaid fraud. I'm not even in that department anymore."

"Isn't that weird?" I asked him unsure of how often people are transferred in the attorney general's office.

"It is," he answered seemingly unsure of what to say. "But I want to wish you luck, and if you need anything you can keep my number."

"You're in medicaid fraud?" I asked him.

"Yeah, why?"

"You should probably check out my half-brother," I told him. I gave him my half-brother's information and hung up. Hopefully that goes somewhere.

After hearing the investigation was going nowhere, I was discouraged. A year later, Mark Shurtleff and his successor John Swallow were charged with ten felony charges that included bribery and taking gifts. They were later cleared of all charges, but like Mark had told me personally, sometimes knowing something and proving it were two different things. Rumors were always circulating about the Order paying people in the government, and this was how they were able to get away with all their crimes. I completely believed this to be true before Mark Shurtleff was arrested. In my mind, this only confirmed my suspicion.

I didn't have too much time to think about it, though. I was in school, running a daycare, and volunteering to help other victims of polygamy. Things were going well in my mind. My husband was working full time and we didn't have a lot of time for each other. We were incredibly distant at the time, and I wasn't making him a priority. I had hired a young girl who had left Warren Jeff's group to work in my daycare and while I knew she was in love with my children, I hadn't realized she was falling in love with my husband as well. My husband treated me well, and most girls from polygamy have never seen that from a man before. My husband was in love with me.

By the time I realized what was going on and came around to asking her, she was honest with me. She had fallen in love with my husband. I wasn't sure what to do, so I asked my husband to limit his time with her, and he complied. When I asked him if there were any feelings there, he assured me there weren't. Unsure of what to do, I contacted Tonia and let her know my concerns. The conversation became heated, and before the end of it, she began making accusations toward my husband based on his lack of faith. I assured her this wasn't true, and I would figure everything out.

She called me back and claimed there were some wild but serious accusations going around. I had grown close to the girl, more so than my husband at the time and didn't know what to think. I've always been a firm believer that if there's smoke, there's fire. If something had happened, it was unacceptable. I contacted the girl directly, and she claimed everything Tonia had said had been a lie and she had never made those accusations. Confused as I could possibly be, I contacted Tonia. Unsure of what to think, tempers flared and her and I exchanged some harsh words. My husband and I contacted the girl's mother and apologized for what was happening. Her mother knew us well, and knew the accusations weren't true. She said that she had never heard the accusations come from her daughter's mouth, so she didn't believe them.

I met with Tonia and explained her mother's perspective. The whole thing seemed to be a tragic misunderstanding. Tonia was unable to let it go and went forward to file a police report. Because the young girl and her mother both denied the claim, they didn't even speak to me or my husband regarding the accusation and Tonia and I both thought it best to part ways.

About a month later, the girl called me to apologize for hurting my husband. She had tried to contact him, but he had changed his number at my request. It was the most difficult thing to listen to her express her feelings for my husband, but I knew this wasn't personal. During the whole charade, it had come out that she had been raped by her father. I hadn't known this when I had been mentoring her and I was not aware that she may form an unhealthy

attachment to a father figure and that's exactly what Alan*
had tried to be for her.

The whole experience was hurtful, but eye opening.
I realized I had not been paying attention to what was
happening in my home, or my marriage. This woman had
formed a stronger attachment to my children than I did at
the time, because she was the one who was with them.
One of our close friends made the comment, "She was
literally trying to replace you in every aspect of your life." I
had enrolled her in a high school program and she had
dreams of going to college. The charity had paid nearly two
thousand dollars for this online High School Degree, but
six months after I quit mentoring her, she gave up, and got
her GED. She later went to college, which I was happy
about, but then she quit. I couldn't help but wonder, was it
worth it? Did I really help her? Or did she nearly ruin
everything good in my life for nothing? I still don't know the
answer, but one thing I was sure of, I wasn't going to risk
that again.

The fact that she was able to affect my marriage so
much, surprised me. I had thought my marriage, though it
was distant at the time, was solid. We were planning to
have another baby when everything blew up, and I had just
had surgery to get my IUD removed. Somehow it had left
my uterus and was lodged in my bowel for the last six
months. When I went to get it removed so we could start
trying for another baby, they couldn't find it. Now, I was
angry with my husband for many reasons. Tonia had been
one of my best friends and her organization had been a
support system for me. Because I defended my husband
against her accusations, we were never able to get past it.
I lost all my friends and a cause I truly believed in because
of a misunderstanding I was blaming him for, despite the
fact, that he hadn't done anything wrong. We had already

been distant, but the whole scandal had made it worse. I had already been close to a mutual friend of ours, Dave, and he became the person I confided in to process what had happened.

Two months later, my headaches that I had dealt with off and on for as long as I could remember only became worse. Doctors did an MRI and thought they found a brain tumor. A week later they found it to be a patch of fluid, but the whole thing was emotionally difficult, and I had no one to support me through it. My husband was there, and he babysat during doctor appointments, but our relationship was not a close or supportive one at the time.

Three months later, I found myself deep into an emotional affair with a male friend, with every intention of turning it physical. I loved my husband, but I resented him for years of hurt that we had never worked through. I had been so busy working on my traumas and triggers that we hadn't had time to invest into our marriage and I wasn't sure how to come back from it. It seemed easier to start over with someone else, so when my friend came back in town for a week, I did what I could to clear my schedule to spend time with him. We went on a couple of dates, and we had the talk about our sexual history and finally, as we were standing on the large deck at the Utah Museum of Natural History, overlooking the Salt Lake Valley, he kissed me.

There was no chemistry. Maybe I was new at this? It had been years since I kissed anyone besides Alan* and I was out of practice. On our second date, we went hiking and tried again. There was nothing. Either he was a bad kisser, or we just didn't have that chemistry for each other. Either way, I was done with this affair. We had plans to see each other that weekend, after he came back from a trip with his family, but I didn't see that happening anymore.

Alan* called as we were driving back to get my car and I agreed to meet him at the gas station close by. I had hired another girl who had left polygamy to work in my daycare because I was still in school and Alan* was working. This would give Alan* and me time to talk and work things out.

When I came to the gas station, Alan* was already there smoking a cigarette. When I showed up, I came clean about everything. He didn't say anything and left. He went catfishing with some friends that night, but we texted back and forth. Throughout our marriage, he wouldn't tell me if I did something that bothered him. I only knew because he would ignore me for a couple of days. He never yelled, and I felt like this meant he didn't care. Once again, he left and wouldn't tell me how he felt. He asked questions, and I answered.

The next day he came back home. It was the fourth of July weekend, and we had plans to go camping. I was surprised when he still agreed to go. Once again, I felt like I had just committed the most hurtful act and he still didn't care. He just asked question after question. I bore my soul as we drove up the mountains.

"Do you think we will make it through this?" I asked as we sat around the campfire after he seemed satisfied with my information.

"I don't think I want to," he said quietly. "I'm not trying to hurt you, but I don't think I can forgive you."

We spent the rest of the night talking, before we finally went into the tent to sleep. I was surprised when he initiated sex, and I warned him that I wasn't on birth control and I could be ovulating. We had been planning to have a baby only months before everything went completely off plan.

The next day as we drove home, he agreed to give us another try. He didn't know if he could come back from everything, but he would try. Three weeks later, a test confirmed I was pregnant with our third baby.

Chapter 23
It's Never Too Late

The next six months were emotionally the most difficult. Alan* quit his job to help me run the daycare, and I fired my assistant and took a break from school. I registered for one class completely online. We were determined to focus everything on giving our marriage one last fighting chance and we spent hours nearly every night talking. Most nights ended in fights and hurt feelings and for so long I thought we were only making it worse.

About three months before I was due to deliver our third son, my brothers and sisters began reaching out to me again. They sent me facebook messages and other small apps to my phone. I loved my siblings, but I promised Alan* I would stay focused on our marriage. I started showing up to my mom's again to drop off presents for birthdays, but I didn't stay long, and I didn't go very often. I realized that if I didn't focus on the family I had tried so hard to build over the years, I would lose them.

Four weeks before my due date, I went into labor. Contractions were very far apart, but they were real. Nothing I did would stop them and they didn't get easier. They didn't seem to be getting closer either. I wasn't worried about delivering four weeks early. My second son had been born at thirty-six weeks and had weighed just over seven pounds. My first was three weeks early and my second had been four weeks early. I thought my third was going to be two weeks early because of the pattern, but I was happy when I went into labor four weeks early. The last month of pregnancy is the hardest.

Three weeks before my due date, I was still pregnant. Contractions were still consistent and they were a little closer together, so I went to the hospital. They confirmed I was in labor, but I was only dilated two out of ten centimeters. Because I was still so early, they wouldn't intervene to speed up the labor. Annoyed, we went home.

Two weeks before my due date, I was still pregnant. My doctor agreed to scrape my membranes because I had been experiencing what they call "prodromal labor" which is pretty much a labor that last more than a couple of days. You're really in labor, but it's moving so extremely slow. Two days after getting my membranes stripped, contractions finally began to speed up. I had been in labor for four weeks and I couldn't believe I was finally in labor. When stood up to make myself a sandwich, my water finally broke.

With my contractions suddenly stronger, I waddled upstairs to change my pants.

"My water broke," I told Alan* who was at in the middle of a dota game.

"Are you sure you didn't just pee yourself?" he asked only half serious.

"That's actually a possibility," I said as I pulled on some clean pants.

"I think I know the noises you make when it's real," he said as he got up from his computer. "It sounds pretty real."

Fortunately, it was late enough in the day that my backup babysitter was already on her way and was able to be there quickly to take over my daycare while I went to the hospital. I thought I still had a lot of time to get to the hospital and I insisted on doing my after-school carpool before heading to the hospital. It would be easier than trying to call my parents and get ahold of them while they were working. My husband was incredible and only rolled his eyes once as I sat to talk for a moment before he reminded me, "Unless you want me to deliver this baby, we should probably get to the hospital." I had been in labor for four weeks. I wasn't in a hurry.

Halfway to the hospital, the contractions were unbearable.

"I don't think we're going to make it," I said as the thought went through my head.

"We'll be fine," my husband said, as he tried to calm me down. "You're still talking through them, right?"

It was a valid point. I hadn't delivered when we pulled into the hospital parking lot and my husband opened my door for me. As soon as I stood up, I felt like my baby was going to fall out and rip me open while he did it.

"I can't walk," I panted through contractions. I literally felt like my baby was going to fall out when I stood up. I saw a wheelchair, but it was too far away.

"What do you want to do?" my husband asked me. I could feel him starting to get nervous as well.

"I can walk," I told him. I took a deep breath and stood up. My baby didn't fall out! "We need to hurry."

I walked as fast as my contracting body could carry me and while the pressure didn't get worse, it did get lower. We made it into the hospital to the front desk.

"I'm in labor," I explained as though it wasn't the most obvious thing in the world. In the past, when I've shown up to the hospital in labor, they ask a bunch of questions at the front desk. This time, they must have realized I was close because they brought a wheelchair right over and wheeled me to an exam room immediately. The doctor was an amazing midwife who stopped touching me every time I was having a contraction and didn't force me to lay flat down when she tried to check me.

After checking me, she immediately called on her phone, calmly but sternly. "Patient is dilated to nine centimeters. Can we get a doctor in here immediately?"

Nine centimeters? By the time we got to the delivery room, the pain had become excruciating.

"I want an epidural," I said as tears welled in my eyes.

"It's too late," the doctor told me as she prepared the bed. "It's time to push."

I suddenly felt as though I had no control over my body and I found my body violently pushing.

"Don't push yet," the midwife said. "We don't have everyone in here."

"I can't control it," I breathed and then screamed as I felt like my body was ripping apart from the bottom up. I thought I was going to die. When I told the doctors, they assured me I wouldn't die, and I was disappointed. I found myself wanting to die. All of a sudden, there was a release, and with it, went most of the pain. Finally, with one more push, my son came out, taking all my pain with him. I still didn't feel much of the placenta delivery despite having no pain medication. There was a slight tug, but nothing more. It was as though I literally felt my body flooding with hormones and I was in a state of euphoria. This natural high was more intense than the epidural had ever been. I didn't know why anyone would use the epidural.

When I said this out loud, everyone laughed.

"Do you remember screaming in pain? My husband asked, and it all came back. Yeah, that sucked.

"Sweets," I said using our nickname for each other.

"Yeah," he asked.

"What are we going to name him?"

We had been arguing over names for months and couldn't agree on one.

"I think that looked like a lot of work," he said. "I'll let you name this one."

"You can pick the middle name," I said.

"Okay."

"Can this also be my punishment for everything bad I did?"

He laughed at that one.

"I think that was pretty damn close."

I had finally achieved my natural childbirth.

For the first time, after childbirth, I didn't call my mom. We had never gotten close again after the incident with Caleb, and I blamed her for his abuse. Caleb had come back from Park Valley, but he never tried to leave the Order again. I was building relationships with all my siblings, but I hated my mom and every time I saw her, I was hurtful. I started seeing my siblings away from my mom's house. I forgave her for what she had done to me, but I couldn't forgive the fact she wasn't changing. If anything, she was worse.

My Mother's Tribute

You brought me into this fucked up world
A perfect, innocent little baby girl.
all your underage friends were having babies too
But you were 21, what was your excuse?
You said you loved me, I was a miracle in your life
Yet you were so preoccupied with your husband's other
wives.
Your daughter was molested, beaten, and raped by your
brothers
you were still so busy with all the other mothers.
You would think one of his whores would put their children
first,
unfortunately, as they all show their colors, they were just
as bad if not worse.

You pathetic little whore
you know that's all you are
why can't it be like it was before?
When you loved him from afar

His damaging words, his hurtful tone
each day, you seemed to break to the bone
I hated your submission, I saw you so weak
Was I really the one who was a freak?
He uses you up, puts on the miles, then puts you out
Do you still not get what this bullshit is about?
He has it all, and you are alone,
You pathetic little puppet drone.

You pathetic little whore
you know that's all you are
Why can't you be like you were before.

You have come so far.

Your eyes fill with tears as you look at your life
All you are is a pathetic polygamous wife.
Are you happy with your mediocre existence?
Are those tears of joy as you are insisting?
Your helplessness angers me
Your pity saddens me

You pathetic little whore
You know that's all you are
Why can't you just see before
This is all you are?

As your soul is drowning and the tears are flowing
The undeniable sadness is finally showing.
As you hold that pistol looking over the edge,
wanting everything to end, filling with dread.
I hope you do it, my precious mother
And when you do, no one will it bother.
You chose someone who could never love you
someone who would never want someone as pathetic as
you.

You pathetic little whore
Everyone knows that's all you are.
There was a chance before.
Now this is all you are.

Chapter 24
Healing

Two and a half years after I had begun therapy, my therapist moved out of state for her husband's job. When she told me she was leaving, I could see her watching my reaction. I felt a slight tug at my abandonment trigger, but I wasn't as broken as I had thought I was. My personalities were back together, and she had given me the tools to handle whatever may come out. I had done a great deal of damage to my marriage during my years of healing. I was not the wife and mother I had gone into my marriage wanting to be, and I had made so many mistakes. When my therapist left, our last session was the question of whether or not I wanted to stay and fix the damage or move on. We never answered that question and my therapist moved on.

My husband had stayed by my side through all the years of my brokenness and had stepped up when I had been unable to parent. As hard as I knew the road back from broken would be, I owed it to my husband to try. I had done a lot of damage in the first four years of our marriage and I put him through more than any person should ever put up with from a spouse. Any other man would have left so many times, but he stayed.

It's now ten years since I left the Order when I was seventeen years old, and I am finally in my happy place. My husband and I are still happily married, though there's still some work to keep moving to an even better place. I'm finally a whole complete person. I'm happy alone and I'm happy with my husband. I've finally let go of all my anger towards everyone in my life, including my mother, and I'm moving forward. I've had some setbacks along the way. My baby brother, Caleb, who I fought so hard for, passed away while I was seven months pregnant with my fourth baby, due to a motorcycle accident. My baby girl was the happiest surprise, while my brother's death was my saddest. Being invited to the funeral allowed me to say goodbye, but also reminded me of the many things I had lost and gained from leaving my old lifestyle. It was incredibly overwhelming.

I was recently diagnosed with Bipolar II disorder from PTSD, after a serious manic episode, but I'm confident I'll make it through this new journey as well. Medication and a healthy lifestyle has kept it under control for the most part, and the more I learn about myself, the better I'm able to identify triggers, and prevent the next episode from happening.

Life continues to be one hell of a roller coaster ride. I've been running my own home daycare for nearly six years now, and I'm finally getting back into writing and fitness. I'm loving being a wife and mom. I'm no longer a survivor. After ten years of trying to survive, I'm finally thriving. What is the saying, "Life's journey is not to the man who arrives at the grave safely, in a well-preserved body, but to the man who slides in sideways, yelling, "Holy shit, what a ride!"

Perfecting Meditations
-Charles Elden Kingston

With my divine birthright, I have unlimited health, knowledge, intelligence, sympathy, tolerance, realization, ambition, courage, patience, vitality, forgiveness, perseverance, energy, obedience, joy, satisfaction, cleanliness, beauty, confidence, determination, and independence, which causes my personality to penetrate and influence all God's creations, because I acknowledge the hand of God in all things making me optimistic, cheerful, helpful, full of love, clean and pure morally, and gives me definite assurance of my continual progress and permanent success.

All is a result of my continued fasting, rejoicing and prayer, which continually fills me with God's desires for divine guidance, making me at ease, at rest, relaxed physically, mentally and spiritually giving me perfect control of my entire being, so that I can work orderly, unceasingly, consciously, unconsciously and subconsciously, always asserting the truth.

I joyfully, continually apply knowledge, seek happiness, assert willpower, living my thoughts, which gives me perfect nerves, muscles and health, keeping me perpetually happy.

Thus God's spirit revitalizes, rejuvenates, cleanses and continues to energize me, keeping me positive and magnetic to all good and truth as it perfects me, making me an eternal, independent, individual being, different from all others, and an essential part of all creation, and creator of my own destiny.

Perfect youth, which is perfection, and all the intelligences governing my mind and entire body, increase, grow and obey me, according to my growth, understanding, and obedience to God.

With my continued determination to succeed, I live, think, work and love ceaselessly, consciously, subconsciously, and spiritually, while asleep as well as awake, God continually keeping me open physically, mentally, and spiritually to success. I realize, assert, create, and achieve success, in return for continually giving all credit to God.

My main object through perfect ideals is to come to a full realization and understanding of all the laws, powers, and privileges of God, as my personality develops and brings me to them exalting all in perfect Order, harmony and love, which completely penetrates and surrounds my entire personality, as I steadily continue to perfect myself, by gradually following God's direction and plans in pushing on up towards the unknown.

ABC Order Standards

A is for appreciation. I appreciate my life and all of the wonderful blessings and gifts my Heavenly Father has given me.

B is for brother. I love my brothers and sisters and never raise my hand against them.

C is for cherish. I cherish my membership in the Order and thank the Lord each day for this gift. Membership in the Order is like a hunting license. It doesn't guarantee anything, but gives you the right to hunt and seek for eternal life.

D is for dress. I keep myself clean and dress in a modest way that is pleasing to my Heavenly Father.

E is for eternal life. I will put gaining my eternal life before anything else in my life.

F is for form. I will wait to form any ties with a boy or girl until i receive my Heavenly Father's direction on marriage. I will save myself for the one I marry.

G is for the golden rule. I will treat other people as I would want them to treat me.

H is for honesty. I never take anything that is not mine. If i ever borrow anything, I ask permission first and then I return it.

I is for incomings. I will let all my incomings and outgoings be in the name of the Lord. I will watch what I spend and avoid extravagance.

J is for janitor. I would rather be a janitor in the house of the Lord than a king in any other kingdom.

K is for kiss. My first kiss will be on my wedding day with my husband or wife.

L is for love. I will strive to love others as Jesus loves me.

M is for marriage. I will ask my Heavenly Father for direction and guidance in choosing my future husband or wife.

N is for natural. A natural man is an enemy to God.

O is for obedience. I will obey my father and mother and those who are over me.

P is for prayer. I begin and end each day with prayer and remember my meditations. Prayer, meditation, and the help of the Lord will help me make my decisions.

Q is for quality. I will improve the quality of my life by using my time for the benefit of others.

R is for resolve. It is my firm resolve and fixed purpose to give my all to the Lord; my time, my talents, all that I am or ever expect to be, to the establishment of Zion and the building up of the Kingdom of God upon this Earth. This is consecration.

S is for speak. When I speak, the words that I say are clean and pure. I will not swear or use my Heavenly

Father's name in vain.

T is for truth. I will always tell the truth.

U is for understanding. I will understand the feelings and actions of others and not be quick to judge them.

V is for voice. I listen to the still small voice within me. It tells me what is right and wrong. If I listen, and obey, it will guide me every day.

W is for the word of wisdom. I obey the Word of Wisdom and eat and drink only the things that are good for me and my body. I will never taste an alcoholic beverage or try any drug. I will never put a cigarette in my mouth.

X is for exercise. I will exercise my mind and body with clean thoughts and wholesome activities.

Y is for youth. I will represent the youth of Zion and keep myself clean with clean thoughts and wholesome activities.

Z is for zest. I do my work with zest and do more than I am asked to do. I thank the Lord each day for my opportunities and blessings.

Memory Gems

It is my firm resolve and fixed purpose to give my all to the Lord: my time, my talents, all that I am or ever expect to be, to the establishment of Zion and the building up of the Kingdom of God upon the earth.

True happiness is not found in doing what one wants to do, but in learning to like to do the things one ought to do.

I will let all my incomings and outgoings be in the name of the Lord.

If the Order doesn't have it, we don't need it.

Seek ye first the Kingdom of God in all its righteousness and all else will be added.

Put your trust in that spirit which leadeth to do good, Yea to do justly, to walk humbly, and judge righteously, for this is my spirit.

About the Author

At age seventeen, Nicole Mafi embarked on her journey to freedom by leaving Kingston Clan. She then married her husband in 2009 and went on to have four beautiful children while attending college classes and opening her own home child care business. She graduated with an associate's degree in health science in 2009 and went on to study business management. She has volunteered with the nonprofit Holding Out Help to help others leave their communities and has guest starred in the TLC television series *Sister Wives*. She has been a guest in other local radio shows as well. When she's not busy with her kids, she enjoys crossfit and reading great novels. She loves hearing from readers and helping others in any way she can. She can be contacted at nicolemafi75@gmail.com

Printed in Great Britain
by Amazon

11218961R00180